The War
Against the Poor

The War Against the Poor

THE UNDERCLASS
and
ANTIPOVERTY POLICY

HERBERT J. GANS

BasicBooks

A Division of HarperCollinsPublishers

Designed by Joe Eagle

Library of Congress Cataloging-in-Publication Data
Gans, Herbert J.
    The war against the poor: the underclass and antipoverty policy /
Herbert J. Gans.
      p. cm.
    Includes bibliographical references and index.
    ISBN 0–465–01990–0
    1. Poor—United States. 2. Public welfare—United States. 3. Economic assistance, Domestic—United States. I. Title
HC110.P6G36 1995
362.5'8'0973—dc20   95–13180
                                                        CIP

95 96 97 98 ◆/HC 9 8 7 6 5 4 3 2 1

For Louise and David

When it shall be said in any country in the world, my poor are happy; neither ignorance nor distress is to be found among them; my jails are empty of prisoners, my streets of beggars; the aged are not in want, the taxes are not oppressive . . . ; when these things can be said, then may that country boast of its constitution and its government.

—*Thomas Paine*

Contents

Preface and Acknowledgments

This book has been germinating in my mind for a long, long time. My involvement in the war against the poor began in the late 1950s, with the war against low-cost housing, also called urban renewal, that I reported in my book *The Urban Villagers*. This led, in the 1960s, to my becoming one of a number of social scientists consulting with civil rights organizations, foundations, and the government on, and writing about, antipoverty policy.

My concern with the dangers of terms and labels like "the underclass" began later in that decade, when academics and policy-makers started assigning the poor to a culture of poverty that in effect blamed them for being poor. At that time, I published some articles and a few satires attacking the stereotypes with which the poor were being saddled.

It was not until the mid-1980s, however, later than several other social scientists, that I became concerned about the harm being done by the word "underclass" as a new label for condemning the poor as undeserving. This led me to the larger question of how and why we, the fortunate classes, unjustly stigmatize so many poor people as undeserving—and from there eventually followed the rest of this book. The final product is a social science essay on the relations between the classes in America, but it is also a social policy tract, to use the language of an earlier day.

One morning in 1989, Eric Wanner, then as now president of the Russell Sage Foundation, listened patiently as I poured out my thoughts and feelings about the term "underclass," and the studies that I thought needed to be done. This initiated a process that eventually led to a Visiting Scholarship at the foundation, in the academic year 1989–90, where I had the chance to begin to plan and research some of the contents of this book. I am grateful to Eric Wanner for that marvelous year of research time, scholarly conversation, and other help. He, and his trustees, deserve thanks also for creating an atmosphere and a place in which I could cheerfully have spent the rest of my working life.

My primary intellectual debt is to one of the visiting scholars from 1989–90, Michael B. Katz, who had earlier carried out pioneer work on what he calls "the language of poverty." Although Katz had by then moved on to other poverty research topics, being with him that year at the foundation enabled me to catch up with all his writings on my topic, and to learn from our frequent discussions. He is no more responsible than Eric Wanner for the direction in which I finally headed or for the book that came out of it, however.

Since university teaching is, the popular belief to the contrary, a full-time job, I had to wait for my next sabbatical from Columbia University to write this book. My work on it was also aided by semesters of research assistance from a number of graduate students, who helped in the library as well as in gathering the Nexis data that I analyze in chapter 2. These included Anthony Browne, Gwendolyn Dordick, Deborah A. Horden, Katherine Hughes, Katherine Kaufman, Helen-Maria Lekas, Andrew Pollack, and Valli Rajah. My son David Gans contributed suggestions and references, first as a college history major and then as a law school student. A number of other helpers—and interviewees—are mentioned in relevant footnotes; yet others remain anonymous because I promised them confidentiality. I am particularly grateful to the readers of the penultimate draft of this book, my wife Louise, always my most incisive reader, Peter Marris, Frances Piven, Lee Rainwater, and Joyce Seltzer; as well as to my editor, Steven Fraser; my copy editor, Ann Klefstad; and my production editor, Matt Shine. Their corrections of ideas, facts, and analyses were numerous; the mistakes that remain are all mine.

The actual writing of the book would not have been possible without some other staff members at the Russell Sage Foundation. These include, among others, Vivian Kaufman, who was my secretary that year, as well as Pauline Rothstein and her staff for superb library and related help. Jamie Gray, Sara Beckman, and Vivian Kaufman of the foundation trained me to write on the computer when I was there; Kun Deng helped further later at Columbia University. Thanks in part to them, I "typed" every draft of the manuscript by myself for the first time in four decades of book-writing, and enabled my manual typewriter to watch from the sidelines.

H. J. G.
February 1995

Introduction

For much of its history, America has been waging war against many of its poor people. It is a war waged with a variety of weapons, such as withholding the opportunities for decent jobs, schools, housing, and the necessities required for a modest version of the American way of life. Sometimes it is also a killing war, but more often, the war kills poor people's spirit and morale, and otherwise adds to the miseries resulting from sheer lack of money.

Since the beginning of the 1980s, the war against the poor has escalated, and it bids to escalate further. Unknowingly repeating old battle strategies, the leaders of this war continue to decrease the welfare benefits that go to poor mothers unable to work or find jobs, threaten to end welfare altogether, increase the punitive conditions under which all help is given, and fan further the hatred of the poor among the more fortunate classes.

Even so, the war against the poor could spread to members of these classes in the future. As more well-paying and secure jobs disappear from the American economy, many Americans will not find new ones, until an ever larger number of such workers, or their children, slide slowly but surely into poverty themselves.

This book reports especially on a part of the war that has not yet received much attention: the war of words—or of pejorative labels—that stereotype, stigmatize, and harass the poor by questioning their morality and their values. The labeling of the poor as moral inferiors, which has also been stepped up in the last fifteen years, blames them falsely for the ills of the American society and economy, reinforces their mistreatment, increases their misery, and further discourages their moving out of poverty.

The generic label is "undeserving," the undeserving poor being thought so morally deficient that they are not deserving of any economic or other assistance. Furthermore, their being labeled undeserving reduces their

chances of becoming either "deserving poor" or of escaping poverty altogether. The political chances of reviving effective antipoverty policy are also
reduced, since politicians or voters are rarely prepared to spend public
money for people who do not deserve help. The phrase "undeserving
poor" originated in England in the 1830s, and is not currently much used
there or here, but I use it because it is clear and brutally frank.[1]

In the past the undeserving poor were called "paupers," "vagrants," or
a "dangerous class," but new labels are invented all the time. Since the
1980s, the reigning label has been "underclass," a redefinition of an economic term originally introduced by the Swedish economist Gunnar
Myrdal in 1963 to describe the workers being forced out of a new economy now often called postindustrial. I shall say little more in this book
about the underclass as an economic term, about the sociological elabora-
tions added by William Julius Wilson and others, or about the extensive
social science research using this term, especially as a synonym for persistent and extreme poverty.[2]

Instead, I write about another "underclass," a behavioral term invented
by journalists and social scientists to describe poor people who are accused,
rightly or wrongly, of failing to behave in the "mainstream" ways of the
numerically or culturally dominant American middle class. This behavioral
definition denominates poor people who drop out of school, do not work,
and, if they are young women, have babies without benefit of marriage and
go on welfare. The behavioral underclass also includes the homeless, beggars and panhandlers, poor addicts to alcohol or drugs, and street criminals. Because the term is flexible, poor people who live in "the projects,"
illegal immigrants, and teenage gang members are often also assigned to
this underclass. Indeed, the very flexibility of the behavioral definition is
what lends itself to the term becoming a label that can be used to stigmatize
poor people, whatever their actual behavior.

The other critical shortcoming of the behavioral definition lies in its
casual assumption about the behavior of the poor. Mainstream culture
believes that the poor people who behave in the ways included in the definition do so because of moral deficiencies or bad values. I argue instead that
the causes of these behaviors, when they do occur, are in fact usually
poverty-related effects; that sometimes poor people are driven by the effects
of poverty to actions that violate their own morals and values. Poverty-
related effects or pressures develop because poor people lack the funds, the
economic security, and sometimes the social supports and emotional

strength, to behave in mainstream ways. This is why antipoverty programs to help them are in the end the only sure remedy for behavior thought to make people undeserving.

Admittedly, doing something about poverty has not been a fashionable idea in recent years, in part because more fortunate Americans demand, as they so often have in the past, that the poor first pull themselves up by bootstraps in reality available only to these same classes. Some also blame the failure of the imagined federal bootstraps of the 1960s, or what those of us involved in it then used to call the Skirmish on Poverty.

While most users of the behavioral underclass terminology believe in a real underclass, I think that there is no such class, and that it is merely today's popular label to stereotype poor people. Consequently, while I will be writing frequently about "the underclass," "the undeserving poor," and related labels, I always do so with the stipulation that I am writing about people *so labeled by others.*

Nevertheless, this is not a book about words and phrases. Words and actions are not the same, and I do not think society is a text. My interest in notions like "the underclass" and the "undeserving poor" is as words that justify actions—mostly those involving mistreatment and punishment of the poor. Still this is also not a book that determines who among the poor is really deserving or undeserving. Stereotypes usually contain a grain of truth amid their untruths, but they survive mainly because people want to believe them even if they are not true. Of course, poor unmarried teenage mothers exist in too large a number, but in most cases, their poverty, their motherhood, and their unmarried state are not the result of their moral shortcomings.

Furthermore, almost all of these teenagers are actually eighteen or nineteen when they become mothers, which is already young adulthood in the chronological world of the poor.[3] Many writers have corrected this and other stereotypes about the poor, but so far to no avail. As long as some people want to believe that the country is full of poor "babies having babies," the comparative handful of fifteen-, fourteen-, and even twelve-year-olds needed to satisfy true believers in the stereotype can be produced. What concerns me is why such stereotypes persist even though they have been corrected many times.

None of this is intended to deny the existence of undeserving poor people, but undeserving people also exist in all of the more fortunate classes and could certainly be identified if a moral census of the entire society were undertaken. I do not feel moral (or morally expert) enough to make judgments about whether entire categories of people are undeserving, and I doubt whether anyone else is either, but I do know that judging the poor in this way is unconscionable as long as the practice is not applied universally. Crime and violence are undeserving behavior whether committed by poor muggers or by manufacturers of defective products. If a poor mother who spends her days watching television instead of taking care of her child is undeserving, then so is the affluent one who shops all day and drags her child with her.

"Bad apples" exist at all social levels, and it takes only a few such apples to create problems for, and hurt the reputation of, the rest. As one moves up the socioeconomic ladder, however, the bad apples and their questionable behavior become less visible. Non-poor alcoholics can drink at home, and sometimes even on the job, but poor ones are often found in the gutter. Moreover, the morally dubious acts of the better-off frequently turn out to be perfectly legal, in accord with the "golden rule": the people who own the gold make the rules. And by the same principle, the people who own enough gold and cheat the Internal Revenue Service are sometimes able to negotiate for only a partial payment of what they owe, while the poor who cheat the welfare department immediately lose their welfare benefits, and may even go to jail.

People who are mistreated by their society are not always particularly nice people, whether they are rich or poor, but the poor are mistreated regularly. Perhaps there is more visible illegality among the poor because they are driven to it by the already mentioned poverty-related pressures. Some poor people do become street criminals, but middle-income people do not. There are, after all, no middle-class muggers. Poverty-related pressures also lead to unmarried motherhood, as they have for centuries, and will as long as poor men and women do not have access to decent and secure jobs and affordable housing so that they can marry. Few muggers really want to be muggers and most unmarried mothers would rather be married. Their values eschew illegitimacy, and most female welfare recipients have gone off welfare even if not permanently, because they found work or employed men to marry in their twenties or thirties.[4]

But perhaps the prime fact about poverty-related pressures is that they sharply restrict the choices of the poor, especially those that better-off people take for granted.[5] Even though poverty-related pressures may not be comprehensible to more fortunate people, they are very real. When poor women grow up among jobless men who cannot support a household, they have babies nonetheless, even if better-off people, who can postpone parenthood until they begin careers, charge them with immorality.

If a thousand poor young people compete for a hundred decent jobs that promise them a secure place in the mainstream economy, some of the remaining nine hundred who will stay jobless may eventually take their economic deprivation and their feeling of social uselessness out on themselves or on the rest of society, but do they really choose these solutions?

Mainstream society insists that they do choose, and that they are therefore, as a result of this presumed choice, unwilling to perform their responsibilities. Irresponsible poor people exist, of course, including some who are irresponsible out of revenge because they feel society has treated them irresponsibly. But others are irresponsible by mainstream standards because the conditions under which they live set different criteria for responsibility, which are imposed by the need to survive under conditions better-off Americans cannot even imagine. It is not always easy to be responsible with economic security and a decent income, but the majority of poor people who seek to abide by mainstream criteria of responsibility have it much harder: they have to do it with fewer material and social resources. Who, then, is morally expert enough to judge whether they are irresponsible because of moral failure, or because they live with poverty-related pressure and its effects?

Poverty-related pressure is in some respects like wartime combat, which almost no one survives without some aftereffects. What these effects are depends on the exact nature of the poverty (or combat), and that elusive human quality popularly called emotional strength, which is why different people come out of the same experience differently. Just as with combat, most poor people go through extreme poverty with only bitter memories, or with personal pains and private demons. Some, however, come out of the experience with levels of hopelessness, anger, or depression that produce publicly visible behavior that others, who may never have had to go through extreme poverty or combat, condemn offhandedly as immoral. Immoral it may be, but to attempt to solve it by condemnation, or by appeals for moral self-improvement, is neither worthy nor useful.[6]

These observations are not meant to justify street crime and other kinds of crime, violent or not, despite their causal ties to poverty-related pressure.

There can be no argument with prosecuting poor people who have broken the law, even if crime would be reduced more effectively if decent jobs and membership in the mainstream economy were available for the poor in the first place.

Indeed, effective crime reduction might help to reduce labeling of the poor as undeserving, for that label is not always just a whim or a prejudice of the affluent population.[7] When street crime is an *actual* threat to the safety of poor and nonpoor alike, the resulting fear of crime is understandable; it is even understandable when it is based on *imagined* threats. But the notion of the undeserving poor spreads like germs, to stigmatize a variety of economic, cultural, and behavior patterns of the law-abiding poor that do not really threaten anyone.

As I read through the literature on which this study is based, an ideology of undeservingness justifying the war against the poor became evident. That ideology, supported by some and perhaps even many Americans, can be summarized, with some oversimplification, in four parts:

1. If poor people do not behave according to the rules set by mainstream America, they must be undeserving. They are undeserving because they believe in and therefore practice bad values, suggesting that they do not want to be part of mainstream America culturally or socially. As a result of bad values and practices, undeservingness has become a major cause of contemporary poverty. If poor people gave up these values, their poverty would decline automatically, and mainstream Americans would be ready to help them, as they help other, "deserving" poor people.

2. The men among the undeserving poor are lazy or unable to learn the cultural importance of work and its requirements; in some cases, their bad values turn them into street criminals. If they really wanted to work, jobs would be available for them, and they would be able to earn their own income like other Americans.

3. The women among the undeserving poor have an unhealthy and immoral taste for early sexual activity and for having babies as adolescents. If they would wait until they were older, sufficiently mature, and ready to find work as well as husbands who wanted to work, they and their children would not need to be poor, and poverty might even end with the current generation.

4. If the undeserving poor do not alter their values and practices voluntarily, they must be forced to do so, for example by ending welfare payments, placing illegitimate children into foster care or orphanages, and by other kinds of punishment. Since some of these punishments can be perceived as benefitting their victims, such as curing their "dependency," likely negative effects, including the breaking up of families, increased homelessness, higher rates of physical and mental illness, can be ignored, even if the better-off population eventually has to pay some of the higher social and economic costs.

Although the more fortunate classes use this ideology to condemn the poor, I discovered that they also find the undeserving poor useful in a number of ways. For example, the very notion of the undeserving poor leads, directly and indirectly, to the creation of new job opportunities for the better-off populations in the many professions and occupations that exist to isolate, control, or punish the poor. Likewise, the undeservingness of the poor is used to emasculate them politically, thus excluding them, and their needs, from political institutions that are supposed to serve all citizens.

Two uses of the undeserving poor are most important. One is their treatment as scapegoats to blame for the social problems of the day. A manifestation of this is the way that benefits and other help to welfare recipients can be characterized as contributing to the high level of taxation, and even to the shortcomings of the economy.

Similarly, poor unmarried mothers can be charged with helping to further the changes in sexual behavior that have taken place in America since the 1960s, which are understood to be immoral and contrary to the values of mainstream Americans." Using "the sixties" as a touchstone also allows radical or "paleoliberal" "elites" to share the blame, as they can be accused of initiating these changes.

By making scapegoats of the poor for fundamental problems they have not caused nor can change, Americans can also postpone politically difficult and divisive solutions to the country's economic ills and the need to prepare the economy and polity for the challenges of the twenty-first century. In fact, many mainstream Americans have persuaded themselves to embrace, at least for the time being, an individualistic and anti-governmental populism that pays homage to traditional mainstream values even as others use these values to redistribute more income, wealth, and power to the classes that are already most affluent in these respects.

The second use of the undeserving poor may be even more critical. In an economy in which there may no longer be enough decent jobs for all who want to work, the people who are labeled morally undeserving can be forced out of the economy so as to preserve the jobs of the deserving citizens. And if the idea of a hereditarian or genetic underclass, which has exploded on the American scene as this introduction is being written, catches on again (no thanks to Richard Herrnstein and Charles Murray's *The Bell Curve*), then people who can be assigned to this underclass may be forced out of the economy on the grounds that they are biologically unable to perform as workers.

The liberal political values that underlie this introduction—and book—should be obvious, although I write with other values as well which seem to me eminently conservative, such as maintaining and maximizing the social peace. Also, I have never understood why trying to head off street crime with effective employment programs is liberal, and failing to do so with ineffective punishment is conservative. By the same token, isn't spending millions for prison-building that does not deter crime a good example of tax-and-spend liberalism—or, more to the point, a foolish waste of the public monies conservatives are supposed to prevent liberals from spending? In any case, the book is partly a work of advocacy, a contribution to antipoverty policy, but advocacy grounded in relevant empirical research whenever possible, eschewing Left romanticism about the poor as much as Right punitiveness.

The Organization of the Book

The book begins with an introduction to the sociology of labeling the poor, including the label-formation process itself, and the similarities evident in the many labels that have preceded the underclass over the last several centuries. Chapter 2 reports on how and why the behavioral underclass label was invented, on the people and processes that made it the buzzword it is today, the professionals who spread it, and the institutions that supported its legitimacy. Chapter 3 analyzes the dangers I see in the labels applied to the poor, both the ones specific to a technical-sounding word like "underclass" and the universal ones shared by most labels for the undeserving poor.

Chapter 4 moves beyond the underclass altogether, and examines the reasons for condemning some of the poor as undeserving, first in terms of the *actual* dangers and threats, such as street crime, that some poor people constitute for those labeling them, and then in terms of *imagined* threats that actually constitute most of the condemnation. The latter half of the chapter is devoted to describing a number of the diverse uses or functions that a notion of the undeserving poor performs for more fortunate Americans, some of which seem designed to guarantee the perpetuation of "the undeserving poor" and similar labels as well as of poverty itself.

Because undeservingness can only be eradicated by ending poverty, chapter 5 reviews the political strategy of antipoverty policy and discusses needed antipoverty programs, especially job-centered ones. Some "debunking" programs are also proposed to fight the labeling of the poor and the notion of "undeservingness" itself—programs that are rarely included in conventional antipoverty policy.

Since the newest changes in American capitalism, sometimes described as "jobless prosperity" or "job erosion," seem likely to generate new impoverished populations, the final chapter discusses job and other antipoverty policies for a twenty-first-century America in which decent full-time jobs could become increasingly scarce. The book ends with a variety of programs intended to maintain a viable American standard of living even when many if not most Americans may be working only part-time.

A final organizational note: in order to keep the social scientist's empirical data, as well as the required qualifications of the findings and the argument, out of the text, I have placed most of these in the endnotes. Some of the endnotes also supply further, sometimes extended, analytic detail about, and commentary on, what is in the text that I have added especially for researchers and students.

CHAPTER 1

Labeling the Poor

Everyday life is, among other things, a never-ending flow of moral surveillance. We all survey each other to see if actions live up to the norms and expectations we carry in our heads, since our subsequent behavior is shaped by our surveillance. That surveillance is also moral, since we judge rather than merely observe or study the situations and the people that make up everyday life.

When it comes to family, friends, co-workers, and others we trust, we normally assess actions. With people we know less well, however, especially strangers and entire groups, we quickly move from judging actions to judging "character," particularly as soon as a given number of their actions strike us as wrong.

With greater social distance, the judgments are apt to be based less on direct actual knowledge and more on indirect knowledge, including that gained from the media. And at times, judgments are based on *imagined* knowledge, which may come from stories and preconceived ideas that accord with the values and prejudices of the judges as well as with their position in society.[1]

TERMS, LABELS, AND LABELING

The resort to imagined knowledge is *labeling*, and the descriptions of people based on it are labels. Labels are used primarily to designate people as "deviant," different in a negative or pejorative sense because "these people," or some of their actions and beliefs, are beyond the pale of our own or even "mainstream" values.[2]

This book is limited to a discussion of negative labeling of, and labels for, the poor, although positive labels also exist for them, such as those used by some Marxists or Christians to romanticize the poor.[3] Moreover, labels have to be distinguished from *terms*, the latter aiming to describe and not to stigmatize.[4] Thus terms are usually less dangerous than labels, although when the same word is used, as in the case of the underclass, writers may mean "term" while readers choose to see "label." And some ostensibly descriptive terms, such as "welfare recipient" or "delinquent," describe people so often maligned that the terms have also become labels.[5]

Labeling and labels are in many respects similar to stereotyping and stereotypes, although many labels may be invented for the same general stereotype. When Walter Lippman first described stereotypes as "pictures in our heads," he conceived them to be positive or negative. In today's conventional usage of the term, however, stereotypes are negative, and so are labels, for the same reason: they may extrapolate from small kernels of truth about some people to large imagined untruths that are applied to everyone in a group. Such stereotypes are applied to many groups in our society, affluent and poor. Thus, for example, used-car sales personnel have long been labeled in this fashion, but as long as used cars are needed, their sellers can cope with their negative image. The poor are far more vulnerable, and racial minorities among them even more so.

Negative labels rarely stereotype only behavior; more often they transform and magnify it into a character failing. As a result, welfare recipients become defective personalities or deficient moral types; that they are also family members, churchgoers, or neighbors is immaterial. Indeed, one of the purposes of labels is to strip labeled persons of other qualities. That a welfare recipient may be a fine mother becomes irrelevant; the label assumes that she, like all others in her category, is a bad mother, and she is given no chance to prove otherwise.

Labels may do worse damage: they may sometimes force the labeled to behave in ways defined by and in the labels. For example, if an adolescent boy comes from a poor single-parent family, he may be stereotyped as having grown up without male supervision and role models, and therefore thought likely to become delinquent. Once he has done something wrong, even as a child, he is labeled as a possible delinquent, is thereafter more apt to be picked up by the police, and, once he has begun to develop the inevitable arrest record that goes with such pickups, may also be labeled as a delinquent by the courts. The more often he is treated as a delinquent, the more likely that nondelinquent opportunities may slowly but surely be closed to him, and he could end up becoming a delinquent because he has no other choices.[6] Ex-convicts who are not hired for respectable jobs face this problem continually.

"Delinquency" is also a penal term and, like some of the other terms and labels assigned to the poor, subjects those so described or labeled to legal punishment as well as stigmatization. In nineteenth-century England and America, people labeled as paupers could be sent to jails or workhouses. Vagrants, vagabonds, and other labels attached to wandering poor people were almost always penal concepts as well. Today, the word "pauper" is antiquarian, but vagrants can still be jailed and welfare recipients can lose their benefits if they disobey the rules or even the government officials on whom they are dependent.

The terms and labels that are assigned to the poor and that designate them as undeserving may be obstacles preventing their escape from poverty. Ironically enough, at the same time as they are held back by labels, poor people are expected to take advantage of job and self-improvement opportunities to which they may not have access, including those from which they have been barred by these very labels. The labels may be only words, but they are words that can become powerful sticks and stones.

Labels are public and private, polite and profane, and tailored to the habits of America's various social classes. The terms and labels to be considered here are primarily used in the public communication of the upper-middle-class and professional strata, for example in magazines such as *Newsweek* or *Time*.[7] Occasionally elite words are adopted by other classes. "Underclass" is a good example, for it appears not only in elite newspapers such as the *New York Times* but in popular ones—*Newsday*, for example.

The public media limit themselves to politely worded labels, but less polite terms and labels for the poor can be found in the private communications of all classes. These are hard to study sociologically, precisely because they are impolite as well as private.[8] This being America, with its taboo against class terminology, popular private communication uses racial and ethnic labels far more often than class ones, although these are usually reserved for low-income people—from "wop" to "spic" and "nigger."[9] Jonathan Rieder reported the middle- and working-class white residents of the New York neighborhood of Canarsie talking about poor blacks—toward whom they were extremely hostile—as "the element," "animals," and "boons."[10]

More polite words are also used, such as the standard in-group/out-group dichotomy of "us" and "them"; indeed, a version of the latter, "these people," is generally used as an only moderately impolite pejorative for disliked minorities. But even such words are not accessible to a study like mine, which is based largely on the professional literature, news stories, and interviews with journalists and others.[11]

Professional researchers, however, try to shun even polite labels, and come to consider their labels to be analytic or technical terms or concepts.[12] Nonetheless, when the terms mainly accuse or celebrate an entire population, they become labels, whatever else they are called.[13]

WAYS OF LABELING THE POOR: A HISTORICAL SURVEY

Labels with which to stigmatize the poor have probably existed since the emergence of hierarchical societies, but it suffices to look back to the end of the medieval era to understand the historical context of today's labels.[14] Since then, the poor have regularly been dichotomized, at least by critics of the poor and formulators of laws about poverty, into two groups. The first encompassed the sick and old, as well as the working poor, and was considered good or worthy of help, while the second, able-bodied nonworking poor people, have been deemed unworthy.

America has inherited much of its labeling tradition from England, which seems to have invented the modern version.[15] The first users of the distinction between worthy and unworthy poor people have never been identified, but it began to be applied regularly when responsibility for the English poor was given over from the centralized church to locally governed parishes starting in about the fourteenth century.[16] The words "deserving" and "undeserving" were actually invented much later, again in England, in connection with discussions concerning the 1834 Poor Law.[17]

Not surprisingly, labels for the various kinds of deserving poor are virtually nonexistent, although at this writing "working poor" is becoming an increasingly positive label in mainstream American culture.[18] Conversely, the supply of labels for the undeserving poor, as of that for stigmatized racial and ethnic groups, is plentiful.

My historical survey of the labels for the undeserving poor is cursory and meant to be merely illustrative.[19] The label with the greatest longevity may be "pauper," although over the years it underwent several changes in meaning. In the fourteenth century it was used to describe the mobile poor.[20] Then it became a synonym for deserving poor women; later the women became undeserving, but in the nineteenth century the word was also used to label the impoverished men and women who would, in today's medical vocabulary, be considered depressed, and in the punitive vocabulary lazy or shiftless.[21]

I will list here only some of the other prominently used labels of the past, with the help of a nineteenth-century classificatory scheme for the undeserving poor: "defective, dependent, and delinquent."[22] The trichotomy is not mutually exclusive, for some of the labels that classified the poor as culturally, morally, and biologically defective also treated them as criminal (or delinquent) and vice versa.

Despite the hostility the better-off classes have long felt toward poor people who were not supporting themselves, there are not many words for those solely or primarily dependent; in rough historical order, these include "paupers," "hard-core poor" (although people with this label are also viewed as stubbornly, almost delinquently poor), and (today) "welfare dependent" and "illegal immigrant." The latter is a good example of a term that has become a label.

The largest number of labels seems to have been invented for the various kinds of poor people deemed defective. These include, again in approximate historical order: paupers (as shiftless); debauched; hopeless classes; "ne'er-do-wells"; dregs; residue; residuum; feebleminded; morons; white trash; school dropouts; culturally deprived or disadvantaged; and poor in the culture of poverty.[23] To this list must be added the class of labels that view the defective poor as dangers to public health, referring to their ragged and dirty state, their living in slums, and the like. This set of labels was particularly important before and during the nineteenth century, although some overtones of past labels survive in today's AIDS victims and needle-using substance-users.

The delinquents include the politically threatening: the dangerous classes, *Lumpenproletariat*, and sometimes, rabble and mob.[24] Charles Loring Brace used the term "dangerous class" in America for homeless children, also called street urchins or street arabs, because he feared what they would do politically when they were adults.[25] The remainder of the labels for delinquents mainly describe street people, criminal and otherwise, although this informal survey found few older words for this label. Today's are all familiar, and include "bums," "substance abusers" (including the earlier "dissolute" and "debauched"), "gang members," "muggers," "beggars," and "panhandlers"—although some of these also double as descriptive terms. In the 1980s, "babies having babies" became popular, and in the 1990s, "illegitimacy" was revived to call particular attention to the poor single-parent family.[26]

Two further types of labels deserve separate attention. The *mobile* or *transient* poor have been considered delinquent since at least medieval times, on the assumption that, being mobile, they were free from local social control, and thus expected to turn to crime, mostly economic but also sexual and political, during their wanderings. The list includes "vagabonds," "vagrants," "bums" once more, "street urchins" or "street arabs," "tramps," "shiftless," "lodgers," "hobos," "drifters," "loiterers," and, more recently, "the homeless."[27] The mobile poor were particularly threatening in the centuries before the invention of the police, and most European languages include labels for them.[28]

The other label type might be called *class failures*, for some labels, including a few already listed above, treat the undeserving poor as being below, or having fallen out of, the class structure.[29] Among these are "residue," "residuum," "dregs," and "lower-lower class"; but the label that banishes the poor from the class hierarchy most literally is "the underclass."

All of the labeled are inevitably charged with the failure to adhere to one or more mainstream values by their behavior, but this is why they are considered undeserving in the first place. The labels lend themselves to many other kinds of analyses and distinctions, for example whether they pertain to individuals, such as school dropouts, or to collectivities, like a mob.[30]

A more significant distinction that deserves systematic study is the extent to which labels are either race-blind or racially pejorative. Although most labels for the poor are literally neutral with respect to ethnicity and race, they have actually been meant mainly for immigrants and dark-skinned people in the United States and elsewhere, even if most of those fitting the labels probably came, and still come, from the majority population. In the nineteenth century, a high proportion of those labeled in England were Irish, while the Americans who were labeled were immigrants, many initially also Irish.[31] Later in the century the labels were transferred to Southern European Catholics and Eastern European Jews, who were typically described as "swarthy races," while Italian immigrants were also called "guineas" because of their dark skin. Even before these immigrants had been administered the intelligence tests that were newly invented to stigmatize and exclude them, many were deemed of low intelligence or even feeble-minded by the eugenicists, who were almost all white Anglo-Saxon Protestants (WASPs). But WASPs were not the only ones to conduct racial labeling; a nineteenth-century American magazine intended for German-Jewish readers described the newly arriving Eastern European Jewish immigrants as "miserable *darkened* Hebrews."[32]

Although some labels have cut across gender, criminal and mobile ones have been mostly, if not completely, reserved for men, while women have been labeled with economic, familial, and sexual failings.[33] Mothers have to be supported with tax funds as paupers or welfare recipients, but despite the existence of home relief for men, poor men are rarely thought to be welfare dependents. There is not even a regularly used label for their inability to be stable breadwinners, probably because the better-off fear them mainly as potentially violent street criminals. Conversely, although the young men are periodically blamed for failing to pay child support, they are rarely labeled for being unmarried parents, perhaps because of the traditional sexual double standard. Those men who impregnate several adolescent women are sometimes labeled "studs," but the women involved have always borne the brunt of exclusively pejorative labeling.[34]

Specific and Umbrella Labels

Labels and terms must also be distinguished by whether they refer to specific shortcomings or to general ones, which might be called umbrella labels because they include a large number of faults under one cover.[35] Umbrella terms are not limited to the poor; more often they are widely known popular words that summarize or lump many technical ones. Thus, "schizophrenia" and "cancer" are widely used umbrellas in popular medical writing even as medical specialists and researchers try to insist on the differences between various kinds of cancers and types of schizophrenia.[36]

Most labels for the poor have been specific, although the people to which they are given are sometimes thought so dangerous or flawed that people labeled with one word are accused of having other faults, until finally the label is broadened into an umbrella one. Michael Katz rightly describes this process as "the interchangeability of defects." "Welfare recipient" is a good example, for while recipients are accused mainly of economic dependency, they are also labeled as lacking "family values"—failing to get married, being sexually promiscuous, raising school dropouts and delinquent youngsters, as well as giving birth to another generation of unmarried mothers who will turn welfare dependence into a permanent state.

Umbrella labels accomplish this process of interchangeability and expansion automatically, for they are of sufficiently vast scope to cover with one word almost all the sins the undeserving poor can be accused of committing. Two other characteristics further distinguish umbrella labels from specific ones. First, they ascribe the behavior of the poor people involved to a prime cause, usually attached to the label itself—for example, genetic impairment in the case of the feebleminded and internalization for the culture of poverty. Second, these causes are powerful enough so that they are perceived to function permanently. As a result, the deficiencies summarized in the label are passed on automatically to future generations. Three major umbrella labels have been popular in the twentieth century: feeblemindedness, the culture of poverty, and the underclass.

THE LABEL-FORMATION PROCESS

Putting an end to the labels unfairly assigned to the poor cannot be accomplished without understanding the origins of labels and the processes, as well as the agents and agencies, responsible for the formation, communication, popularity, and eventual disappearance of these labels.[37]

The process begins with the *label-makers*, who invent the label, or reinvent, redefine, or refine an old one, and the reasons, as well as precipitating events, if any, that lead them to do what they do. Many label-makers may actually intend to describe rather than to label, but later historical hindsight makes it clear that they played a major role in making the label, and that the reasons they chose to use new words help in understanding why these labels are then used by others.

In this day and age, most label-makers are professionals: academics and other researchers, journalists, or practitioners working with the poor—or against them. In fact, a significant number of the label-makers recent enough to be identifiable have been social scientists.[38] The most famous of these is undoubtedly Karl Marx, who translated the Victorian phrase "ragged poor" into *Lumpenproletariat.*

Effective label-makers need to perform, or delegate, two other tasks. They have to be alarm-raisers or *alarmists,* able to persuade their audiences that their new word identifies a population that that audience already thinks or is prepared to believe is responsible for alarming problems.[39] Alarmists are most effective when they are good at attention-seeking and -getting, which is why they often come from storytelling occupations such as writing, journalism, reform, and politics.[40] Label-makers also have to be or have access to *counters,* who can supply numbers indicating that the labeled population is sufficiently large to be alarming. Such famous nineteenth-century students of the London poor as Charles Booth and Henry Mayhew are classic figures in the history of alarmist counting.

Like other producers of symbolic goods, label-makers have to put together, intentionally or otherwise, the right ingredients to result in a popular label, and not all these ingredients are under their control. The label must alarm or at least gain the attention of many people, "grabbing" them, as journalists like to put it.[41] In order to grab, the label must possess metaphoric and perhaps graphic qualities that signify or symbolize danger, either to personal safety or to mainstream values.

Also, labels should refer to the failings of already feared or disliked people, and not to processes or concepts—which is why "feebleminded" was a long-lasting label, and "culture of poverty" was not. Above all, successful labels must be credible, and while believability is up to the believer, a vague label is more popular than an unambiguous one. Today, so is a single-word label, short enough to fit a headline. "Underclass" fits all these requirements nicely.

Different times probably require different labels, and there may even be times when no label for the undeserving poor is needed, either because an old one is being used or because full employment and affluence eliminate poverty as a subject of public or private concern. Perhaps other pressing social problems then preoccupy the general public, although there seem to be few problems for which the poor cannot be blamed.

At times, a new label only becomes popular after an old one has lost favor, and at times there is competition between alternative labels. Most often, however, the *sorting* or *replacement* process is gradual enough to be less than openly competitive, and in most cases it is probably invisible, with the people who do the sorting testing new words they have heard on each other before using them in public. If the tests are successful, public tryouts can begin.[42]

Normally, the new label is of the same genre as the old one, as when post–Civil War America invented "tramp" to replace earlier European words such as "vagrant" and "vagabond." At times, however, there is a change of genre as well, when changing conditions, or innovations in scientific or popular ideology, are expressed in label replacements. This is demonstrated, for example, in the shift from labels like "pauper" and "tramp" to those in the "feebleminded" genre, reflecting the new belief that the undeservingness of the poor was caused mainly by heredity, and not just by morality or lack of it.

Even the most popular labels do not remain static. In our time at least, they are communicated mainly by various kinds of journalists, who, unlike academics, rarely look up or cite established definitions, and must also adapt their definitions to the particular stories for which they use the label. A vicious mugger cannot be defined into the same underclass as a welfare dependent.[43] As a result, labels undergo *broadening,* in which they may develop subsidiary meanings, or be attached to other populations.

The actual survival of labels depends on communicators and willing media.[44] Journalists, from reporters to columnists and editors, also need events and news "pegs" to justify use of a label. There is no a priori reason why labels should be communicated mainly by journalists, however, since experts, popularizers, church-related or secular moralists, politicians, penal and other officials dealing with the poor, and writers of print or electronic fiction could also do so. In fact, most successful innovations are actually communicated by word-of-mouth, even if now also electronically transmitted on computer networks, among professional and lay opinion leaders— and by opinion "followers" who make word-of-mouth actually work.

Above all, establishing new labels in popular communication requires the willingness of *label users,* who are in this day and age often audiences, to attend to a new word and sometimes to give up old labels to which they may have become accustomed. But the greater the willingness of audiences to pay attention to the innovation, the greater also the subsequent efforts of communicators to use the label repeatedly, in the hope of holding on to the audience's often elusive attention.

Ancillary to but important in the label-making and communicating processes are *legitimators,* whose pronouncements and credentials justify the use of the label, particularly if it is brand new or controversial.[45] Legitimators are now often researchers or other experts, but they can also be lay people, particularly if they are popular politicians, best-selling authors, or, in the 1990s, radio talk show hosts.

Direct legitimators participate personally, by speaking, writing, or letting their words be used directly for justification purposes.[46] Indirect or supportive legitimators do the research that can be used to count the labeled, or to suggest that they are alarming. In some ways the most important supportive legitimators are the funders, who pay for the research, conferences, and publications that allow researchers, and the direct legitimators used by journalists, to do their work. The funders may be rich private individuals, foundations, and the government, and their power and prestige can add to the effectiveness of their other legitimating efforts.

The ever-present participants in all of these processes are the *labeled*, the poor people who are the silent, unasked, unwilling targets of the label.

Label formation does not operate in a vacuum, and the ultimate explanation for the success of a label must eventually include what I think of as *contextual conditions*. These range from individuals to powerful agencies to impersonal forces, but also include those set in motion by traumatic events such as plagues, depressions, and wars. These often create worries that make a population susceptible and receptive to a label. To return once more to that distinctively American word "tramp," it was first invented to describe the ex–Civil War soldiers "tramping" around the country looking for work.

The forces, agencies, and individuals that make up contextual conditions can come from a variety of sectors of society, but they are usually the sufficient factor in the label-making process. Without contextual conditions or changes in them that lead the better-off to worry, they will not resort to labeling the poor. And when these conditions stop operating, the label dies. Thus "residuum," the prevailing turn-of-the-century English label for the persistently jobless and poor that crowded the cities, disappeared almost instantaneously at the beginning of World War I, when the labeled people found jobs in the war economy.[47]

The "residuum" vanished with the arrival of full employment, but new labels for the poor arise from time to time and others disappear without such dramatic changes in contextual conditions. Typically labels collect enough enemies—who might be called "label-killers"—over time so that they eventually lose their credibility.[48]

Strangely enough, dead labels are occasionally revived, decades later, by *romanticizers* who resurrect and transform them to celebrate one or another virtue, imagined or real, of the past, at which point once-negative labels become positive. Tramps and hoboes are now viewed as romantic figures, and slowly but surely, so are hippies, once the undeserving middle-class poor of the 1960s. Popular American writers and filmmakers have also romanticized foreign preindustrial people and cultures—the Bushmen of the Kalahari, for example, who are victims of labeling at home, and their peers in the Amazon who are, like the Bushmen, being killed or driven out of their jungle homes.[49]

LABEL FORMATION BEFORE "UNDERCLASS": "FEEBLEMINDEDNESS" AND "THE CULTURE OF POVERTY"

The label-formation process that eventually led to "feeblemindedness" had its beginnings with Francis Galton, Charles Darwin's cousin, who initiated family heredity studies in 1860 in part because of his concerns about the survival of the white race.[50] Galton used the studies to justify his advocacy of eugenic policies to protect the racial, and presumably the cultural and political, dominance of the English elite.[51] His concerns and terminology also caught on quickly in America, where a number of amateur researchers and social workers (in today's terminology) took over from English biologists and statisticians, conducting genealogical studies of very poor families who appeared to demonstrate the disastrous moral effects of heredity.[52]

The first American genealogical researcher, Richard Dugdale, was mainly concerned with identifying hereditary criminal and sexually deviant tendencies. A well-born reformer, Dugdale began his family research serendipitously, for while on an official prison reform project, he met several members of a rural upstate New York family he called the Jukes. This encounter persuaded Dugdale to find as many Jukes as possible, and to enumerate what he viewed as their hereditary defects. He published his results in 1875, and the case history research method he used would be followed by his successors for the next half century.[53]

Unlike the self-styled "scientific reformers" of the period, Dugdale does not seem to have been particularly interested in punishing the poor. He considered himself a sociologist, but not a eugenicist, identifying himself as a Lamarckian who thought that environmental reforms, especially moral and educational ones, could somehow help the poor. "Heredity," he wrote, "is the preponderating factor . . . but it is, even then, capable of marked modification for better or worse by the character of the environment."[54]

The term "feeblemindedness" was not introduced until the twentieth century, toward the end of the family studies period. First used in England, the term was made famous in America by Henry Goddard, a Ph.D. in psychology who worked part of his life as a superintendent of facilities for the retarded, and may have become a label-maker as a result of his best-selling books.[55] Goddard is probably best known for his extensive study of a New Jersey family whose alleged feeblemindedness he traced from the time of the Revolutionary War to the twentieth century, and which he published in 1912 as *The Kallikak Family*. He considered his major opus, however, to be his 1914 book, *Feeblemindedness*.[56] It sought to demonstrate the feeblemindedness of criminal and deviant Southern and Eastern European immigrants, and it appeared just as America's anti-immigrant sentiments were reaching a peak.[57] In the book, Goddard gave the term its umbrella quality, tracing all of the period's "dependent, defective, and delinquent" behavior patterns and people to feeblemindedness, using simple correlational statistics to make broad causal claims. As a result, Goddard could justify feeblemindedness as an umbrella label for the undeserving poor.

Needless to say, Goddard did not consider himself a label-maker. He saw himself as doing scientific research and was described as a dedicated researcher by those who later wrote about him. He was also, however, a dedicated member of the eugenicist movement advocating policies to root out biological inferiority, which may have helped taint his research. For example, Goddard's major fieldworker, being as ignorant of proper fieldwork methods as she was of proper clinical diagnosis, later reported that she had determined feeblemindedness from the appearance and the living arrangements of the Kallikaks; and she constructed the family genealogy and the alleged misdeeds of its members, not to mention the mental state of the dead ones, mainly from area gossip.[58] Many years later, Stephen Jay Gould discovered that Henry Goddard had doctored the photographs of the Kallikaks that he included in his book to make them look deranged and threatening.[59]

Whether as label or "scientific" term, "feeblemindedness" had an immense effect on America. It, and the eugenicists who publicized it, helped bring about, among other things, intelligence tests used to exclude poor people from a variety of opportunities, sterilization of allegedly feebleminded people, and the 1925 legislation that virtually ended immigration from countries other than Northern and Western Europe until 1965.[60]

The feeblemindedness label, like the eugenics movement itself, lasted until the end of World War II, when its claims were rejected by systematic research and its ideas by the revulsion against Nazi race ideology and policy, although sterilization of the poor continued in some American states until the 1970s. Several class-biased intelligence tests have survived until today, and semblances of old racist thought returned in the 1960s with the attempt by scattered psychologists and others to find genetic evidence attesting to differences in intelligence between blacks and whites. The development of sociobiology, and then of basic and applied genetic research, has subsequently resulted in a variety of claims about the genetic causes of poverty-related behavior patterns.[61] In the fall of 1994, the publication of several books correlating, like Goddard's, poverty, crime, and a variety of poverty-related behavior patterns with intelligence, heredity, and even genes, and then treating these correlations as causes, has broadened the underclass label to invent a hereditary or genetic underclass.[62]

The Culture of Poverty

The history of the culture of poverty, the other umbrella label to precede the underclass, is very different. Although it also had scholarly beginnings, it was associated with a single researcher, the anthropologist Oscar Lewis. He defined it as a quasi-pathological culture besetting an estimated 20 percent of America's poor that consisted of sixty-two "traits," among them all of the typical behavioral and personality characteristics used to describe and label the undeserving poor. In a much-quoted phrase that highlights his conception, Lewis pointed out that "The culture of poverty . . . tends to *perpetuate itself from generation to generation because of its effects on the children.* By the time the slum children are age six or seven, they have usually absorbed the basic values . . . *and are not psychologically geared to take full advantage of . . . increased opportunities that may occur in their lifetime.*[63]

Lewis had originally developed what he thought to be a concept in connection with, and to pull together, his research in Mexico.[64] By the mid-1960s he had become world-famous for *La Vida* and other books, and the response to his public lectures on his work in Mexico and Puerto Rico, which he undertook at the time of the War on Poverty, encouraged him to

Americanize his idea, and to repeat it frequently.[65] Partly because of his responsiveness to journalists, he saw it turn into a pejorative label in the 1960s. Perhaps because it was an impersonal phrase rather than a single word, it never became widely used, however, and both it and Lewis's original concept began to fade away after Lewis's premature death in 1970.

Nonetheless, during the 1960s it played a major role in the ideological and policy battles over the causes of poverty and over the deservingness of the poor among liberals and conservatives. At the end of that decade, and after the ghetto uprisings of the period, Lewis's phrase may have helped to influence the arrival of the academic term "lower-class culture," which became an occasional label for journalists in the 1970s as a synonym for "the undeserving poor," until it was replaced by "underclass" in the 1980s.

The contextual conditions that created a demand for a new label during the turbulence of the 1960s was mainly responsible for turning "the culture of poverty" into a pejorative label. Lewis was helpful, however, though perhaps unintentionally, in the transformation, for he never turned the culture of poverty into a tested scientific concept. Being unable but also unwilling to analyze the immense amount of data he had collected to develop his concept, but also being reluctant to drop the term, Lewis relied instead on dramatic illustrations from his case studies—just what journalists and his lecture audiences needed to use it as a label.[66] "The culture of poverty" also lent itself to becoming a synonym for undeservingness, because Lewis could be read to claim, as in the above-quoted excerpt, that the culture made the poor responsible for remaining poor, and he could thus be interpreted, as he often was, as blaming the victims for their own poverty. Lewis did not help matters by the resemblance of many of his sixty-two "traits" to features of earlier labels, including "feeblemindedness." Moreover, Lewis seemed to compare the poor in the culture of poverty invidiously to an unmentioned middle class, and to several (named) foreign poor populations. Once, he even claimed that "most primitive people have achieved a higher level of socio-cultural organization than our modern urban slum dwellers."[67]

Whether or not Lewis intended to be deliberately pejorative, he also described himself as a socialist, who believed that the culture of poverty could only be eradicated by socialism.[68] But on the other hand, like some other anthropologists of his time, Lewis was fascinated by psychiatry, and thus Lewis believed that the culture could also be eradicated by stationing psychiatric social workers in the homes of the poor living in the culture of poverty.[69]

Ironically enough, the first writer to use Lewis's phrase to describe American poverty was an active socialist, Michael Harrington, who referred to it several times in his best-selling 1962 book, *The Other America*, which helped to initiate the War on Poverty. Harrington's "culture of poverty" was an economic term, however, which paid little attention to "culture" or to its transmission to later generations. Instead, Harrington indicated emphatically and repeatedly how the economy and social structure limited the opportunities of the poor and produced a culture of poverty they could not choose and did not want.[70] While Harrington said what the socialist part of Lewis might have wanted to say, giving Lewis the opportunity to use Harrington's analysis to support his own term, Lewis himself was angry at Harrington for borrowing and "misinterpreting" his concept, and instead dwelt on its cultural—that is, behavioral—features.[71] As the next chapter suggests, "underclass" also first came to public attention as an economic term and then became a behavioral label.

CHAPTER 2

The Invention of the
Underclass Label

The story of the making of "the underclass" into a behavioral term and label is worth telling because it can supply information about much of the label-formation process not available for past labels: who made it happen, how, and why. The basic story is that of a professor's newly minted term being transformed into a popular label in a process that was helped along by social scientists and journalists, among others. Although the label "grabbed" nearly everyone it touched, including social scientists and journalists, it would not have become as widely known as it has become without a variety of contextual conditions, including changes in the U.S. economy and political climate during the 1980s. The end product was the reinvigoration of an ancient stereotype of the poor that only needed to be stimulated by a new label to grab the better-off population.[1]

The term "underclass" was coined by Gunnar Myrdal, the Swedish (or, more correctly, multinational) economist, who used it in a small book for the general American public, *Challenge to Affluence*, published in 1963.[2] In predicting a pessimistic future for the American economy, Myrdal used "under-class" as an economic term to describe the victims of deindustrialization and what would later be called the postindustrial economy, but both Myrdal's use of the term and the analysis of these economic victims was brief.

Myrdal's fullest definition of "under-class" is "an unprivileged class of unemployed, unemployables and underemployed who are more and more hopelessly set apart from the nation at large and do not share in its life, its ambitions and its achievements."[3] Myrdal did not describe this population's race, its gender, or its cultural behavior other than to imply its lack of hope. Myrdal mentioned "the under-class" directly only three further times in his book—and indirectly twice more—and each time mainly to repeat his initial thesis: an under-class, consisting of people forced out of the labor market by the changes in the economy he foresaw, was being created. The book's main agenda was to propose economic reform to solve the problems he saw in the American future; only one of these perceived problems was the formation of an underclass.

Myrdal actually reinvented "under-class," borrowing a now obsolete nineteenth-century Swedish word for lower class, *underklass*, and adding a hyphen.[4] Myrdal said nothing pejorative about the under-class, although many nineteenth-century Swedish writers had used the term as a synonym for the undeserving poor. There was one major exception to this prevailing usage: the most famous writer to use *underklass*, the playwright August Strindberg, stressed the virtues of its members as those of his mother, who came from it.[5] Strindberg also offered a more general and sociological conception of the term, writing, for example, "Society is an invention of the *overklass* in order to keep the *underklass* below it."[6]

Challenge to Affluence was published during the post–World War II era of affluence. Also, Myrdal was then writing mostly about international economic issues, which may explain why he, and his book, received little notice in America.[7] Myrdal used "under-class" only once more after *Challenge to Affluence*, in 1970, and died in 1987, just before it reached its peak as a pejorative behavioral term.[8]

"UNDERCLASS" TURNS RACIAL AND BEHAVIORAL

In 1963, there seemed to be no demand for a new label for the undeserving poor. The eugenicists' writings had been firmly rejected, and the European immigrants so feared by them had become Americanized and were for the most part ensconced in the middle class. Michael Harrington's *The Other America* had been published in 1962, but any comparison of his notion of the culture of poverty to Myrdal's under-class could only have suggested that the two writers agreed almost entirely on the nature, causes, and effects of poverty. And since Harrington's book was widely reviewed even before President Kennedy read it, it should not be surprising that Myrdal's term was virtually unknown.

That situation continued for about the next decade. The mid-1960s, however, brought the ghetto uprisings in Watts, and then in Newark, Detroit, and elsewhere, and the subsequent liberalization of welfare eligibility and welfare benefits. These events and others generated a backlash, one element of which was a new phase of writing critical of the black poor. It set the groundwork for the emergence of "the underclass" as both a racial term and a pejorative label.

Actually the shift from a nonracial underclass to a racial one took place as early as 1964, when Tom Kahn, an associate of Michael Harrington, used the term, now without Myrdal's hyphen, to write about poverty and inequality.[9] But Kahn, Lee Rainwater, I, and a few others who wrote in passing about the black underclass either followed Myrdal's definition of economic victimhood, or treated "underclass" as a new term for extreme or persistent poverty.[10] That "underclass" also made occasional appearances in a handful of other publications, including the February 1969 issue of the social science magazine *Trans-action,* a publication written to reach a popular audience.[11] As a result, the word may have begun to become known to some journalists and other readers, although there was little evidence of any wider use.

Actually, three other terms were more often used in reaction to the civil disorders of the 1960s—and all were behavioral, pejoratively used labels that blamed poor blacks for their actual or imagined behavior. Two first appeared in, and were borrowed from, Daniel P. Moynihan's 1965 "Moynihan Report." Moynihan used the first, "the female-headed black family," to identify a major cause of wider black problems.[12] The second term was a phrase, "tangle of pathology," which Moynihan took from E. Franklin Frazier's analysis of the black poor.[13]

The third term was an old sociological concept, "lower class," which Edward Banfield redefined as a behavioral label in 1968 in a frequently mentioned article entitled "Rioting Mainly for Fun and Profit."[14] In addition to the theme announced in the article's title, Banfield wrote critically about a "lower class" that lacked especially the ability to defer gratifications and to plan for the future.[15] These shortcomings were of venerable vintage; they had been mentioned as behavioral failures by British and

American writers at least since the nineteenth century.[16] Banfield's term probably never moved far out of the academy, although journalists occasionally used it in their articles in the 1970s until they discovered "underclass."[17]

In 1973 Myrdal's word reappeared but with a further transformation: it became a *behavioral* term as well as a racial one. The new definition first appeared in an article in the conservative journal *The Public Interest*, in a wide-ranging and often thoughtful description of the physical and social deterioration of the South Side Chicago neighborhood of Woodlawn.[18]

Most of the article concerned the out-migration of Woodlawn's middle-class and working-class blacks, the unprofitability of housing the black poor, and the arson that was slowly destroying the area. In addition, it focused on the gang activity, violence, and "criminal terror" carried out by young black males, especially those active in violent criminal gangs, whom the article called a "destructive residual underclass."[19] The authors did not supply a formal definition or a more detailed description of the underclass, and sometimes also used the term to refer to unspecified others. They supplied little empirical evidence about this underclass other than telling the story of the best-known criminal gang, the Blackstone Rangers.[20] Nonetheless, they felt confident in explaining that the underclass was "largely the product of urban welfare policies, which institutionalize poverty, stifle upward mobility, and discourage stable family formation for a large number of blacks."[21]

With hindsight the article can be considered a first step in the label-making process that took place later in the decade, although unlike the later label-makers its authors resorted only tangentially to the rhetoric and stereotyping associated with labeling per se. These authors were Winston Moore, a correctional psychologist, who then worked as an executive in Chicago's correctional system; Charles P. Livermore, a Chicago youth-work executive with a social work background and previous familiarity with Chicago gangs; and George F. Galland, Jr., a law student at the University of Chicago, which abuts Woodlawn.[22] Livermore had chosen the term "underclass"—he had read or heard it somewhere—although none of the authors knew any of the local social scientists and journalists subsequently identified with the term.[23]

As Livermore pointed out, not only did the term appeal to him—"a light went on" is how he put it—but he felt it fit the Woodlawn criminal gang scene better than Banfield's "lower class," which he also used in the article. In fact, he added "residual" to "underclass" because he felt a class term, and class analysis in general, were insufficient to explain the violent and terrorizing behavior of a small group of young criminals. For Livermore, then, "underclass" was a new term, previously unknown and undefined, and thus useful for understanding what he felt to be a distinctive situation.[24]

The article's publication in a prominent conservative journal was no accident. Not only did its critique of government welfare-state policies follow the basic *Public Interest* line, but Livermore was familiar with the journal and some of its editors, including Daniel P. Moynihan, whom he described as an "acquaintance."[25]

With this article, the double transformation of Myrdal's economic and race-blind term into a behavioral and pejorative label for a poor racial minority had begun. Looking backward, such a transformation should not have been unexpected, because it has happened to many of the terms that preceded "the underclass." "Pauper," for example, was a synonym for the poor supplicant and thus a term of economic victimhood before it turned into a synonym for dependency and shiftlessness. Likewise, Michael Harrington had written about the American culture of poverty as an effect of poverty only a decade earlier, but later it was turned into an at least partly behavioral label for some of America's poor.

Nonetheless, the history of "underclass" did not proceed in a straight line or on a logical path. At about the same time Myrdal's term underwent its behavioral redefinition, it also surfaced as a synonym for black poverty in the June 17, 1974, issue of *Time*. The occasion was a cover story on the successes of the growing black middle class, but it included a brief boxed story entitled "The Underclass: Enduring Dilemma," which made a reference to the one-third of the black population living below the poverty line and described it simply as a "troubled underclass," as if the term was sufficiently well known not to need definition.[26]

The Behavioral "Underclass" Enters the Mainstream Media

Three years after *Time*'s box and four years after Moore's article, the behavioral black underclass suddenly reappeared. Once more, the place was *Time*, but now the term was far more broadly defined than in the *Public Interest* article.[27] It was also more prominently displayed, appearing in the title of the cover story for the August 29, 1977, issue of a magazine with a readership of millions. The appearance of this article, and the way it defined the underclass, began the process by which it replaced all the earlier behavioral terms, was turned into a label, and became the popular label it is today.

Titled "The American Underclass: Destitute and Desperate in the Land of Plenty," the article defined the label in alarmist language in the first paragraph, describing "a large group of people who are more intractable, more socially alien and more hostile than almost anyone had imagined. They are the unreachables: the American underclass." *Time* indicated that this underclass "is made up mostly of impoverished urban blacks who still suffer from the heritage of slavery," and emphasized their poverty, addiction, and their status as "victims and victimizers in the culture of the street hustle."[28] That "the underclass" was meant to be a racial term was already suggested on the cover page, where it was subtitled "Minority within a Minority."

The rest of the article was a review, in *Time*'s typical hyperbolic language but without much supportive evidence, of the poverty and isolation of the underclass as well as its anger and dangerousness, although the various elements of the story were not entirely consistent.[29] Thus the text and pictures in the article focused to a considerable extent on the underclass as a group of victims, without detailing who or what was victimizing it. Likewise, the cover drawing was a mixture of black and Hispanic faces, male and female, with the strongest figure, the one in front, seeming to signal defeat rather than anger.[30]

The more dramatic language was reserved for the victimizers: "the rampaging members [who] carried out much of the orgy of looting and burning that swept New York's ghettoes during the July blackout."[31] In addition, *Time* made its own attempt to count the underclass (one of the first such attempts), suggesting that "it must number at least 7 million to 8 million Americans—perhaps even 10 million."[32]

The people *Time* assigned to the underclass were familiar from earlier labels: using the magazine's language, they were juvenile delinquents, school dropouts, drug addicts, and welfare mothers (also "welfare dependents"), as well as looters, arsonists, violent criminals, unmarried mothers, pimps, pushers, panhandlers. The most interesting characteristic of the list is that it included almost everyone who was subsequently labeled as underclass up to the mid-1990s.

Time's underclass cover, and its prescient label, almost did not see the light of day. Elvis Presley had died after the story had been scheduled for the cover, and only an order—itself unusual—from Hedley Donovan, the editor-in-chief of all Time Inc. publications, prevented its being replaced by a Presley obituary cover.[33]

Even if Hedley Donovan had not vetoed the Presley obituary, chances are that the underclass material would have appeared subsequently, for the story had been written in response to "the feeling that things were getting worse." "Things" referred to black youth crime, which had been a July 1977 *Time* cover, as well as what was perceived by the people who had worked on the underclass story as the more general discomfort of the magazine's readers, and thus the country's middle classes, with the problems and the behavior of some poor black Americans.

Another influential voice in support of the underclass cover was the highest placed of *Time's* black journalists, who was then the Chicago bureau chief. He lobbied for stories about the black poor, and had instigated *Time's* first use of "underclass" in 1974, feeling urgently that *Time's* white readers should learn about black poverty as they were reading a cover story about the achievements of the black middle class.

Still, a postponed or revived underclass article would not necessarily have used the term "underclass," for none of the principals involved in producing the cover story had any investment or even particular interest in the term. The black journalist wanted *Time* to run more stories about black poverty, but he was not interested in terminology.[34]

Furthermore, in *Time's* organizational structure at the time none of the reporters were responsible for the cover story's text or its title. Even the writer of the cover story text, a young Canadian-born journalist, was not much interested in the term "underclass." For him the cover was then just an assignment.[35] The senior editor in charge of supervising the cover claimed credit for the use of the word, but he recalled that his main interest in it was as another example of *Time's* invention of new terms.[36] Actually, no one at *Time* seems to have been aware that the term was not new, even if *Time* was the first large-circulation magazine to use it.[37] In any case, "underclass" arrived in the magazine and therefore in the major public media almost by accident.

The last stage in the label-making process took place four years later, with a set of articles in the *New Yorker*. Ken Auletta, their author, was a journalist with an M.A. in political science, and his three 1981 articles as well as his 1982 book were entitled *The Underclass*.[38] Auletta's writings established "the underclass" as a behavioral term that lent itself to being used as a label, beginning with weekly journals of opinion and monthly

magazines catering to "educated" (read mainly upper-middle-class) readers, until it diffused into general use in the media over the next ten years.

Auletta's work had a number of parallels to the *Time* article. To begin
with, he too was reacting to the worsening of "things." As he put it, "I
wanted to go beyond what I had done in the book on New York City's fiscal
crisis, the social aspect, something about the homeless and lost people I was
seeing in the subway."[39] He expressed his reaction to the worsening of
"things" in an alarmist tone, beginning with a reference in his second paragraph to "the bulging crime, welfare and drug statistics—and the all-too-
visible rise in anti-social behavior—that afflicts most American cities."[40] He
also counted the underclass, reporting nearly a dozen then available estimates of its size, although he wisely did not commit himself to any single figure.[41] And like the *Time* article, Auletta placed a long list of people in the
underclass, each of whom, he argued, "feels excluded from society, rejects
commonly accepted values, suffers from *behavioral* as well as *income* deficiencies."[42] Accordingly, he lumped together under a single umbrella term
street criminals, drug addicts, hustlers, alcoholics, drifters, the homeless—
including the women who were called shopping-bag ladies in those days—
and the mentally ill, as well as the welfare recipients, ex-addicts, ex-convicts,
school dropouts, and delinquents on whom he reported in detail.[43]

It is tempting to speculate whether the term "underclass" would have
been forgotten again after *Time*'s 1977 cover if Auletta had not used it, but
while his choice of terms was hardly predetermined, it was by no means
arbitrary. For one thing, Auletta, like *Time*'s reporters, had ties to the Urban
League. In fact, Auletta thought he might have found the word there, or
from Manpower Demonstration Research Corporation staff he interviewed
for his book. Later, he thought that he might have seen it in *Time*'s cover
story, in which case that magazine is ultimately the primary label-maker. In
the second chapter of his book Auletta discussed the reasons for turning
down competing terms, one factor being that he needed a "flexible" term to
cover the various kinds of people he was writing about.[44] And finally he
wanted a term that "would get people to listen . . . that resonated."[45]

In effect, the die may have been cast. Auletta's subject, as he saw it,
required an umbrella term, and his role, that of a professional writer who
wanted to attract readers and buyers, sent him toward an attention-getting
term. And Auletta, like others before him, sensed that "underclass" already
grabbed or would grab people.

Although Auletta believed himself to be writing about a descriptive term, his "underclass" could often be read as a pejorative label. Hindsight also suggests, however, that Auletta's work ended the label-making process, virtually all major popular uses of "underclass" as a behavioral label since then being derived from his or earlier definitions. Thus the label-making process was over by 1982, although the term has been broadened and otherwise extended subsequently.

Perhaps Auletta became the decisive maker of this label because he had more time and words at his disposal than his colleagues at *Time*. That he expanded his articles into a book may be even more significant, for a book is always a more permanent statement than an article. Perhaps most important, he conducted extensive research, supplying enough data to allow subsequent journalists to feel that "underclass" was a term that could be used to label poor people by reporters and columnists who had to write 800-word stories, sometimes with little time for fact gathering or reflection. In effect, then, Auletta may have pretested the label for later writers. Also, Auletta had quoted enough experts to convince those readers (and journalists) who needed convincing that a behavioral term fit the poor people he was writing about better than a purely economic term modeled on Myrdal's original analysis did.[46]

Label Replacement

The making of the underclass label may be distinctive because it does not seem to have been preceded by a period of label replacement. Between the early and late 1970s, when "underclass" had begun to surface, journalists who had heard the word asked relevant or accessible scholars for their reactions, but apparently they came with few existing terms or labels.[47] Banfield's "lower class" was the principal one, perhaps even the only one.[48]

From the mid-1970s on, at least, journalists used "lower class" as a synonym for poor, low-status, and politically powerless people. Nor did "lower class" disappear when "underclass" became prominent; it continues to be used by journalists alongside other terms to this day, maintaining minor but steady annual use figures since the mid-1980s, as shown in table 2.1.[49] The most likely reason that "lower class" never became a behavioral term or label is that when the demand for a new label emerged in the early 1980s, "underclass" had become available. Furthermore, a class *under* all of the others was clearly a more dramatic term than a class merely lower than some others.[50]

Broadening the Underclass

Once "underclass" had been established as both an economic and behavioral term and label in the news media, it underwent the rapid broadening that had taken place among earlier terms and labels to make them fit the needs of their moments.

An important broadening of the behavioral term has been to increase the list of the stigmatized, including homeless people and panhandlers, as well as crack users and sometimes dealers, who were practically unknown when the label-makers were at work in the late 1970s and early 1980s. In some communities, the term has been extended to public housing tenants, and since the early 1990s it has spread to immigrants, notably illegal ones.[51] In addition, welfare recipients have been featured more prominently as members of the underclass than when *Time* and Auletta were inventing the label, as have poor unmarried teenage mothers.

An equally prominent form of broadening is to add elaborating or qualifying adjectives to create new meanings, or to further emphasize the dangerousness of the underclass. Such adjectives include several with essentially the same ominous meaning: "permanent," "intergenerational," "biological" (or "genetic") and "hereditary," and, less often, "entrenched." Sometimes the underclass is seen as desperate and dependent or hardened and "hard-core" (a term first applied to the poor in the 1960s), and it is often assumed to be growing. Several observers have suggested that some of the labeled are so stigmatized as to constitute a sub-underclass, "the lowest of the underclass, or those who have fallen out of it."[52] And with the same point in mind, President Clinton altered the term somewhat in 1993, saying "it's not an underclass anymore. . . . It's an outer class."[53]

A third broadening applies more to the underclass as an economic term. For example, "permanent" and "trapped" have been used since the late 1970s with "underclass" to describe a permanently poor and jobless population. The economic term is also broadened whenever the poor are being deprived of the newest goods and services in the mainstream consumer package, as when "information underclass" is used to point out that the poor are unable to afford access to the "information superhighway."

Another broadening expands the term beyond the stigmatized and the poor. Some writers call attention to a "political underclass" to emphasize its powerlessness, although usually the group in question is either the poor or poor blacks.[54] Another kind of powerlessness associated with the underclass is gendered, so that sometimes even affluent women are thought to be part of a gender underclass.[55]

A final broadening borrows the popularity of the economic or behavioral term, and thus its attention-getting power, for other times, places, and species. Historians have begun to write retroactively about underclasses in earlier centuries, sometimes using the term as a label, sometimes as a neutral or celebratory term, but in any case separating it from the late-twentieth-century conditions that spawned it.[56]

Unusual forms of broadening may take place when an American term or label is shifted to another country and altered to fit local conditions.[57] The term has even been broadened beyond the human species, in one specific case to baby iguanas "placed in a competitive laboratory environment" as turning either into "tyrants" or a "deprived underclass."[58] And sometimes "underclass" appears in the title of a book or article without also appearing in its text, supporting Mercer Sullivan's claim, in a discussion with the author, that "underclass" is often used as a marketing term.

THE JOURNALISTIC DISSEMINATORS OF "UNDERCLASS"[59]

Labels are communicated by many people in many ways, but until an intensive interview study asks people whether and how they have talked about the underclass, the analysis must be limited to data gathered from data bases that track the journalistic communication of the term by major print media.[60] In what follows, the data base Nexis is employed to see how many stories using the term have appeared in various major print media, and to analyze some stories to determine when and where "underclass" is used as an economic or political term or as a behavioral one.

A sampling of three major newspapers and newsmagazines indicates that the use of "underclass" rose from less than 6 stories per year in the middle 1970s to about 40 in the early 1980s, rising to over 100 (and in some cases 130) for the first time between 1985 and 1990, and then declining to about 90 annual uses in the first three years of the current decade.[61] The year of highest use for "underclass" generally came in 1988 or 1989 (see table 2.1).

Even the peak-use numbers may not seem impressive considering that newspapers are published 365 days a year, but stories about the poor have never been plentiful, especially in the newsmagazines, which serve a more affluent and less urban readership.[62] As table 2.1 indicates, "underclass" is used in about half as many stories per year, on the average, as other labels that also serve as descriptive terms, such as "welfare recipient" and "school dropout," at least in the sampled newspapers and newsmagazines.[63] "Underclass" appeared more often, however, than "welfare dependent" (and "welfare dependency"), which are more pejorative than "welfare recipient" and are used almost entirely as labels. Judging by its years of highest use, and the popular appeal of welfare "reform," however, "welfare dependent" could become more widely used in the middle 1990s. The newsmagazines, which appeal to national audiences, did not use specific terms as often as newspapers, but they did use "underclass" almost as often, perhaps because the word fits the more opinionated newsmagazine style. "Underclass" also appeared more often than "lower class."[64]

Table 2.1 also indicates the year of highest use for each term during the period of the study, and suggests that specific terms, like "underclass," generally peaked in the late 1980s. This reflects, perhaps, a wider public concern about the poor as well as journalistic concern, and, as I suggest later, the greater visibility of poverty-related crime and nonmainstream behavior in the media and among the public.

Looking at *how* "underclass" has been used suggests that journalists decided or assumed almost from the start that the underclass is black. This has been true whether they wrote about an economically exploited population or a morally undeserving one. Poor whites have almost never been described as underclass in the national media, and when they are it is generally as an exception proving the rule of the blackness of the underclass.[65]

The sampled newspapers and magazines provide no evidence that journalists have copied the definitions of the label-makers or any other definition, including academic ones. Ken Auletta's *The Underclass* received reviews in all the major print media, but his use of the term and his conclusions about the underclass were cited only once or twice.[66] Most likely, Auletta, and *Time*'s cover story before him, exerted their influence on journalists indirectly, by creating interest in the new labels among such journalists and among their readers. Journalists are not given to definitions anyway, and the way they use terms or labels can be (or have to be) gleaned from linguistic context.

Table 2.2 reports various types of uses in *Newsweek* and *U.S. News & World Report* by five-year periods. From 1975 until the mid-1980s, "the

TABLE 2.1

Average Annual Number of Stories Using "Underclass" and Related Terms, 1985–93
(Year of Highest Number in Parentheses)

Terms	Newspapers			Newsmagazines[a]	
	New York Times	Los Angeles Times	Chicago Tribune	Time	Newsweek	U.S. News & World Report
Underclass	90.1 (1989)	83.9 (1989)	89.2 (1985)	84.0 (1988)	70.1 (1988)	68.4 (1989, '91)
Lower class	40.5 (1990)	56.0 (1992)	41.7 (1987)	35.8 (1985)	21.8 (1990)	18.7 (1985)
Welfare recipient	100.1 (1987)	126.6 (1992)	68.1 (1987)	26.5 (1991)	31.1 (1992)	48.2 (1992)
Welfare dependent[b]	19.2 (1992)	22.6 (1993)	19.7 (1988)	7.0 (none)	26.4 (1993)	14.0 (1992, '93)
School dropout	117.9 (1987)	183.2 (1990)	113.7 (1993)	51.3 (1992)	36.6 (1990)	61.4 (1990)
Drug addict	193.1 (1990)	193.7 (1990)	116.8 (1990)	70.0 (1988)	60.0 (1987, '88)	48.2 (1986, '88)

[a] All weekly newsmagazine stories were multiplied by seven to make them comparable with the number of daily newspaper stories.

[b] Also includes stories using welfare dependency.

underclass" appeared primarily as an economic term, mainly to refer to a population being excluded from the labor market.[67] During that period, as the tables suggest, the term was also used politically, generally to describe immigrants, especially illegal Latin American ones.[68] At that time, then, the underclass was viewed as a group of victims of political oppression or economic exploitation. Broadening was also evident in that early period: in 1979, *U.S. News & World Report* already worried about the possibility of a permanent underclass.

A dramatic change in the usage of "underclass" occurred around 1985, when it began to be used more and more often as a behavioral term, a practice that had not yet ended by the close of 1993. As table 2.2 indicates (as well as does table 2.3, which reports the distribution of uses in *Newsday* since 1988), the proportion of stories using a behavioral definition, or mixed behavioral and economic definitions, increased regularly and steadily over the years, outnumbering all others. By that time, immigrants termed or labeled "underclass" were in the news for behavioral shortcomings far more often than for their economic or other difficulties.

Content analysis cannot be used to determine the motives of the journalists, or to determine whether they used behavioral terms for the underclass in order to label it as undeserving. Some of the behavioral terminology was ostensibly neutral, or at least intended to be so by journalists, insofar as it simply observed that the underclass included single-parent families or school dropouts, even though the writers had no data either on the number of actual parents in the families or whether the school leavers had been pushed out of school. Many more, however, did not use neutral language. And some journalists made it obvious from the kinds of adjectives and elaborating clauses or sentences they used that they were engaged in explicit condemnation of a population they called "the underclass."

Evidently, by the mid-1980s the rules of journalistic objectivity had been relaxed with respect to the underclass, as they frequently have been for other "public enemies" of mainstream America, so that the writers (or their editors) did not have to think about being detached or fair, even in the news columns. And by the late 1980s, both of the newsmagazines analyzed here had writers and columnists who repeatedly attacked the underclass in virtually the same way, focusing particularly on unmarried mothers. One journalist called them the "hard-core no-father ghetto poor."

Why the shift to a behavioral "underclass" after 1985? A reliable answer is impossible without comprehensive interviewing of the journal-

TABLE 2.2

Distribution of Underclass Definitions, by Years,
Newsweek and *U.S. News & World Report*

	1976–80	1981–85	1986–90	1991–93	Total
Economic	44	38	18	9	22
Behavioral	4	6	30	44	26
Political[a]	32	19	6	2	10
Economic and behavioral[b]	0	8	8	2	6
Behavioral and economic[c]	0	0	3	4	2
Undefined	20	23	29	38	29
Other	0	6	6	2	5
N (100%)	25	48	107	66	246

[a] Definitions emphasizing the powerlessness of the underclass, either because of poverty or race or both.
[b] Mixed or multiple definitions, beginning with an economic one.
[c] Mixed or multiple definitions, beginning with a behavioral one.

TABLE 2.3

Distribution of Underclass Definitions, by Years, *Newsday*

	1988	1989	1990	1991	1992	1993	TOTAL
Economic	24	2	14	22	20	16	17
Behavioral	21	27	34	29	25	32	28
Political[a]	6	6	13	10	8	16	9
Economic and behavioral[b]	6	6	2	2	3	3	4
Behavioral and economic[c]	3	2	1	2	5	0	2
Undefined	35	50	30	33	35	29	35
Other	5	8	6	2	3	5	5
N (100%)	75	52	85	51	60	38	361

[a] Definitions emphasizing the powerlessness of the underclass, either because of poverty or race or both.
[b] Mixed or multiple definitions, beginning with an economic one.
[c] Mixed or multiple definitions, beginning with a behavioral one.

ists involved in the shift, especially since no dramatic changes took place in the news stories being covered at the time. Most likely, the increasing visibility of street crime, drug use, and single-parent families played a role in the definitional shift, but this does not explain why these phenomena, themselves hardly novel or suddenly rising numerically, were now becoming more visible.

The journalists also used "underclass" in another way, which can only be called *undefined,* since the journalists supplied neither definitions nor elaborating words and phrases that would enable readers to figure out what they meant. Indeed, they used "underclass" as if its meaning were beyond question, or universally agreed on. Nonetheless, this undefined category came with four different implied meanings. First, "underclass" appeared to be a synonym for the poor, as when stories compared the middle class and the underclass. Second, "underclass" seemed to refer to the nonworking poor. In the third usage, the underclass was compared with the poor, but the stories did not offer any clues as to the basis of the comparison, for example whether the underclass had lower incomes or were less deserving than the poor. Finally, some journalists hinted that the underclass was a separate category from the poor, but how and why was not indicated.[69] Perhaps news writers assumed that their readers knew what they meant, or they chose to let their readers define the term for themselves.[70]

Different types of print-media journalists and nonjournalistic contributors used "underclass" in widely different ways.[71] Sometimes the numerical differences between types were small, but reporters and other contributors to the news pages were most likely to use the economic term, or if they used two, the economic-behavioral combination. They used proportionally more behavioral terminology at the newsmagazines, but then the newsmagazines maintain their economic niche in the news industry with "vivid" writing.

Columnists, who are in the business of offering opinion but are usually free to choose their own, wrote almost exclusively about a behavioral underclass, and were given to pejorative terminology in the newsmagazines and in *Newsday*. So were politicians, when stories quoted them directly, as well as letter writers, who complained when stories were neutral about or not condemning of the underclass.[72] Experts were somewhat more likely to use an economic definition, but perhaps the reporters who had a choice of experts quoted those who saw the underclass as a poor or jobless population rather than as a misbehaving one.

TABLE 2.4

Distribution of Underclass Definitions, by Journalistic Roles,
Newsweek and *U.S. News & World Report*, 1976–93

	News writer	Columnist	Reviewer[a]	Expert	Official[b]
Economic	23	6	15	44	7
Behavioral	25	67	5	6	21
Political[c]	9	0	10	11	43
Economic and behavioral[d]	7	0	0	6	0
Behavioral and economic[e]	4	0	0	0	0
Undefined	26	27	70	28	29
Other	6	0	0	6	0
N (100%)	162	30	20	18	14

[a] *U.S. News & World Report* does not review books, but during 1976–80 asked three authors of books to contribute stories tabulated here.

[b] Includes elected and appointed officials.

[c] Definitions emphasizing the powerlessness of the underclass, either because of poverty or race or both.

[d] Mixed or multiple definitions, beginning with an economic one.

[e] Mixed or multiple definitions, beginning with a behavioral one.

TABLE 2.5

Distribution of Underclass Definitions, by Journalistic Roles,
Newsday, 1988–92

	News writer	Columnist	Reviewer	Expert	Official[a]	Letter writer
Economic	21	10	18	25	13	9
Behavioral	15	42	30	21	32	36
Political[b]	14	4	10	12	4	5
Economic and behavioral[c]	3	7	5	3	4	0
Behavioral and economic[d]	4	1	0	4	4	5
Undefined	41	29	35	32	43	27
Other	1	6	2	4	0	18
N (100%)	71	86	40	73	47	22

[a]Includes elected and appointed officials.
[b]Definitions emphasizing the powerlessness of the underclass, either because of poverty or race or both.
[c]Mixed or multiple definitions, beginning with an economic one.
[d]Mixed or multiple definitions, beginning with a behavioral one.

These days, conservative columnists dominate many op ed pages, either because the political climate is viewed as conservative, or because conservative readers are more vocal than liberal ones, and commercial news media please them by gravitating to conservative columnists.[73] *Newsday*'s columnists and reviewers are especially interesting, for they were the dominant users at that newspaper of "underclass" as well as of its behavioral definition. Since most of these are syndicated national figures, they may be bringing a national term, and one more often associated with the elite media than with the popular ones, to a local newspaper that caters primarily to New York's lower-middle- and working-class populations.

Political and Governmental Users of "Underclass"

Politicians and government officials have not been eager users of the word, and those among them who used "underclass" as a behavioral term and as a pejorative label have been mainly social and religious conservatives rather than defenders of free enterprise.[74] Most of the "underclass" users in the political and governmental category who were quoted in, or otherwise showed up in, the *Newsday* analysis were New York union officials and liberal black politicians who treated "underclass" as a term relating to economic and occasionally political domination.[75]

Members of Congress have not resorted to the term very often either, but when they have done so they have clearly not followed media trends. A Lexis analysis of the *Congressional Record* from 1985 to 1993 showed an average annual use of 40.3, with only minor yearly fluctuations.[76] Perhaps more important, the lawmakers did not copy the media shift to the behavioral underclass, for over the years the economic definition has been used most often—40 percent of the time, exactly twice as much as the behavioral one.[77] Like journalists, the lawmakers began to eschew definitions more often over time.[78]

At times, it seemed as if the members of Congress were teachers rather than politicians, because they spoke frequently about an educational underclass, or about education as the solution to the difficulties of the economic underclass.[79] True, the speeches reported in the *Congressional Record* do not constitute American policy or politics, but they are a rough indicator, particularly since almost all the references to the underclass came from the elected officials themselves, rather than from texts of others inserted in the *Record*.[80]

The government bureaucracy has been comparatively uninterested in the term. Over the years, "underclass" surfaced, as title or text or both, in a 1980 Department of Commerce report, a 1982 Urban Policy Committee study, a May 1989 hearing of the Joint Economic Committee, a 1990 General Accounting Office (GAO) report entitled "The Urban Underclass: Disturbing Problems Demanding Attention," as well as on one page of the 1991 federal budget.

The governmental body least likely to follow the crowd has been the U.S. Supreme Court, which used "underclass" only once, in 1982, in a path-breaking case in which it described illegal immigrants as a "permanent caste . . . denied the benefits that our society makes available to citizens and lawful residents."[81]

LEGITIMATING "THE UNDERCLASS"

Legitimators are the people and institutions cited by label-makers and communicators to justify their terms and ideas as credible, and to supply expert evidence for the relevance of a new term. Before journalists took over the communication role, it, as well as label-making and legitimation, were often carried out by the same people. Frequently they had vested organizational interests in the labels as well as credentials that allowed them concurrently to publicize the labels and to endow them with credibility and legitimacy. In the fifteenth century, for example, when responsibility for the poor began to be transferred from the Church to public agencies, authorities from Martin Luther to Emperor Charles V of Germany invoked the labels of the time in identifying those who did not deserve help.[82]

The best-known legitimators of the nineteenth century were the practitioners and researchers of the so-called scientific charity movement. They sought to put the poor under their control, in charities as well as in prisons and mental hospitals, using and legitimating pejorative terms to help justify punitive measures against the poor.[83] Later on, legitimacy also was supplied by famous WASP writers and civic leaders, as well as leaders of the newly emerging academic social sciences, also WASP, who helped to legitimize the attack on the poor immigrants whom they labeled as feebleminded.[84]

The major legitimators for "the underclass" as a behavioral term have been academics, researchers working for public or private agencies, and other experts—at times even without their intending to do so, since journalists are free to quote whatever they write or say on the record.[85] Legitimators were used particularly during the label-making process. The analytic portions of *Time*'s underclass cover story quoted fifteen people, ten of whom were social scientists and other professionals and government, civil rights, or other officials; almost half of Auletta's fifty-five references in his chapter about the underclass were social scientists or related researchers. Both *Time*'s and Auletta's experts were cited mainly for their analyses rather than in defense of the magazine's and the writer's definitions of "the underclass."

When "the underclass" was a new label, the well-known magazines and publishing houses that first published materials about it also functioned as legitimators. Publishers may not normally be considered as legitimating what they publish, but in the 1970s and early 1980s, the reputations of *Time*, the *New Yorker*, and Random House supplied some early credibility for the new underclass label.[86] Also, in the journalistic world if not in the academic one, authors published by the major mainstream publishers are sometimes treated as experts and legitimators.

The speakers appearing in the *Congressional Record* referred only rarely to social scientists to justify their conception of the underclass, but William Julius Wilson led the list of the social scientists who were so cited.[87] Inside the Beltway, Washington's principal social scientist legitimators of the behavioral underclass have been the sociologist Erol Ricketts and the well-known Washington economist Isabel Sawhill. Her definition of the underclass, which invokes four norms whose violation marks "behavior . . . that often harms the rest of society," has been made known in her writings, interviews with journalists, congressional committee testimony, and numerous appearances in Washington and elsewhere.[88]

Journalists do not usually quote social scientists to legitimate their definitions, but like elected officials they use similar or simplified definitions, frequently without attribution. When they do cite social scientists' definitions and include attribution, they indicate, or perhaps believe, that scientists' definitions are scientific.

Perhaps expert reference to the underclass that is cited or quoted by journalists helps to legitimate the term or label further, but once a term is widely used its legitimacy no longer needs support.[89] In fact, at that point, newsworthiness can take a very different turn. When William Julius Wilson announced, in his 1990 presidential address to the American Sociological Association, that he was dropping the term "underclass" and replacing it with "ghetto poor," the story appeared in all three newsweeklies and major national newspapers, including the *New York Times*, the *Washington Post*, and the *Wall Street Journal*. None of the journalists at these and other publications, however, followed Wilson's lead.

In retrospect, the more important legitimation functions taken on by academics and other researchers have been two of the traditional supportive ones: that of alarmists and counters. Americans have here followed the English survey tradition of alarmist counting of the poor, especially those they considered undeserving. Henry Goddard not only estimated the total number of feebleminded people in America but also estimated what proportions of all street criminals, prostitutes, and other lawbreakers and the like were feebleminded. In the 1960s, Daniel P. Moynihan's alarmed reporting of the increase in female-headed black families in the "Moynihan Report" undoubtedly contributed to the public concern that subsequently led to the assigning of such families to the behavioral underclass.

The first counters of the underclass defined it as an economic term, including Frank Levy, whose 1977 study measured persistent poverty even though he referred to the people he measured as a behavioral underclass.[90] Since then, many counting exercises have been conducted, with wildly differing results, depending on the underclass definition used and the way in which that definition was operationalized so as to make use of already available data.[91] A good deal of social scientific counting is alarmist in nature, because social scientists are rarely asked to count anything unproblematic. Moreover, even if counters do not necessarily report their findings in alarmist tones, journalists and others using their numbers are free to add their own spin, turning scientific counting into alarmist prose.

The Funders

Researchers, like other legitimators, have sometimes been individuals working on their own, but since the underclass generated public interest, they have usually been funded. Funders become especially important legitimators if and when the researchers' work cannot proceed without money, for example in the case of counting. Thus, the funding the eugenicists required for their counting and other work came from rich private philanthropists, the predecessors of today's foundations.[92]

By the time the underclass terminology appeared, the private philanthropists had been largely replaced by conservative foundations (and associated conservative research institutes) that support labeling the undeserving poor and advance arguments for the reduction of antipoverty and related welfare state programs. Among the better-known foundations, some of which actually obtain most of their money from a few private philanthropists, are family foundations such as Bradley, Coors, Olin, Scaife, and Smith Richardson. In addition, the Heritage Foundation, the American Enterprise Institute, and the Manhattan Institute raise funds, frequently from the above-named funders, that they use for preparing and disseminating research reports and ideological tracts.[93]

While conservative foundations fund intellectuals and others who propagate the idea that poverty is largely the fault of the poor, there are no equivalently affluent liberal foundations devoted to propagating the idea that poverty is mainly the fault of the economy. The so-called liberal foundations such as Ford or Rockefeller are ideologically better described as centrist, and are called liberal because they are viewed as overtly and officially nonideological.[94]

These foundations have not sought to participate directly in the political debate over the underclass and the welfare state. Instead, they have mainly funded research, conferences, and scholarly publications that add to the knowledge about both the underclass and poverty. Sometimes, however, the monies they have made available for counting, or for influential conferences, and the prestige that attaches to their names, have played an indirect role in the legitimation of "underclass" as a behavioral term, and thus also in its persistence and its use as a label.

Of these foundations, the Rockefeller Foundation was central during the years in which "underclass" emerged as a popular behavioral term. Indeed, the foundation's brief foray into "underclass research" illustrates that a nonideological foundation can sometimes help to legitimate a label, and not intentionally so, even as it works to advance antipoverty research and policy.[95]

The Rockefeller Foundation's major underclass-related activities, which began about 1987, were centered in its Equal Opportunities Division, which gave research money to social scientists via the Social Science Research Council (SSRC) until 1993, and program money to private community action agencies in six communities, which have continued beyond 1993.[96] According to a senior foundation staff member who had contact with the board of trustees, the Rockefeller Foundation's interest in the underclass, and its emphasis on the term, was initiated by the appointment to the board of civil rights leader Eleanor Holmes Norton and the election of a new board chairman, Richard Lyman.[97] The board's interest in the underclass was also said to have been influenced by the "powderkeg concerns" of more conservative board members, who were worried about increased social unrest in the black community and the mounting financial problems of the cities.[98]

Nevertheless, the specific focus on the term "underclass" was also indirectly encouraged by the wide use of the term in the mass media. The previously mentioned senior staff member thought that "poverty didn't sell," and that "underclass" had become an "energizing" term that restored the foundation's interest in poverty research and policy. The media's influence also made itself felt on the scholars at the Social Science Research Council. Its staff initially favored research on "persistent poverty," and the SSRC Committee for Research on the Underclass, the group of academics that supervised the research, had at first had mixed feelings about the word "underclass." But an SSRC staff memo explaining the council's eventual decision to use the term pointed out, "The urban underclass is a concept that grabs people's attention in ways that poverty no longer appears to do," adding that the term "underclass" had been "popularized by the media."[99]

Media considerations did not, however, shape the activities of the two organizations.[100] Instead, some of the signals emanating from the Rockefeller Foundation's board to the SSRC were interpreted by the latter as expressing the foundation's interest in looking at the underclass from a behavioral perspective. For example, the foundation's liaison with the SSRC's underclass research unit was Erol Ricketts, who had worked with Isabel Sawhill in developing the behavioral definition of the underclass most widely accepted by scholars.[101]

The SSRC remained free, however, to develop its own research agenda and terminology, even if many of its research committees included "underclass" in their titles.[102] Their research interests were much like those of social scientists doing poverty research elsewhere, and the resulting topics were often about the poor rather than about the agencies, structures, and processes that produce poverty.[103] Researchers who were careless in their language sometimes reported their findings about the poor as their faults, or used language associated more often with labeling than with scientific writing. Such a perspective was at least implied by a head of SSRC's Committee for Research on the Underclass, who in his introduction to an SSRCsponsored book on the underclass defended the term by arguing, among other things, that " 'under' suggests . . . the disreputable, dangerous, dark, evil and even hellish."[104]

Despite the SSRC researchers' new contributions to knowledge about poverty, the Rockefeller Foundation became impatient with the research program, particularly its failure to produce innovations in antipoverty policy, and the foundation's financial support ended in 1993.[105] The community action programs continued, but their leaders, responding to community opposition, took "underclass" out of their organizational names at the earliest opportunity.[106]

Government as Legitimator

The administrations of presidents Reagan and Bush, which resorted to energetic actions to punish the poor financially and otherwise, evidently did not need words to back up their actions, and thus neither made any use of the then new underclass label to justify its policies.[107]

Perhaps the Bush administration's feeling about the term, if in fact it had one, was best expressed after a meeting of the Domestic Policy Council in July 1990 that seems to have referred, without attribution, to an "unofficial underclass."[108] President Clinton, on the other hand, used "underclass" occasionally, often with direct reference to the ideas of William Julius Wilson, and his secretary of labor, Dr. Robert Reich, suggested in 1994 a tripartite American class hierarchy, the lowest portion of which consisted of an "underclass quarantined in surroundings that are unspeakably bleak, and often violent."[109]

The Distinctive Roles of Black Officials and Researchers

Finally, the emergence and legitimation of "underclass" as term and label were aided in a distinctive fashion by the black community, particularly the Urban League, as well as by black professionals. Although it is not a foundation but a "defense organization," the league, which has traditionally spoken for black business and other black elites as well as for the larger black community, was a legitimator of "underclass" as a behavioral term. This role of the Urban League was unintentional, but some other black organizations and researchers later played a more willing role in legitimating "underclass."

The Urban League's unintentional legitimating role derived directly from two already noted phenomena: that as early as the mid-1960s, the underclass was viewed as mainly black; and that in the 1970s, the Urban League was the only national organization with a research department that kept track of federal and other statistics about the black population. Consequently, journalists and others generally turned first to the league for information about the black community and thus quizzed it about the underclass.

In addition, some league officers and staff were a source for legitimating quotes. The second quote in the 1977 *Time* cover story came from the director of the Chicago Urban League, who was reported as saying, "If the cities erupt again, we will find no safe place on either side of the barricades."[110]

In this quote as in most others, Urban League officials did not use the term "underclass." For example, the league director, Vernon Jordan, and others such as the researcher Robert Hill, sought to persuade journalists that the term was empirically invalid.[111] Some other black officials and researchers have been quoted using the term, however, as have black newspaper columnists—and not all of them have been political conservatives. Black labeling of poor fellow blacks reflects an old class conflict in the black community; in black social science research, this pattern can be traced back at least to W. E. B. Du Bois, and later to E. Franklin Frazier, among others, who looked askance at the lifestyles of poor blacks. The same intragroup class conflict has taken place in white ethnic communities, with middle- and upper-class members publicly expressing hostility toward their poor co-ethnics, including recent immigrants, whom they consider undeserving.

An internal ethnic class conflict has also been operating in the black community, with West Indian–born professionals criticizing the behavior of the African-American poor. Indeed, some of the most prominent black writers about the black underclass who are advocates of a behavioral definition are of West Indian origin. Such class conflict also parallels a white pattern. Among European immigrants it existed between affluent northern Italians and poor southerners, affluent German-born Jews and poor Eastern European ones, and many others; and it now exists among current immigrant groups. Nonetheless, there is something particularly ironic and tragic about black organizations and researchers supplying data and comments to white America that can be used to label and stigmatize other blacks.

WHY THE SUCCESS OF "UNDERCLASS"?
CONTEXTUAL CONDITIONS

Despite the participation of these diverse experts in the creation of "the underclass," their activities are ultimately a necessary but not sufficient explanation of the existence of this label. Labels become influential not only because they are available but also because they become meaningful to enough people to encourage their further use by journalists, politicians, researchers, funding agencies, and others. The result is a vicious circle that may not be broken for a long time.

Obviously, gestation periods are required for this process, which may help explain both why Myrdal's 1963 conception was not transformed into a behavioral term until 1973, and why it did not reach the mainstream media until *Time*'s 1977 cover story. Another ten years intervened before "underclass" became an everyday media term; presumably, the combination of several conditions in the country in the middle and late 1980s are partly responsible.[112]

The 1960s gave rise to the renewed use of term and label "rioters," especially in cities that had ghetto disorders.[113] In the 1970s, when journalists were first learning about the underclass, the black poor were not receiving much attention, however, in part because the increase in oil prices and the subsequent general inflation dominated public attention. The beginning of interest in the underclass at the beginning of the 1980s, after Auletta published his work, coincided with the arrival of Ronald Reagan and the replacement of high inflation with increased unemployment.

If the general public paid sufficient attention to the White House and its ideological supporters, the hostile actions of the Reagan administration against the poor, as well as those of the conservative intellectual and other forces with which it was allied, should have made people aware of the "underclass." But what appears instead to have turned the term into a widely used label, beginning in the mid-1980s, was the rising visibility, and in some cases the rising numbers, of welfare recipients, unmarried mothers, street criminals, crack users and sellers, homeless people, and panhandlers.

Perception is as important here as reality, since the increasing visibility of these poor people and the problems ascribed to them probably reflected yet other conditions. The most immediate of these were the entry of the children of the postwar black migration and Latino immigration into a labor market that really could not use them; a political economy dominated by interests who saw no reason to do anything about or for them; and an increasing number of Americans who were beginning, as the 1990s would reveal, to worry about their own economic future.

As a result, many of these Americans were ready to be alarmed. For example, while researchers were reporting that actual rates of teenage motherhood had been declining for years, most white journalists and their audiences were just learning about "babies having babies." Some of the alarms were first sounded on television, with pictures to accompany them, and often they were reported from the ghettoes of New York City and other major northeast cities to a country in which most whites—except poor ones—were now suburbanites.[114]

Not only were the newly visible forms of ghetto behavior alarming in themselves, but they may have indicated the inability of politicians, officials, experts, and others to control the threatening (read black) poor. Indeed, the rise of a new label may itself be an indicator of this inability.[115]

Last but not least, "underclass" may have special qualities as a term that meet the demands of today's alarmed Americans. Unfortunately, nothing is known about how they visualize the underclass, but the behavioral term has three potentially powerful semantic qualities. First, "under" could signify to lay people what it did to the Harvard political scientist I quoted earlier: "the disreputable, dangerous, dark, evil and even hellish." Second, the fact that the behavioral "underclass" was defined as applying to all of the newly visible black and Hispanic poor made a diverse population of troubled and troublemaking poor people into a single class, which only increased its tendency to alarm. Third, the combination of "under" with "class" may have expressed the feeling of the alarmed that any population that displays the threatening qualities associated with "underness" should be placed under, and if possible isolated from, the rest of society.

The Role of Social Scientists and Journalists

This analysis of "underclass" is a case study, and only a study of many terms and labels would make it possible to determine the causal influence of varying types of contextual conditions and the responsibility of various types of label-makers in bringing about and legitimating behavioral labels such as "underclass."

As the history of the past decades suggests, Myrdal's original concept could not have become a behavioral term and label without the participation of some social scientists and journalists.[116] Whether they could also have prevented the rise of the underclass label and the stigmatization accompanying it is more difficult to say; if they had tried, another behavioral term and label might have sprung up instead.

Enough social scientists who favored, were not opposed to, or were indifferent about stigmatizing terms, but who were professionally ready to be helpful, were available to assist in the rise of "the underclass," and so were legitimators and funders to support them. Being members of their own society, after all, they were influenced by the popularity of "underclass" as a media term, sometimes without knowing it. Sometimes social scientists also acted as label communicators themselves, as well as legitimators.[117]

The participation of journalists in the spreading of the underclass label could almost be guaranteed, since they are expected to help attract an audience and are thus virtually required to use labels that grab it. Even if they were not impelled by commercial considerations, they would nonetheless want as large an audience as possible for their work.

Journalists are supposed to avoid thinking about the effects of their work; otherwise they could never report the news. They are also supposed to be overtly nonideological, and are thus discouraged from thinking about the ideologies buried in the terms they use. Lacking the protection of tenure, journalists also have less freedom to object to labeling than social scientists, and can thus do less to prevent it. Social scientists are freed from these commercial obligations, but the ethic of value-free social science and disinterested research also frees them from thinking about the effects of both their research and their concepts.

Had social scientists thought about these effects, they might not have suppressed their ideas about the underclass but they might have undertaken research to look into the effects of the use of the term, once its popularity as a stigmatizing label became apparent. Such a redirection of research efforts, however, would probably have required an empathy toward the poor that too few social scientists of any era have so far displayed.[118] The rise of the underclass label was not inevitable, but looking back, it had few hurdles to get over among either social scientists or journalists.

THE FUTURE OF THE UNDERCLASS LABEL

Labels to stigmatize the poor have appeared and disappeared for a long time. Presumably, "underclass" will eventually suffer the same fate, either when poverty has been eliminated or is no longer on the public agenda, or when new conditions create a demand for new labels. If a particular set of behaviors, actual or imagined, on the part of the poor or officials dealing with them becomes an urgent enough public issue in America, or if new policies become popular (or unpopular), specific labels may once more replace the umbrella term.

For example, the Clinton administration's attempts to bring about a liberal version of welfare reform, and before that the 1988 Family Security Act, began to put the spotlight on welfare recipients and encouraged hostile political forces, elite and popular, to help revive labels such as "welfare dependent" and "illegitimacy." Judging by the major speech-makers, these forces included Catholic and other Christian defenders of traditional "family values," as well as secular conservatives who realized that welfare reform and even "workfare" would mean an increase in welfare state activities to supply public jobs and public day care. These are expensive, and are apt to increase the power of liberal professionals, whereas a moral campaign against illegitimacy would be neither.[119]

David Matza's hypothesis that labels are eventually killed off by being stigmatized has not so far been supported by the case of "the underclass." Despite attacks on the behavioral term by black social scientists and others since the 1970s, and by white ones since the early 1980s, the label has flourished.[120] It is young, however, and it is too early to tell whether it will have a long life.

Under normal circumstances, "underclass" should not be expected to join the list of labels that have been romanticized. Of course the future could always produce another Kurt Weill and Bertoldt Brecht, who, it may be remembered, romanticized the urban murderers, thieves, and other criminals of another century in the *Dreigröschen Oper,* albeit in protest against poverty and the capitalism that brought it about. Leonard Bernstein could romanticize the 1950s gangs of New York's West Side, and turn his nostalgia into a commercial success that has become a classic. Even the "underclass," then, could be romanticized someday.

The Dangers of "Underclass" and Other Labels[1]

One of America's popular pejorative labels is "slum," which characterizes low-income dwellings and neighborhoods as harmful to their poor occupants and the rest of the community. In the nineteenth century, slums were often faulted for turning the deserving poor into the undeserving poor, but in the twentieth century the causality was sometimes reversed, so that poor people with "slum-dweller hearts" were accused of destroying viable buildings and neighborhoods.

After World War II, "slum" and "slum dweller" as well as "blight" all became more or less official labels when the federal government, egged on by a variety of builder and realty pressure groups, started handing out sizeable sums for the "clearance" of low-income neighborhoods unfortunate enough to fit these terms as they were defined in the 1949 U.S. Housing Act.[2] Although by and large only slums located in areas where private enterprise could build luxury and other profitable housing were torn down, more than a million poor households lost their homes in the next twenty years, with almost nothing done for the people displaced from them.

This chapter is written with that much-told history in mind, in order to suggest that the underclass label—as well as all but the most neutrally formulated behavioral term—can have dangerous effects for the poor and for antipoverty policy. While the emphasis will be on "underclass," the dangers of related labels will be discussed as well.

Labels may be only words, but they are judgmental or normative words, which can stir institutions and individuals to punitive actions. The dangers from such labels are many, but the danger common to all behavioral labels and terms is that they focus on behavior that hides the poverty causing it, and substitutes as its cause moral or cultural or genetic failures.[3]

"THE UNDERCLASS" AS CODE WORD

The term "underclass" has developed an attention-getting power that constitutes its first danger. The word has a technical aura that enables it to serve as a euphemism or code word to be used for labeling.[4] Users of the label can thus hide their disapproval of the poor behind an impressively academic term. "Underclass" has also become morally ambiguous, and as it is often left undefined, people can understand it in any way they choose, including as a label.

Because "underclass" is a code word that places some of the poor *under* society and implies that they are not or should not be *in* society, users of the term can therefore favor excluding them from the rest of society without saying so.[5] Once whites thought of slaves, "primitives," and wartime enemies as the inhuman "other," but placing some people under society may not be altogether different.[6]

A subtler yet in some ways more insidious version of the exclusionary mechanism is the use of "underclass" as a synonym for the poor, deserving and undeserving. While not excluding anyone from society, it increases the social distance of the poor from everyone else. This distance is increased further by the contemporary tendency of elected officials and journalists to rename and upgrade the working class as the lower middle class—or even the middle class.

Because "underclass" is also used as a racial and even ethnic code word, it is a convenient device for hiding antiblack or anti-Latino feelings. As such a code word, "underclass" accommodates contemporary taboos against overt prejudice, not to mention hate speech. Such taboos sometimes paper over—and even repress—racial antagonisms that people do not want to express openly.

Ironically, the racial code word also hides the existence of very poor whites who suffer from many of the same problems as poor blacks. When used as a racial term, "underclass" blurs the extent to which the troubles of whites and blacks alike are generated by the economy and by classism or class discrimination and require class-based as well as race-based solutions.

Like other code words, "underclass" may interfere with public discussion. Disapproval of the actions of others is part of democracy, but code words make covert what needs to be overt in order for the disapproval to be questioned and debated. If openly critical terms such as "bums" and "pauper" were still in use, and if umbrella terms such as "underclass" were replaced with specific ones such as "beggars" or "welfare dependents," upset citizens could indicate clearly the faults of which they want to accuse poor people. In that case, public discussion might be able to deal more openly with the feelings the more fortunate classes hold about the poor, the actual facts about the poor, and the policy issues having to do with poverty and poverty-related behavior.

THE FLEXIBILITY OF THE LABEL

Terms and labels undergo broadening in order to adapt them for use in varying conditions. Broadening also makes labels flexible so that they can be used to stigmatize new populations, or accuse already targeted ones of new failures.

One source of harm to such populations is flexible *meaning*, which stems from the vagueness of a new word, the lack of an agreed-upon definition for it. Since Oscar Lewis once identified nearly sixty-five "traits" for his culture of poverty, there is apt precedent for the flexibility of the underclass label that replaced Lewis's term. Flexibility becomes more harmful when pejorative prefixes can be added to otherwise descriptively used terms; for example, a female welfare recipient can also be described as a member of a permanent underclass, which suggests that she is incapable of ever escaping welfare. An underclass of young people becomes considerably more threatening when it is called "feral," and even worse is the idea of a biological underclass, which implies a genetic and thus permanent inferiority of a group of people whom public policy can render harmless only by sterilizing, imprisoning, or killing them.

Another serious danger follows from the flexibility of *subjects*: the freedom of anyone with labeling power to add further populations to the underclass, and to do so without being accountable to anyone. The poor cannot, after all, afford to bring libel and slander suits. If tenants of public housing are also assigned to the underclass, they are even more stigmatized than when they are coming from "the projects." Illegal immigrants who are refugees from a country not favored by the State Department or the Immigration and Naturalization Service are more likely candidates for public harassment or deportation if their native-born neighbors decide that their behavior marks them as members of the underclass. That they may be doing work that no one else will do or collecting entitlements for which they have paid their share of taxes becomes irrelevant once they have been assigned the label.

THE REIFICATION OF THE LABEL

A further source of danger is the reification of the label, which takes place when a definition is awarded the gift of life and label users believe there to be an actually existing and homogeneous underclass that is composed of whatever poor people are currently defined as underclass. Reification, which turns a definition into an actual set of people, hides the reality that the underclass is an imagined group that has been constructed in the minds of its definers. Once a stigmatized label is reified, however, visible signs to identify it are sure to be demanded sooner or later, and then invented, so that people bearing the signs can be harassed more easily.

Furthermore, once the signs are in place so that imagined groups can be made actual, the labels run the danger of being treated as causal mechanisms. As a result, the better-off classes may decide that being in the underclass is a cause of becoming homeless or turning to street crime. Homelessness then becomes a symptom of underclass membership, with the additional danger of the hidden policy implication: that the elimination of the underclass would end homelessness, thereby avoiding the need for affordable housing or for jobs and income grants for the homeless.

Even purely descriptive terms referring to actual people, such as "welfare recipients," can be reified and turned into causal labels. People may thus persuade themselves to believe that being on welfare is a cause of poverty, or of single-parent families. Once so persuaded, they can propose to eliminate both effects by ending welfare, and without appearing to be inhumane—which is what conservative politicians running for office, and the intellectuals supporting them, have been doing since the early 1990s. They ignore the fact that in the real world the causal arrow goes in the other direction, but they achieve their political aim, even if they also harm poor mothers and their children.

Since popular causal thinking is almost always moral as well as empirical, the reification of a label like "the underclass" usually leads to the assignment of *moral* causality. If the underclass is the cause of behavior that deviates from mainstream norms, the solution is moral condemnation, behavioral modification, or punishment by the elimination of financial aid. Thus people are blamed who are more often than not victims instead of perpetrators, which ignores the empirical causes, say, of street crime, and interferes with the development of effective anticrime policy. Blaming people may allow blamers to feel better by blowing off the steam of righteous (and in the case of crime, perfectly justified) indignation, but even justified blaming does not constitute or lead to policy for ending street crime.[7]

A scholarly form of reification can be carried out with labels that are also scientific terms, so that the former are confused with the latter and thus obtain the legitimacy that accompanies scientific concepts. Conversely, the moral opprobrium placed on the labeled allows social scientists either to incorporate overt biases in their concepts or to relax their detachment and in the process turn scientific concepts into little more than operationalized labels.

A case in point is the operational definition of "the underclass" by Erol Ricketts and Isabel Sawhill, which has been widely used by government, scholars, and in simplified form even by popular writers.[8] The two social scientists argue that the underclass consists of four populations: "high school dropouts," "prime-age males not regularly attached to the labor force," welfare recipients, and "female heads."[9] Ricketts and Sawhill identify these populations as manifesting "underclass behaviors," or "dysfunctional behaviors," which they believe to be "at variance with those of mainstream populations."[10]

The two authors indicate that they can "remain agnostic about the fundamental causes of these behaviors."[11] Nonetheless, they actually adopt an implicit moral causality, because in defining the underclass as "people whose behavior departs from (mainstream) norms" and remaining silent about causality, they imply that the behaviors result from the violations of these values.[12]

Ricketts and Sawhill provide no evidence, however, that the four behaviors in question are actually the result of norm violation. More important, their operational definition does not consider other causal explanations of the same behavior. No doubt some poor young people drop out of school because they reject mainstream norms for education, but Ricketts and Sawhill omit those who drop out because they have to go to work to support their families, or because they feel that their future in the job market is nil, as well as the youngsters who are forced out by school administrators and who should be called "pushouts."[13]

Likewise, in addition to the "prime-age males" Ricketts and Sawhill believe to be jobless because they do not want to work, some of these men reject being targeted for a career of dead-end jobs, and others, most in fact, are jobless because there are no jobs for them. Indeed, the irony of the Ricketts-Sawhill definition is that when an employer goes out of business, workers who may previously have been praised as working poor but now cannot find other jobs are then banished to the underclass.

Poor mothers go on welfare for a variety of reasons. Some are working mothers who need Medicaid for their children and cannot get health benefits from their employers. Female family heads are often single because jobless men make poor breadwinners, not because they question the desirability of mainstream marriage norms.[14]

If I read the two authors correctly, they are conducting essentially normative analyses of the four types of underclass people they have defined, even if they may not have intended to be normative. Thus, the measures they have chosen to operationalize their definitions bear some resemblance to popular pejorative labels that condemn rather than understand behavior.[15] Conversely, Ricketts and Sawhill do not appear to consider the possibility that the failure of the mainstream economy is what prevents people from achieving the norms they are setting for the poor.

As a result, the two authors make no provision for data that measure the failures of the mainstream economy, and they do not include—or operationalize—a good deal of other information. For example, they could count home, school, and neighborhood conditions that interfere with or discourage learning, and the economic conditions that cause the disappearance of jobs and frustrate the desire for work. In addition, they might obtain information on job availability for jobless prime-age males, as well as for women on welfare—just to mention some of the relevant data that are publicly available. Until they include such data, their definition and operationalization of "underclass" are scientific only because and to the extent that their counting procedures observe the rules of science.[16]

A different approach to the indiscriminate mixing of science and labeling, and to the reification of stereotypes, emerged in some proposals in the

late 1980s to measure underclass status by poor people's answers to attitude questions: on their willingness to plan ahead, for example. Such attitude data could be found in the widely used Panel Survey of Income
Dynamics. This type of question assumes not only that people should plan
ahead, but that their failure to do so reflects their unwillingness, rather than
their inability, to plan ahead, which has been documented in many empirical studies. Nonetheless, people whose poverty prevented them from planning ahead and who answered honestly that they did not so plan, would
have been assigned a stigmatizing label—merely on the basis of their
response to superficial and general questions.[17] Fortunately, this approach
to "measuring" the underclass appears not to have been used so far by anyone in an influential position.

A final reification is spatial, an approach in which behavioral labels are
applied to census tracts to produce "underclass areas." Such areas derive
from statistical artifacts invented by the U.S. Bureau of the Census. The
bureau developed the concept of "extreme poverty areas" for those places
in which at least 40 percent of the people were poor.[18] While this is inaccurate enough—especially for the 60 percent not poor—Ricketts and Sawhill
subsequently identified "underclass areas," in which the proportion of people exhibiting all four of their behavioral indicators for being in the underclass was "one standard deviation above the mean *for the country as a
whole.*"[19] The two authors did not explain why they chose this measure,
even though poverty is not dispersed through the country as a whole but is
concentrated in the cities of the northeast, midwest, and south, the latter
being also the location of the most severe rural poverty.

Most people lack the methodological skills of social scientists, and do
not see the assumptions that underlie the approaches to underclass counting. Once word gets out that social scientists have identified some areas as
underclass areas, however, these neighborhoods can easily be stigmatized,
the population labeled accordingly and accused of whatever local meanings
the term "underclass" may have acquired.[20]

When areas become known as underclass areas, local governments and
commercial enterprises obtain legitimation to withdraw or not provide
facilities and services that could ameliorate the poverty of the area's inhabitants. Labeling areas as underclass can also encourage governments to
choose them as locations for excess numbers of homeless shelters, drug
treatment centers, and other facilities that serve the very poor and that are
therefore rejected by other neighborhoods.[21]

In fact, "underclass area" is basically a current version of the old label "slum," which also treated indicators of poverty as behavioral failures. In the affluent economy of the post–World War II era, similar defining and subsequent counting activities were used to justify "slum clearance," and the displacement of poor people for subsidized housing for the affluent. And as in all labeling, the poor people who are labeled are left to fend for themselves.

THE DANGERS OF THE UMBRELLA EFFECT

Since "underclass" is an umbrella label that can include in its definition all the various behavioral and moral faults that label-makers and users choose to associate with it, two further dangers accrue to those it labels.

The sheer breadth of the umbrella label seems to attract alarmist writers who magnify the many kinds of moral and behavioral harmfulness attributed to people it names. A correlate of the umbrella effect is amnesia on the part of writers about the extreme and usually persistent poverty of the labeled. Thus, the more widely people believe in the validity of the underclass label, and the broader its umbrella becomes, the more likely it is that political conditions will not allow for reinstituting effective antipoverty policy. If the underclass is dangerous, and dangerous in so many different ways, it follows that the government's responsibility is to beef up the police, increase the punishments courts can demand, and create other punitive agencies that try to protect the rest of society from this dangerous class.

Umbrella labels also do harm when they lump into a single term a variety of diverse people with different problems.[22] This ignores the reality that the people who are assigned the underclass label have in common only that their actual or imagined behaviors upset the mainstream population, or the politicians who claim to speak in its name. Using this single characteristic to classify people under one label can be disastrous, especially if politicians and voters should ever start talking about comprehensive "underclass policies," or what Christopher Jencks has called "meta solutions."[23] For one thing, many of the people who are tagged with the label have not even deviated from mainstream norms, and yet others have done nothing illegal. An underclass policy would thus be a drastic violation of civil rights and civil liberties.

At this writing, electioneering politicians as well as angry voters still remain content with policies that harm the people who bear specific labels, such as welfare recipients, illegal immigrants, and the homeless. In the past, however, the makers of earlier umbrella labels have proposed extremely drastic policies. In 1912, Henry Goddard suggested dealing with the feeble-minded by "unsexing . . . removing, from the male and female, the necessary organs for procreation." Realizing that there would be strong popular opposition both to castration and ovariectomies, he proposed instead that the next best solution was "segregation and colonization" of the feeble-minded.[24] A few decades earlier, Charles Booth had offered the same solution for an equivalent category of poor people, and not long before he was forced to resign as vice president of the United States in 1974, Spiro Agnew suggested that poor people accused of behavioral shortcomings should be rehoused in rural new towns built far away from existing cities and suburbs.

Even a thoughtful underclass policy would be dangerous, because the people forced under the underclass umbrella suffer from different kinds of poverty and, in some cases, poverty-related problems, which may require different solutions. Reducing poverty for able-bodied workers requires labor market policy change; reducing it for people who cannot work calls for a humane income grant program. Enabling and encouraging young people to stay in school requires different policies than the elimination of homelessness, and ending substance abuse or street crime demand yet others. Labelers or experts who claim one policy can do it all are simply wrong.

THE HUMAN DANGERS OF LABELING

Most immediately, the underclass label poses a danger for poor people in that the agencies with which they must deal can hurt clients who are so labeled.[25] For one thing, agencies for the poor sometimes build labels into their operating procedures and apply them to all of their clients. As a result, either evidence about actual clients is not collected, or the label is assumed to fit regardless of evidence to the contrary. Agencies responsible for public safety typically resort to this procedure as a crime prevention or deterrence measure, especially when those labeled have little legal or political power. For example, in 1993, the Denver police department compiled a roster of suspected gang members based on "clothing choices," "flashing of gang signals," or associating with known gang members. The list included two-thirds of the city's young black men, of whom only a small percentage were actual gang members.[26]

Labeling also creates direct punitive effects of several kinds. Bruce Link's studies of people labeled as mentally ill have found that the labeling act itself can lead to depression and demoralization, which prevent those labeled from being at their best in job interviews and other competitive situations.[27] Likewise, when poor youngsters who hang out on street corners are treated as "loiterers," they may end up with an arrest record that hurts them in later life—which is probably why middle-class teenagers who also hang out are rarely accused of loitering.

Some effects of labels are felt even earlier in children's lives. Teachers treat students differently if they think they come from broken homes.[28] A long-term study of working-class London has found that labeling effects may even be intergenerational. Labeling of parents as delinquent makes it more likely that their children will also be labeled, adding to the numbers in both generations who are accused of delinquent or criminal behavior.[29]

Sometimes the effect of labeling is more indirect: agencies cut off opportunities and the label turns into a self-fulfilling prophecy. When teachers label low-income or very dark-skinned students as unable to learn, they may reduce their efforts to teach them—often unintentionally, but even so students then become less able to learn. If poor youngsters accused of loitering are assumed to have grown up without the self-control thought to be supplied by male supervision, they may be harassed—sometimes to tease and entrap them into an angry response. The arrests and arrest records that inevitably follow may deprive youngsters from fatherless families of legal job opportunities, and help force them into delinquent ones. In all these cases, the self-fulfilling prophecy is used to declare the labeled guilty without evidence of misconduct.

Another variation of the entrapment process takes place in jails. John Irwin's study of San Francisco courts and jails reports that these sometimes punished defendants whether they were guilty or not, and adds that "the experience of harsh and unfairly delivered punishment frequently enrages or embitters defendants and makes it easier for them to reject the values of those who have dealt with them in this way."[30] In this instance, as in many of the other instances when the labels are applied by penal institutions, the labeled are not necessarily "passive innocents," as Hagan and Palloni put it.[31] Instead, labeling sometimes generates reactions, both on the part of the police and of those they arrest, that push both sides over the edge.

The direct and indirect effects of labeling even hurt the poor in seeking help, because when they evoke labels in the minds of service suppliers they may be given inferior service, the wrong service, or none at all. Services for the labeled are normally underfunded to begin with and service suppliers are frequently overworked, so that the agencies from which the poor seek help must operate under more or less permanent triage conditions. One way of deciding who will be sacrificed in triage decisions is to assume that most clients cheat, use every contact with them to determine whether they are cheating, and exclude those who can be suspected of cheating. Since clients are of lower status than service suppliers and lack any power or influence over them, the suppliers can also vent their own status frustrations on clients. An arbitrary denial of services to clients not only relieves such frustrations but also enables suppliers to make the needed triage choices. For that reason alone, poor clients who object to being mistreated are usually the first to be declared ineligible for help.

Labeling clients as cheaters encourages service suppliers to distrust them, and that distrust is increased if the suppliers fear revenge, particularly violent revenge, from these clients. Consequently, suppliers hug the rules more tightly, making no leeway in individual cases, and even punishing colleagues who bend the rules in trying to help clients. When clients, who presumably come with prejudices of their own about agency staffs, develop distrust of the staff, a spiraling effect of mutual distrust and fear is set up. This creates data to justify labeling on both sides. The mutual distrust also encourages the exchange of violence, or the preemptive strikes of staff members who fear violence from angry clients.[32]

Admittedly, labeling of clients is only a small part of staff-client misunderstandings and client mistreatment. The previously noted lack of funds and staff, the stresses of operating in stigmatized agencies and with stigmatized clients, normal bureaucratic rules that always put the demands of the agency and its staff ahead of the needs of clients, as well as differences of class and race between staff and clients, wreak their own cumulative havoc.

The added role of labeling in reducing services is particularly serious for poor people who live at the edge of homelessness or starvation or ill health. Yet another cause for the reduction or ending of already minimal services may push them over the edge, into the streets or an emergency clinic, into chronic illness or permanent disability, or into street crime.

Nevertheless, agencies sometimes actively discourage labeled people from escaping their stigmatized status. Liebow reports a dramatic but typical incident from a women's shelter: two women were trying to escape homelessness by taking second jobs, which they were forced to give up in order to attend obligatory but aimless night meetings so as to retain their beds in the shelter.[33] In unlabeled populations, taking second jobs would have been rewarded as upward mobility; among labeled ones it is identified as evasion of agency rules or flouting of service supplier authority, as well as evidence of the client troublemaking that is often associated with the label.

Consequently, one major ingredient in successful efforts to help the labeled poor is to remove the label. For example, scattered site housing studies suggest that such housing is successful in changing the lives of the rehoused when their origins and backgrounds are kept from their new neighbors, so that these cannot react to pejorative labels about slum dwellers.[34]

The labels that have produced these effects are not created solely from overheated mainstream fears or imaginations. Like all stereotypes, such labels are built around a small core of truth, or apply "to a few bad apples," as lay psychology puts it. Labeling, however, punishes not only the bad apples but everybody in the population to whom the label is applied. By labeling poor young black males as potential street criminals, for example, the white and black populations fearful of being attacked may feel that they protect themselves, but at the cost of hurting and antagonizing the large majority of poor young black males who are innocent. Inevitably, however, a proportion of the innocent will react angrily to the label, and find ways of getting even with those who have labeled them. In the end, then, everyone loses, the label users as well as the labeled.

Nonetheless, labeling is only a by-product of a larger structural process that cannot be ignored. In any population that lacks enough legitimate opportunities, illegitimate ones will be created and someone will take them. When the jobs for which the poor are eligible pay such a low wage that even some of the employed will turn to drug selling or other crime to increase their incomes, the labeling process is set in motion that finally hurts many more people, poor and nonpoor, whether or not they are guilty or innocent. Still, the real guilt has to be laid at the door of the employers that pay insufficient wages and the market conditions that may give some of them little other choice.

THE INACCURACIES OF LABELS

Last but not least, labels are dangerous simply because they are inaccurate. "Underclass" is inaccurate if interpreted literally, because there can be no class that exists *under* society, as the class hierarchy extends from the top of society to its very bottom. Indeed, "underclass" is like "underworld," which is also part of society, and in fact could not long exist if it were not supplying demanded goods or services to an "overworld."[35]

"Underclass" is also an inaccurate label because it so vague that there is no agreement on a single or simple definition. Several other labels, however, which have evolved from descriptive terms about which there is widespread consensus, offer good illustrations of how much the portraits of the labeled vary from data on actual people.

"Welfare dependent," "single-parent family," "teenage mother," and "the homeless" are relevant examples. "Welfare dependent" is a corruption of "welfare recipient," which assumes that recipients become dependent on the government by virtue of obtaining welfare. In fact, however, only 30 percent of all recipients who begin a period on welfare will stay on for more than two years, and only 7 percent will be on more than eight years, although some of those who leave it also return to it later.[36] Further, about 20 percent of all welfare recipients report non-AFDC income, although if off-the-books employment is counted, nearly half of all recipients are working.[37]

Some recipients would leave welfare and take their chances in the labor market if they could obtain medical insurance for their children. Still, many poor women clearly rely on AFDC and are thus dependent on the government program; what is noted less often is that often they are even more dependent on staying in the good graces of their welfare agency, which can decide to cut them off arbitrarily without a great deal of accountability.

Ironically enough, only welfare recipients are accused of being dependents; others who are subsidized by government without adding something to the economy in exchange for their subsidy are not so labeled. Students with government fellowships, home owners who receive federal tax and mortgage interest deductions, corporations that receive subsidies to stay in existence, as well as unproductive civil servants and the workers on superfluous military bases kept open to prevent the elimination of jobs, are not thought of as being dependent. Thus the economic dependency of welfare recipients is not the real issue, and the label is misnamed as well as partly inaccurate.

"Single-parent family," or at least the label, is also partly or wholly incorrect. For one thing, some families have a man in or near the household de facto if not de jure; more are embedded in an extended family in which mothers, grandmothers, and others share the parenting.[38]

The notion that the children of such families are subject to undue school leaving, joblessness, and poverty, as well as crime and various pathologies, because they did not grow up in two-parent households is similarly incorrect. Since the modern family is not an economically productive institution, single-parenthood per se cannot logically cause poverty in the next generation, any more than growing up in a two-parent family can cause affluence. This helps to explain why well-off single parents are rarely accused of raising children who will grow up with economic or other problems. And since single-parent households are almost always poorer than other poor households, at least when their economic condition is measured properly, whatever economic effects children from such households suffer can be traced to their more extreme poverty or greater economic insecurity.

In addition, while the children of happy two-parent families are best off, all other things being equal, the children of single parents are sometimes emotionally and otherwise better off than the children of two parents who are in constant conflict.[39] If parental conflict is more detrimental to children's well-being and performance than is single parenthood, it would explain the results of studies concluding that children of divorced parents are not uniformly worse off than those from intact families.[40] Since the scarcity of money is a major cause of conflict—and spouse battering— among poor parents, this also helps to explain further the unwillingness of pregnant young women to marry their partners if they are jobless. None of this argues that poor single-parent families are desirable and should be encouraged, because if there is only one parent, the economic and other burdens on her and the children are often too great, and all may suffer. But the single-parent family structure and the burdens that come with it are usually the result of poverty.

The same conclusions apply to teenage pregnancy. Unmarried adolescents who bear children constitute about half of all adolescent mothers and 8 percent of all welfare recipients, although some adult welfare recipients also became mothers in adolescence.[41] The younger among them may be reacting to school failures as well as family conflict, which can increase the urgency of the normal desire to feel useful to and loved by someone. More to the economic point, many scholars, beginning with Frank Furstenberg,

Jr., have pointed out that the babies of such mothers will be in school when their occupational chances are better.

These observations are no argument *for* adolescent motherhood, especially since many of the babies are actually unwanted at time of conception, and may even be the product of a young woman's defeat by her sexual partner in a power struggle over wearing a condom, or over having sex at all. Unwanted fetuses, however, seem to turn into wanted babies, partly because of lack of access to abortion facilities but perhaps also because low-income families have traditionally welcomed new arrivals. Given the limited chances for upward mobility among the poor, additional babies do not represent the same obstacle to higher status that they sometimes do among the more affluent classes.

There is not even reliable evidence that poor women in their twenties are automatically better mothers than poor girls in their teens, especially if the teenagers have already been responsible for taking care of their younger siblings. Older mothers are probably more mature, but if adolescent mothers receive more help from their mothers and grandmothers than they would if they were older, then adolescence may sometimes be an advantage.[42] It could also be an advantage on health grounds, if the hypothesis that poor mothers are healthier as teenagers than as adults turns out to be supported by sufficient evidence.[43] Conversely, today's poor teenagers are in the unfortunate position of becoming mothers when America's culturally dominant female role models—upper-middle-class professional women—postpone motherhood as long as possible in order to put their careers on a secure footing. Thus what may be rational behavior for poor young women is decidedly irrational according to cultural norms these days. Teenage motherhood does not thereby become desirable, but once more, the fundamental problem is the poverty that helps to make it happen.

Finally, even the homeless label can be incorrect. For one thing, label users tend to combine panhandlers with the homeless, even though the former are frequently housed. Furthermore, homeless populations differ from community to community depending on the nature of the low-income labor and housing markets, and particularly of housing vacancy rates for poor nonwhites in these communities. Even the rates of mental illness and substance abuse vary.

More important, since the mentally ill and addicted homeless were poor to begin with, curing them would not by itself significantly increase their ability to find affordable housing, or jobs that would enable them to afford such housing. Most lack occupational skills and skin colors that are needed on the job market these days, the obvious virtues of mental health and freedom from addiction notwithstanding. Jencks argues that money spent on substance abuse could be used instead for shelter, but in most communities, it is both easier and cheaper to get hard drugs and alcohol than low-income housing.[44] It is not yet even known how many homeless people turned to alcohol or drugs because of economic problems or familial ones—or just lack of family—and then became homeless, and how many became homeless first and addicts subsequently.

While dealing with mental illness and addiction are vital, homelessness is a disease of the housing market, just as being on welfare is a disease of the job market. The mentally ill and the addicted are the most vulnerable to both of these economic diseases, but as long as there are not enough dwelling units and jobs for the poor, someone will have to be homeless and on welfare. Whether intentionally or not, the most vulnerable are almost always "selected" for most deprivations, among other reasons because they are the least able to protest or to defend themselves.

Labels, whether applied to welfare recipients, the homeless, and other poor people, cannot ever describe the labeled, because labels mainly describe their imagined behavioral and moral deviations from an assumed mainstream. Justified or not, labels express the discontents of the mainstream and those speaking for it, not the characteristics and conditions of the labeled themselves. When label users are discontented and seek people on whom they can project their frustrations, the accuracy of the resultant labels is not a major consideration. In fact, accuracy may get in the way if frustrated people want to be enraged by poor people and thus able to blame them.

Ultimately, however, even accurate labels for the poor are dangerous because the labels cannot end poverty or the criminal and offending poverty-related behavior of some of the poor, or the fear, anger, and unhappiness of the labelers. In the long run, these latter may be the most dangerous effects of labels.

CHAPTER 4

The Undeservingness of the Poor

Eliminating "underclass" as a label will not eliminate its dangers, history having shown that if one label loses its appeal, another is likely to emerge sooner or later, new and old labels being merely new words for the undeserving poor. The more basic problem lies elsewhere: in the underlying idea of the undeserving poor. Behind that idea is the power of the stereotypes expressed in it, and even more important, the structural sources and reasons for that power, which are located in the larger society. The hatred aroused by the poor accused of being undeserving really has to do with more basic faults and social fault lines in America.

Why, for example, are politicians able to score symbolic triumphs by inveighing against alleged dangers from the imagined undeservingness of welfare recipients? What economic and moral problems in the country lead them to fall all over themselves to propose ending welfare, or to invent new ways of making it ever more punitive? Why do some intellectuals feel that illegitimacy is a more serious American problem than violent crime, the failure of the economy to generate enough jobs, or the country's need to come to terms with worldwide wars and civil wars? Why does the country even need such scapegoats as the undeserving poor?

UNDESERVINGNESS

Perhaps because it is such a powerful label, undeservingness is not assigned only to the poor. During or just before a war, inhabitants of the prospective combatant country have to become undeserving in order to become enemies, in order to persuade every citizen of the need for their defeat and destruction.[1] Enemies are just one category of the threatening outgroup of strangers, however, and it is the threatening outgroup that is always, or almost always, thought undeserving, whether its threats are actual or imagined.

Such outgroups are created everywhere in American society. Parts of the political and economic elite are perceived to be corrupt or greedy by the rest of the population, while most of the working poor and working-class people who earn their living through manual labor consider white-collar, professional, and managerial workers to be undeserving because they sit on their behinds instead of working. The old rich perceive the new rich to be undeserving, and vice versa, for the ways they earn or spend their money. In residential areas, old-timers look down on newcomers, and newcomers scorn old-timers, but some of the strongest hatreds are found between seemingly similar ideological groups, especially on the far right and far left.

All class strata seem agreed, however, on the undeservingness of the poor they judge to be criminal and deviant. Moreover, since the characterization of the undeserving poor has changed remarkably little over at least the last five hundred years, the undeservingness of the poor is not simply a problem of modernity or postmodernity; capitalism, classical and advanced; or socialism, state and otherwise.[2]

Similar events may recur for a variety of reasons; today's notion of undeservingness is created by two factors. The undeserving poor constitute a perceived threat to the better-off classes; and judging some poor people as undeserving has positive uses or benefits for various institutions and interest groups in society. If the causes of the threats, and the incentives behind the uses, can be understood, policies to do away with undeservingness can at least be proposed.[3]

THE THREATS OF UNDESERVINGNESS

"Threat" is a strong word, but it is apt because the intensity of feelings harbored by the more fortunate classes about the poor thought to be undeserving is so strong.[4] Indeed, the liberal politicians and policymakers of the 1980s and 1990s have paid a heavy price for underestimating it. In reality, the feelings are a mixture of fear, anger, and disapproval, but fear may be the most important element in the mixture. Such feelings are expressed not only in the political rhetoric of increasing numbers of seekers for public office but in news, entertainment, and other outlets of public communication. These all tell alarmist stories in which the villains often have neither motive, reason, nor any redeeming human features. Whether they are street criminals or young mothers without husbands, they are in effect demons, usually black, who have been let loose on an innocent country. And the privately told stories are much worse than the public ones.

The threats of undeservingness can be divided into four modes, here called actual, imagined, exaggerated, and displaced. These threats can also be classified into a number of substantive categories that have changed little over the centuries. The primary ones are threats to safety, cultural standards, economic position, and moral values or norms, although these often blend into one another. Only the intensity of the various fears and the urgency of the demands for ending them vary with the times.

Actual threats are empirically verifiable by an outside observer, by scientific, journalistic, and lay methods. Most actual crime threats reflect personal experience, or what people hear from relatives, friends, and neighbors, and see on TV.

Imagined threats are those for which reasonable evidence of an actual threat does not exist; a typical and recurring example is alleged but untrue police killings of blacks that have often set off urban uprisings.[5] People who are upset may not recognize or even care that the threats are imaginary, but the researcher and policymaker must care. They cannot ignore the power of imagination; indeed, the raw material for the making of stereotypes and labels is imagination, although the imaginary threat almost always has a prior cause. That cause does not always stem from the people felt to be threatening. Thus, imaginary threats must be understood and dealt with by seeking their causes and sources in the imaginations and fears of the threatened. These are sometimes found in past actual incidents that fire up imaginations, rather than fictional ones that never happened, but sometimes the causes and sources have nothing to do with the poor, and the threats that result are displaced ones.

Exaggerated threats are hyperbolic versions of actual threats, creating a mixture of actual and imagined threats—the best example is the white fear of all poor, black, young males, which exaggerates the statistical fact that black young males commit a disproportionately high amount of street crime. Many of the anecdotes and even news stories about the misbehaviors of the undeserving poor are probably exaggerated threats, having been enhanced by hyperbole in their telling and retelling. They are also in some respects the most difficult to reduce or eliminate, because the threatened may see only the actual threats while in fact they have put their imaginations to work to exaggerate the danger or to increase the anger they feel. Imagined threats can sometimes be debunked because they have no basis in reality; exaggerated ones are more dangerous because they do have such a basis, even if it is often far-fetched.

Persuading people that their fears are imaginary or exaggerated is immensely difficult, for facts and rational arguments are effective only under conditions of calm and trust. When fears take over, citizens who are bitter opponents of additional taxes open their pockets to build expensive new prisons, and predictions based on past experience that they will not reduce street crime are ignored. Politicians who must know that public miserliness is often the best road to reelection may try to fight such building schemes, but when a significant number of people believe imagined threats to be actual no one can stop them, and politicians who want to be reelected do not try.[6] Analytically, the best solution may be to forget the difference between imagined and exaggerated threats, and to assume that the same kinds of upsets fuel both of them.[7]

Displaced threats are those imagined and exaggerated ones that fearful people project on the poor but which they have displaced from the conditions that actually generate them. When affluent people fear what they call the dependency of welfare recipients, perhaps they feel that their own economic independence is threatened, or that the political value system that enabled them to become economically independent, even affluent, is under attack, and could place them in the same dependent role that they view welfare recipients as occupying. In this case, the affluent may be displacing anxieties about the economy and society on welfare recipients, although usually not consciously so. Since one of the major uses or functions of the undeserving poor is to serve as scapegoats, they are, by definition, targets of displaced threats.

At some point, systematic research on *why* the better-off stereotype the poor as undeserving and *why* they perceive imaginary threats from them as actual will have to be undertaken. The results will probably show that many such threats are in fact displaced, and that the problems lie elsewhere in the society. Historians have supplied evidence of how colonial America's problems were projected on witches, such as in the Salem cases, but preventive policy-making requires more contemporary analysis. This is desperately needed, particularly in a society that builds more prisons than any other to cope with threats of which only some are actual. And until the process by which a handful of actual threats are turned into a flood of imagined and exaggerated threats is understood, little can be done to end fear of threats unfairly blamed on the undeserving poor.

Crime, Fear of Crime, and Other Threats to Safety

Currently, the threat to safety is the major fear associated with undeservingness. For the better-off classes, the primary actual threat is street crime, such as mugging, burglary, and pickpocketing, which are particularly threatening because even when the crimes are not violent, they are always invasions of personal privacy.[8] Conversely, auto theft, probably the most pervasive of urban and suburban crimes, seems to be treated as less threatening.

Street crime is threatening as well because its occurrence is essentially unpredictable, thus making defense against it seemingly impossible. The fears generated by unpredictability also make people less willing to distinguish between actual and imagined threats, and more willing to listen to politicians who promise to take harsh measures against suspected street criminals. Because street crime is so widely feared, local news media rarely miss the most dramatic incidents, especially in white neighborhoods, which provides further raw material for the widespread fear of crime.[9] The fact that the news media rarely explain why specific crimes have taken place may add to the unpredictability of street crime, and, when the crime is violent, increase perception of it as "random" or "senseless."

Although the fear of crime is said to be high in many places, even outside the cities, information about it is tragically sparse. Crime shows up high on the pollsters' lists of major national problems only sporadically, and even though it is a productive election campaign issue, and an even more productive topic for radio talk show hosts, how many people actually respond and how typical they are of voters remains unclear. Past studies suggest that women, senior citizens, and people in high-crime areas generally are more fearful than others, but that in other such areas, lively and effective neighborhood participation can reduce the fear of crime.[10] Statistical data about trends in the frequency of street crime seem to bear little relation to the fear of crime, that fear being evoked instead by nearby incidents that are endlessly repeated and probably exaggerated in local grapevines, and by dramatic incidents that become major news stories and are later also repeated and exaggerated by word-of-mouth.

Feelings about neighborhood social control would suggest that the fear of crime is partly imagined, and some could actually be displaced fear. This is backed up by national poll data reporting that the percentage of people feeling safe in their own neighborhoods has not changed since the mid-1970s, even though the same people believe that crime has increased significantly both in the country and in their own community "over the past year."[11] Clearly people are fearful of something, which they express as fear of crime in strange neighborhoods but which may be in part displaced fear, perhaps about where the nation and local communities are going in a time of economic uncertainty, social division and political inefficacy, and increased cultural conflict.

In effect, given the very real fears they evoke, perceived threats to safety easily spread elsewhere. Before they move to the level of community and nation, they first spread to poor people who are not criminals. For example, when and where homeless people and panhandlers increase in number, begging and acting-out are often perceived as threats by the better-off, even if they are often imagined threats, since the homeless are largely passive or victimize other homeless people. Beggars rarely attack the people from whom they beg. Unfortunately, the better-off classes observe what they consider to be misuses of *their* public space and invasions of *their* privacy by beggars and the homeless as equivalent invasions by dangerous street criminals. As a result, it is easy for them to imagine that beggars and the homeless inevitably mean street crime. Since beggars generally outnumber street criminals, a possible actual threat from the latter is thus turned into a more frequent and visible imagined threat from the former. Vagabonds and tramps probably evoked similar imagined threats in the rural communities of past centuries.

Moreover, the perception of threat attaches to innocent people who look like street criminals to the better-off: to poor, black, young males especially, who are probably the major focus of imagined threat in America today.[12] In the 1980s, fear for personal safety became pervasive enough that poor unmarried mothers were viewed as breeders of delinquents and street criminals, thus becoming indirect threats to safety themselves, even though there is no reliable evidence that such mothers, on or off welfare, produce more children that become street criminals than other very poor people. Poor unmarried mothers were, however, also viewed as sources of other threats, like American witches, nineteenth-century British paupers, and the husbandless German and Irish women whom Charles Loring Brace thought to be the mothers of the homeless "street urchins" of post–Civil War New York.[13]

Furthermore, personal safety is of such intense concern to people that the need to ward off potential criminals spreads the safety fears further, for example to "gangsta rap," male teenage dress codes, adolescent swagger, and other lifestyles of the poor, all diverging ever more from those of the adult mainstream. From the point of view of the adults in the nonpoor population, these are essentially *cultural* safety threats.[14] These and other such threats to cultural standards are sometimes described as oppositional culture, or a culture of "resistance" or "refusal." Such terminology may overpoliticize the fads and fashions of poor adolescents, when much of it is conventional youth culture of the poor that seeks to keep mainstream adults at a distance by frightening them.[15]

Political safety threats used to be a concern, albeit a minor one, in America, but the days of the politically dangerous classes seem to be over. Poor anarchists and other radicals, immigrant or native-born, are a historical memory, and the previously noted culture of resistance or refusal is only rarely viewed as a significant threat to political safety. Some black nationalist militants may employ revolutionary rhetoric, but most white Americans miss the political intent. Furthermore, Americans are so unused to political violence that no one ever considers the possibility that street crime contains elements of an unmentioned and perhaps unconscious political protest against the lack of decent jobs and other economic inequalities, as well as political injustice.

Indeed, the concern with personal safety and its identification with street crime and the undeserving poor has set aside, or even suppressed, most threats to safety stemming from so-called white collar crime. The occupational safety threats created or condoned by employers of farm workers or factory workers do not seem to touch the people who worry about street crime. Atmospheric pollution, environmental destruction, and the production of unhealthy foods and other consumer goods all impinge on personal safety, but they are not classified as safety *threats* by most people. For one thing, the risk is shared by large numbers of people so that such dangers, like earthquakes and other natural disasters, are not felt as personal threats. For another, many people think dangers to health can be reduced by personal choice—by choosing certain foods or abstaining from smoking, for example—so that they are felt as less unpredictable and therefore less threatening than crime.

Undoubtedly, some of the parents whose children suffer from toxic poisoning and some of the people who have lost their savings to stock manipulation do consider polluting manufacturers or unscrupulous savings and loan associations as threatening. Still, no one has yet created stereotypes of the undeserving members of the chemicals industry, insufficiently safety-conscious automobile companies, careless government regulating agencies—or of irresponsible politicians seeking to end regulation altogether. Consequently, safety threats connected to street crime must also be understood as particular cases of more general class and race fears that go far beyond issues of personal safety.

Economic Threats

From a cost perspective, the losses exacted by street criminals, even including drug sellers, are minor economic threats, at least when compared to the huge sums taken out of the economy by failed savings and loan associations or giant corporations relocating to Mexico. The costs of street crime only increase when the money spent for protection against it is added, expenses such as the funds allocated to police, prisons, courts, private police and related security measures, and insurance. The costs rise further with the addition of replacement costs incurred by thefts and burglaries, and the proportion of the price of goods that pays for shoplifting, other crime, and insurance against crime in the production and distribution of these goods.

Ironically enough, while people may be aware of these costs through paying their home or auto insurance or replacing a stolen car, they do not seem to blame the undeserving poor for them. Although the annual cost of crime, protection, and associated expenditures during the 1990s has been estimated at $163 billion, the better-off classes do not appear to worry about street crime primarily as an economic threat.[16] Instead, this sort of threat is seen as coming from other kinds of poor people. These include illegal immigrants thought to take the jobs of legal residents during periods of high unemployment, and poor people moving into and "taking over" the neighborhoods of the better-off, although then fears about the loss of property values are combined with fears of status loss and fears for personal safety.

By far the greatest economic threat associated with undeservingness, however, seems to be "welfare dependency," including large sums imagined to be spent by governments on payments to welfare recipients. Better-off people feel that these come directly, and in large amounts, from their own taxes—almost as if they were personally subsidizing poor women on welfare. The felt intensity of this economic threat is increased by the notion that welfare recipients are so dependent on welfare that they become permanent burdens to the taxpayers. In fact, of course, the public monies, federal and local, spent on welfare (and food stamps) amounted to slightly less than $40 billion in 1992. This is less than 15 percent of the post–Cold War annual defense budget; about $10 billion less than the mortgage interest tax deductions available to home owners that benefit mainly the rich, and only about one-sixth of the corporate subsudies and tax breaks considered to be "corporate pork."[17]

The taxpayers' anger toward welfare is not generated by the numbers, however. They are angered at least in part by the belief that they get nothing in return for the monies spent on the poor. Their reaction is exaggerated in an economy in which they worry about their own position, and where many are asked to work harder than in the past, which also helps to explain the desire to put recipients to work even when there are no jobs for them. One reason economic threats are not always viewed from a "rational" economic perspective is that they are accompanied by and interwoven with threats to values—actual, imagined, and displaced. In the case of welfare recipients, one perceived threat is the belief that they deliberately thumb their noses at marriage and two-parent families. The disinclination of whites to spend money that goes proportionally more often to poor blacks cannot be ignored either, although in areas of the country with many white young unmarried mothers, race takes a back seat to class hostility.

Moral Value Threats

Moral value threats are perceived dangers to what is believed to be culturally and morally proper. Behavior viewed as threatening people's moral values is felt as a personal attack, especially by those who assiduously practice mainstream values, and who may do so on religious grounds. Threats to values can thus be as actual as threats to safety.

Even so, since better-off people react mainly to stereotypes and know nothing about the values of the poor, the moral value threat appears to be largely imagined. In fact, however, it accords with a general theme of American popular ideology, which assumes that most behavior is caused by the holding and practicing of values, with good behavior resulting from good values and bad behavior from bad values. That behavior is also very largely generated by the economic, political, and other structural conditions to which people must react, sometimes sans choice, is rarely recognized.[18] As a result, if poor people behave in ways that diverge from those thought to be mainstream, it is ascribed to their rejection of mainstream values and not to their inability to act in accord with these values. Larry Backer puts the lay axiom well when he writes that "indigence is produced not by the social or economic system, but by the deviance of the poor. The necessary punishment for deviance is poverty."[19]

There is considerable evidence—but not very much in the popular media—that, when asked about their values, poor people sound as much or more mainstream than most better-off Americans. There is, however, not much evidence in the popular or professional literature about if, when, and how much the better-off themselves abide by mainstream values, how strongly they feel about these values, and whether their adherence to mainstream values is actually any greater or stronger than even the poor they consider undeserving.

Moreover, the people who feel themselves to constitute the mainstream also feel sure that their values are mainstream, and since they know nothing about the actual values of the poor they call undeserving, they also do not know that what they perceive as moral value threats from the poor have nothing per se to do with values.

Instead, the feeling of threat results from the fact that, unlike the affluent classes, the poor cannot mask their occasional inability or unwillingness to practice mainstream behavior, which is why the more affluent imagine the poor have bad values. For example, while middle-class people who become jobless generally have family connections, networks, and other resources to fall back on and usually even remain home owners, while the working poor who lose their jobs often go on welfare, and some eventually become homeless, or show up in the street crime statistics. If the better-off use drugs, they do so in their living rooms. And if the more fortunate fail repeatedly in their marriages, they can still hope that the next one will succeed. Poor women who have rarely met men with decent and secure jobs learn to expect from the start that marriage is not in the cards for them, and government data collectors frequently make sure that the illegitimacy of their children becomes public knowledge. Poor women who sour on marriage are stigmatized while their middle-class peers become the stuff of TV sitcoms, not evidence of moral failure.

In short, the more fortunate classes can keep their deviations from alleged or real mainstreams private, or can frame them as nonmoral, which is why they rarely become value threats. In addition, they can fight government invasions of privacy that could make their behavior public, even as they support more government intrusion into the lives of the poor that will be sure to make *their* behavior public.

This pattern also extends to organizations. While weapons producers may be as dependent on the Pentagon as poor women are on welfare, that dependence is less visible, so that they do not arouse fears that they are violating the norms of American economic individualism. Their dependence is less visible also because almost no one is looking; being respectable private corporations that issue shares traded on the major stock exchanges and that supply well-paying jobs, their dependency is noticeable mainly to radical observers.

That some rich people actually live the lives of hedonistic leisure of which the jobless poor are wrongly accused is also thought irrelevant, even if their income derives directly or indirectly from past gains once thought ill-gotten—for example, war profiteering or slave ownership. Membership in the mainstream permits such contradictions, just as it permits deviations from behavioral and value mainstreams if they remain hidden. Should they be made public by journalistic exposés, criticism may follow until the exposés are forgotten, but the deviations of the poor become public more often and more quickly and are seemingly remembered forever. Visibility of behavior, not adherence to values, turns out to be the de facto test of the existence of value threats.

Threats to moral values may even be felt as safety threats, again of the imagined variety, because of a kind of domino effect. This effect, also an outgrowth of popular ideology, assumes that if poor people are guilty of one deviant behavior or value they are probably guilty of others. Thus the more fortunate classes see themselves threatened by a mass of deviant behavior and values that may put an end to social order and the public peace. The domino effect is reflected in umbrella labels, enabling people to believe in, as did Oscar Lewis, a culture of poverty with over sixty "traits," or an underclass that can become entrenched and permanent.

Representative Newt Gingrich, the Republican party leader, may have had this domino effect in mind when he proposed, in 1993, that adolescent deviance could lead to social breakdown, although his examples were statistical outliers and not representative even of the alleged villains he identified. As he put it in a speech that he has since given many times, "You can't *maintain civilization* with twelve-year-olds having babies and fifteen-year-olds killing each other and seventeen-year-olds dying of AIDS."[20] The misbehavior of the poor can, however, be persuasively demonstrated by statistical or other hyperbole if enough people are ready to believe in that misbehavior a priori.

The Possibility of Displaced Threats

Displaced threats originate from various problems in society but are projected on the undeserving poor, who become scapegoats. Thus Mark Stern writes that "if economic dislocation . . . and urban restructuring were taking their toll on all of us, perhaps it was reassuring to imagine that there was a class at the bottom of society . . . whose vices made us look virtuous."[21]

Most displaced threats fall into two categories: either the poor are blamed for creating or worsening problems in the society with which they have little or nothing to do, or they are accused of setting bad examples for mainstream young people who diverge from mainstream ways. The problems for which the poor are blamed have often been economic; they have been held partly responsible for the decline of the American economy.[22] For example, to accuse the poor of being lazy or unwilling to adhere to the work ethic and its dress and time codes is easier than to confront the inability of the economy to create enough jobs, especially for unskilled people.

It is also easier to believe welfare recipients and, since the mid-1990s, immigrants to be a serious drain on the federal budget than to think about the Pentagon's still-massive drain on that budget. Displacing government inability to provide onto the poor also enables the more fortunate classes to continue to enjoy middle- and upper-class tax loopholes and other "welfare" that is virtually invulnerable to political attack. Corporate employees can feel sorrier for the challenges their employers face in surviving in the economy if they can blame welfare recipients for helping to impoverish that economy.[23] Those employees who have already been fired by their corporate employers and who know that they cannot fight either them or the global economy can at least pressure government to reduce their taxes, so they have more spending money, by demanding that government spend less on the undeserving poor.

Admittedly, some of the accusations leveled at the poor are stirred up by conservative interest groups and populations who have been fighting for higher military expenditures ever since the end of the Cold War, against the welfare state since the 1930s, and for minimal income taxes since before then. In hard times, anti–welfare state messages that concentrate on the financial threat of money spent for the poor become more persuasive. The Moynihan Report, often associated with the current alarm about welfare, did not make much of a stir, at least about welfare, on its publication in 1965 when the economy was still basically healthy.

The displaced threats attributed to the undeserving poor when they are imagined to be subverters of mainstream values are more often sexual or cultural than economic.[24] Adolescent motherhood among the unmarried poor began to rise in the 1950s, but it did not cause concern in white mainstream society until later, at about the time of the general increase in sexual activity among mainstream teenage girls, when it was feared that poor teenagers were becoming sexual role models for all adolescents. Even if working-class or middle-class girls should personally meet poor teenage mothers at school, however, their lives are so different that they have no incentive either to imitate the sexual practices of the latter or to become pregnant. Not only can mainstream girls be sexually active with young men who do not want to become fathers, but middle-class and upper-class youngsters can prevent premature parenthood by their easy access to birth control and abortion.

If the poor are role models, they may be more likely to be so in the youthful consumer culture, for more affluent youngsters seem to patronize manufacturers that borrow some of their fashion ideas in clothes and music from the poor.[25] A further general fear—that the "culture of the streets" may be so attractive as to subvert middle-class teenagers—is less credible, since the harshly enforced conformity demands of that culture are not even attractive to many of the poor youngsters caught in its trap because of their desperate search for excitement, support, and respect.[26] But the fictional version of that culture available in the news and entertainment media enables middle-class parents to blame the poor if their own adolescent children fail to accept parental advice and authority.

When native-born poor people refuse to perform unpleasant work for wages being paid to recent immigrants, and are thought to be insufficiently dedicated to the work ethic, they may serve to displace the doubts that better-off people have about their own devotion to unsatisfying work, workplaces, or employers. It is almost as if everyone feared that if better-paid workers copied the jobless poor and stopped performing unpleasant work the economy would immediately come to a grinding halt. Consequently, the poor can be imagined to be a real threat.

Envying the poor for seemingly living a life of full-time leisure may be easier than questioning the working conditions and job satisfactions available to the better-off in the modern economy.[27] Sometimes that envy is also sexual: the poor are imagined to devote themselves to sexual pleasure and other kinds of hedonism while the better-off have to work. Since such envy—usually male—is combined with anger about the poor enjoying this libidinal utopia at the taxpayers' expense, some better-off men may also be stigmatizing the poor as undeserving for having freed themselves from mainstream sexual norms that such men would sometimes like to jettison themselves.

There is even the possibility that the undeserving poor provide a national enemy when the better-off population lacks a foreign one. It may be coincidental, but anger at the undeserving poor began to rise in the mid-1980s when it looked as if the Cold War would soon end.

The hypothesis of displaced threats must, however, deal with two complications before it can be treated more seriously. One complication is historical: the overt fears expressed about today's welfare recipients, unmarried mothers, and the homeless, among others, resemble some of the fears of paupers, unmarried mothers, vagrants, tramps, and other poor people in past centuries, when society and economy were different. But if society and economy have changed since the nineteenth century, one must ask why fears of the undeserving poor and the hostility toward them have not changed more drastically as well.

To be sure, today's fears, however imaginary or exaggerated, do not result in the brutality with which the undeserving poor of the nineteenth century were treated. Despite their myriad faults, today's welfare officials are more civilized than the charity officials even at the turn of this century, and contemporary jails and prisons do not mistreat their occupants as much as did nineteenth-century workhouses. Perhaps the fears themselves

have actually changed. Or perhaps only the technology and the organization of the economy have changed; and the rest, the everyday economy
and society in which the rank-and-file population is embedded, remains
the same even if pundits now say "the postindustrial economy" and "the
postmodern society." Still, being jobless in the postindustrial economy is
no different than being jobless in the past, and homelessness remains homelessness, even if the death rate of today's homeless is lower than that of the
homeless of the past.

The other complication is methodological and political: it is difficult to
demonstrate the existence of displaced threats. Intensive questioning of the
better-off classes asking people whether, how, and why they are fearful of
and angry at the poor they themselves consider particularly undeserving
may supply clues concerning how their feelings about the undeserving poor
relate to, and stand as proxies for, other kinds of fear and anger, including
fear and anger about the state of the economy and the society.[28]

The Epidemiology of Threats

For policy purposes, information is badly needed about who feels what
threats about whom, and how intensely. If welfare recipients are stigmatized by economic elites who want to pay fewer taxes, a very different politics and policy is needed than if the stigma comes from poorer taxpayers,
or from people who envy recipients for not working or for participating
regularly in orgies.

Unfortunately very little such data has been collected, and most of this
information is survey data about how the better-off classes feel about the
homeless. Many of the studies also ask either-or "attribution" questions—
whether respondents blame "behavioral" shortcomings by the homeless, or
whether they put the blame on "structural" causes in the economy. Such
questions are actually ideological in intent, and answers to them can reveal
little about which parts of the better-off population are most threatened by
and most hostile toward the poor.

Bruce Link and his colleagues have, however, studied the poor as threat,
for they asked a 1,500-person national sample to agree or disagree with
statements about whether they considered the homeless to be dangerous.
Whichever way these statements were worded, only about 5 percent of the
total polled population thought these were "definitely true," while 25 to 40
percent said they were "probably true."[29] When the same respondents were

asked about the dangerousness of the mentally ill, the percentage responding "definitely true" rose to about 15 percent.[30]

The respondents who most often answer "definitely true" to questions asking if the homeless are dangerous were the oldest, least educated, and poorest members of the sample.[31] Presumably this group includes people who live in areas where they see homeless people or who feel themselves to be most at risk from street crime. But they are also the people whom one would expect to be most at risk from the troubled economy and changing society, and therefore also likely to displace their worries on the homeless poor.[32]

The attribution data are ambiguous, for most people mention both behavioral and structural causes. In the previously mentioned study by Link and his colleagues, the most often mentioned causes, all thought to "contribute a lot to homelessness" by at least half the sample, were, first to last, "drug and alcohol abuse," "an economic system that favors the rich over the poor," and "a shortage of affordable housing." All of the other stated causes, whether behavioral or structural, were thought to contribute "a lot" by a quarter to a third of the respondents, whether the statement referred to "laziness" or "irresponsible behavior on the part of the homeless," or "the shortage of government aid for poor people."[33]

Similar attribution patterns are reported in the other studies.[34] Generally, the oldest, least educated, and lowest-income respondents are most likely to see the poor and homeless as at fault behaviorally, but they also blame government the most for not helping with money, affordable housing, and other forms of aid. Moreover, the attitude variations between socioeconomic, educational, and age groups are often not very large.[35]

Although in theory the highest-income population, and especially the most highly educated one, should be most knowledgeable about structural causes, this is not the case, meaning either that they are too far from the homeless either spatially or ideologically or that they are unwilling to indict the economy and the government.

Do these data suggest that the oldest, lowest-income, and least well educated Americans are most threatened by the poor, most hostile to them, and most likely to consider them undeserving? Unfortunately, the surveys do not undertake sufficiently detailed questioning to supply a reliable answer to this question.

What most of the polls *do* show is a kind of generalized desire to help the poor and homeless, and even a subdued eagerness to pay more taxes.[36]

Link's own study, however, found that only 40 percent were willing to pay $25 a year or more extra in taxes to help the homeless.[37]

Surveys may not be the best source of data on how people feel, partly because better-educated respondents are apt to appear more tolerant to interviewers than they might be under other situations—for example, when politicians make strongly worded appeals to their fears, to vested interests, or even to displaced threats.[38] They are also more likely than other people to become politically involved, and perhaps to support actions that contradict their survey responses.

Even so, no one knows exactly who among the American people is supplying the political support to the Republican, religious conservative, and corporate leadership that is spearheading the escalation of the war against the poor in the mid-1990s. Analysts of the November 1994 elections found no visible voter mandate for that escalation. The first opinion polls taken since then also suggest that large numbers of poll respondents disagree with the meanness of the war against the poor and even the intense punitiveness of the otherwise popular "welfare reform" measures that are part of the Republican "Contract with America." Still, the many people who tell pollsters that they favor helping the poor and the overt defenders of the poor are practically without voice, at least for the moment.

Undeservingness: The Bottom Line

It is even possible to guess that the final bottom line or sufficient cause of the undeservingness of the poor is not their threats, actual or imaginary, to the mainstream population. Instead, what may energize feelings of undeservingness above all is the perceived insolence of the poor in behaving as they do while being supported by public funds. Deviation from the mainstream, crime, and even some threats to personal safety are tolerated if they emanate from people who are wealthy or earn their own living, but all are always damned among welfare recipients and others who have to be supported from taxes.

For example, even bearing illegitimate children is permissible on the part of the better-off, but the poor must be married and working so that the state need not spend money on their children. Nonetheless, punishment is reserved for the mothers who get welfare benefits, not the fathers, who get no public funds.

These seeming inconsistencies in the handling of deviance are in part the normally differential treatment of those high and low in the class and gender hierarchies. The undeservingness of the poor is punishment not only for their lowly state, however, but for the existence of poverty itself. The ideology of undeservingness holds that if people were without the moral and other deficiencies that make them poor, there might be no poverty; and if the jobless were not lazy there would be virtually no unemployment. In both instances, the public monies now used to support the poor and the jobless could remain in private purses. That may be the greatest moral failing attributed to the undeserving poor.

THE USES OF UNDESERVINGNESS[39]

Better-off Americans may consider the poor undeserving because of the threats associated with them and the public funds allocated to them. In fact, however, labeling the poor as undeserving also has some uses, or positive functions, or beneficial consequences, for more fortunate Americans. Strange as it may seem on first thought, these functions are very real, resulting in material and immaterial benefits, even though many are not immediately apparent, particularly to the people who benefit from them.[40] This is because functions are not purposes. They are not what people intend to do, but are the consequences of what they actually do, whatever their initial purposes. Consequently, functions are usually neither intended nor recognized when they first emerge, and some are unintended but unavoidable because they follow from the demands of politically important groups.[41] Whatever their origin, however, once these functions exist and produce benefits, their beneficiaries may develop an interest in them and even establish interest groups to defend them.[42]

Needless to say, that undeservingness has uses does not justify it; the analysis of its functions just helps to explain why it persists. In addition, functions for the better-off often entail, or are accompanied by, dysfunctions for the poor, which become economic, social, and political costs not only for them but also for some of the nonpoor. (The disadvantages of labeling for the poor have already been discussed in chapter 3 and the first half of this chapter, and need no further discussion here.)

Of the many positive functions of labeling the poor, thirteen will be discussed here, classified into five interrelated sets.[43] The first eleven functions are not listed in order of importance, but the final two are of greater importance than the others, because they appear to benefit virtually the entire society of the nonpoor.

Two Microsocial Functions

RISK REDUCTION. Perhaps the primary use of the idea of the undeserving poor—primary because it takes place on the microsocial scale of everyday life—is that it distances the labeled from those who label them. By labeling some people as undeserving, label users protect themselves from the risk of getting close to them and being hurt by the encounter. Risk reduction is a way of dealing with threats of all kinds, actual and imagined. The decision to consider a group of people undeserving absolves one of the responsibility to associate with them or even to treat them like morally equal human beings. This absolution can increase feelings of personal safety. All pejorative labels and stereotypes serve this function, which may be why there are so many of them.

SUPPLYING OBJECTS OF REVENGE AND REPULSION. The scapegoating function that the undeserving poor perform has already been discussed in connection with displaced threats, but the poor are also useful as general objects of revenge. They can become such objects because their undeservingness justifies feelings of superiority on the part of the better-off classes. In a society in which punishment is reserved for legislative, judicial, and penal institutions, the *feelings* of revenge and punitiveness that can be directed toward the undeserving poor may offer at least some emotional satisfaction to those lacking the power to punish.

Since labeling poor people undeserving makes nearly unlimited scapegoating possible, the labeled can also be used for distinctive kinds of displacement. For example, many years ago, James Baldwin argued that the undeserving black poor could provide a locus for displaced feelings of repulsion and self-hate that a majority population may have difficulty admitting to itself. Broadening a point first made by Baldwin in *The Fire Next Time*, Andrew Hacker suggests that whites "need the 'nigger,' because it is the 'nigger' within themselves that they cannot tolerate. . . . Whatever it is that whites feel 'nigger' signifies about blacks—lust and laziness, stupidity or squalor—in fact exists within themselves. . . . By creating such a creature, whites are able to say that because only members of the black race can carry that taint, it follows that none of its attributes will be found in white people."[44]

Baldwin's analysis is easily transferable to "the undeserving poor" within the mainstream American, for a number of the traits Oscar Lewis identified in the culture of poverty could be found in that person: "mistrust of government and those in high position," for example, as well as "widespread belief in male superiority" and "provincialism," among others.[45] Moreover, Lewis himself initially felt that some of the culture of poverty's traits were positive, thus implying that they deserve being copied by better-off Americans. These included what Rigdon described as "family loyalty, generosity and sharing, spontaneity, gaiety, courage and the ability to love."[46] Thus it seems as if the undeserving poor could also perform positive displacement functions, being put forth as role models for the driven and pressured members of the more prosperous classes.

Three Economic Functions

CREATING JOBS FOR THE BETTER-OFF POPULATION. Perhaps the most important contemporary economic function of the undeserving poor is their mere presence, which creates a large and increasing number of jobs for the deserving poor and almost all strata of the better-off classes, including professionals. Since the undeserving poor are thought to be dangerous or improperly socialized, their behavior has to be modified so that they will learn to act in socially approved ways. Alternatively, they have to be policed and controlled, or isolated from the deserving sectors of society. The larger the number of people who are declared undeserving, the larger also the number of people needed to modify, police, control, or guard them. These include the police, judges, lawyers, court probation officers, guards, and others who staff the criminal courts and prisons, as well as the social workers, psychiatrists, doctors, and others—and their support staffs—in "special" schools, drug treatment centers, homeless shelters, mental hospitals, and the like. And they also include the teachers and trainers who try to retrain the undeserving.

Other jobs established to deal with the undeserving poor include those held by professionals, investigators, and clerks who administer welfare. Yet other jobs go to officials who look for poor fathers and the child-support monies they often do not have, as well as to the additional welfare office staff needed to remove recipients in violation of welfare rules from the rolls. It could be argued that some of the rules for handling the undeserving poor are more effective at performing the latent function of creating jobs for the working and middle classes than achieving their stated goals of enforcing the laws.[47]

Further jobs are created in the social sciences, journalism, and literature, to conduct research and to write about the faults of the undeserving poor for the more fortunate who want to read about the actual or imagined misbehaviors of those they have stigmatized. Moreover, the undeserving poor supply work for the "salvation industries," religious and secular, which try to save the souls and alter the behavior of the undeserving. Not all such jobs are paid, for the undeserving poor also constitute objects of charity and thus mean volunteer work for those providing it, as well as paid jobs for the professional fundraisers who pursue charitable funds these days. Among the most visible volunteers are the members of cafe and high society who organize and contribute to benefits. While they seek mainly to help the deserving poor, some hold charity balls or collect money in other ways for the homeless and unmarried mothers.

SUPPLYING ILLEGAL GOODS. The undeserving poor who have trouble finding other jobs, even in the informal labor market, are available for work in the manufacture and sale of illegal goods, including drugs. Although it is estimated that 80 percent of all illegal drugs are sold to nonpoor whites, the street sellers are often drug users and others forced out of the formal labor market.[48] Parts of the informal economy that make or sell legal goods or supply legal services but do so under illegal conditions may also attract the undeserving poor, such as welfare recipients or ex-convicts. Garment industry sweatshops and other below-minimum-wage employers often hire illegal immigrants or other people about whose backgrounds they ask no questions.

STAFFING THE RESERVE ARMY OF LABOR. Traditionally, the poor, including even the deserving ones, served the function of staffing the "reserve army of labor." As such they were available to be hired as strikebreakers; they were also invisible presences who could be used to break unions, harass unionized workers, or just scare them into working for less, and thus drive down wage rates. Today, however, with a plentiful supply of jobless people, underpaid full-time and involuntary part-time workers, as well as immigrant workers, a reserve army is less often needed—and when it is needed, it can be recruited from other sectors than the undeserving poor.

Welfare recipients may remain in the reserve army, for many work part-time, in some places in "workfare" programs. They are also encouraged to stay out of the official labor market by being eligible to obtain Medicaid only if they remain on welfare, so that many who need extra money have to work "off the books."[49] If future health insurance programs should ever enable welfare recipients to obtain medical care without staying on welfare, or if future welfare reform programs establish minimum-wage workfare programs on a national basis, larger numbers of welfare recipients will be exerting downward pressure on the wages of the employed. The same effects will occur even more frequently, and drastically, if and when poor women lose their eligibility for welfare or if the welfare program should be abolished entirely. In that case, the victims will once more be full members of the reserve army of labor.[50]

Three Normative Functions[51]

MORAL LEGITIMATION. The same laws that determine what is illegal and criminal also define what is law-abiding, if only by implication and elimi-nation. Likewise, the definition of undeservingness indirectly determines the definition of deservingness. As a result, all institutions and social struc-tures that stigmatize and exclude the undeserving concurrently offer moral and political legitimacy to the institutions and structures of the deserving.[52]

Of these, the most important structure is the class hierarchy, for the exis-tence of an undeserving class or stratum legitimates the deserving classes, and much if not all of their class-related behavior. The alleged immorality of the undeserving also surrounds the class hierarchy with a moral atmos-phere, which may help to explain why upward mobility itself is morally praiseworthy. The fact that the people assigned to "the underclass" and several earlier labels are thought to be déclassé only emphasizes further the moral and political legitimacy of the rest of the class system.[53]

VALUE REINFORCEMENT. When the undeserving poor violate, or are imag-ined to be violating, mainstream behavioral patterns and values, they help to reinforce and reaffirm the desirability of these patterns and values. As Emile Durkheim pointed out nearly a century ago, norm violation is also norm preservation. As a result, a variety of norms, including those some-times dismissed as "motherhood" values, gain new prestige when they are violated and their violators stigmatized or punished.

If the undeserving poor can be imagined to be lazy, they help to reaffirm the "Protestant work ethic"; if poor single-parent families are officially condemned, the two-parent family is once more legitimated as ideal. In the 1960s, "middle-class morality" was sometimes criticized as culturally narrow, and therefore inappropriate for the poor, but since the 1980s, "mainstream values" have again been considered vital sources of behavioral guidance for them.[54]

Norm reinforcement also facilitates the active preservation of values. Before the undeserving poor can obtain financial help, one of the conventional prerequisites is visible indication of their readiness to practice the mainstream values. These values may include some that members of the mainstream may not practice themselves. Consequently, values that might otherwise die out can be preserved. For example, welfare recipients and the jobless must behave deferentially in government agencies even though public officials can insult them freely. Promptness, dress codes, and other work rules that can no longer be enforced in many parts of the economy can be maintained in the regulations for workfare. Economists like to argue that if the poor want to be deserving, they must help "clear the market"—take any kind of job, regardless of its low pay or demeaning character. The economists' argument reflects a work ethic that they themselves do not have to practice and might object to practicing if they had to do so.

Conversely, the undeserving poor may even be punished for behaving in by now conventional ways that diverge from traditional values. A welfare recipient can now be removed from the rolls if she is found to be living with a man without benefit of marriage, but the social worker who removes her has every right to do so without endangering his or her job. Welfare recipients can also be punished for violating rules of housecleaning and child care that middle-class people are free to ignore without being punished. More correctly, while there are many norms and laws regulating child care, only the poor are monitored to see if they obey them. If they fail to do so, or are perceived as using more physical punishment rhan social workers consider desirable, they can be charged with child neglect or abuse and could lose their children to foster care. Likewise, in a society in which the advocates of traditional values remain divided about abortions, the poor, but only the poor, can be prevented from obtaining them. In the political controversy around this issue, the fetuses of the poor seem at times to become especially deserving precisely because their mothers are thought undeserving.

In fact, the defenders of such widely preached if not always so widely practiced values as hard work, thrift, monogamy, and moderation need people who can be accused, accurately or not, of being lazy, spendthrift, promiscuous, and dissolute. All in all, the normative need for misbehaving people creates the exaggerated and imagined behavioral threats of which the undeserving are often accused.

Whether or not very many poor people actually behave in this way is irrelevant if they can be imagined as doing so, and once imaginations take over and the poor can then be labeled undeserving, empirical reality becomes superfluous or not credible. By the 1990s, the beliefs that unmarried motherhood caused poverty, or that young men from poor single-parent families were likely to become street criminals, could appear in the news media without requiring an expert's quote to affirm their accuracy.

Actually, most of the time most of the poor do not violate the fundamental moral values; thus the proportion of welfare recipients who cheat is below the percentage of taxpayers who do so.[55] Moreover, survey after survey has shown that the poor, including most criminals, want to work in secure, well-paid, and respectable jobs like everyone else; hope someday to live in the suburbs and generally pursue the same American Dream as most other Americans of their income level.[56]

POPULAR CULTURE VILLAINS. The undeserving poor have also played a continual role in supplying America with popular culture villains. For many years before and after the Second World War, Hollywood's crime villains were largely drawn from the ranks of poor European immigrants, particularly Sicilians. Then they were complemented for some decades by Cold War and other Communist enemies who were not poor, but even before the end of the Cold War, these were being replaced by black and Hispanic drug dealers, gang leaders, and random killers.

The primary role of these villains is value-reinforcing, showing that crime and other norm violations do not pay. Street criminals and other lawbreakers are shown dead or alive in the hands of the police on the local television news programs every day, and with fictional exaggeration, in crime and action movies and television series. At the same time, however, the popular culture industry has also found popular culture heroes, and villains from the ranks of the undeserving poor, who supply cultural and political protest that criticizes some mainstream values or their alleged hypocrisy. The protest is limited, however, to that which is particularly marketable among white record buyers, who may be using black performers, especially "rappers," to express what they dare not say themselves.

Whatever the content of popular music, its creators and performers have always been recruited to some extent from the undeserving poor, for some of the blues, country music, cowboy songs, jazz, and most recently "rap" were composed and originally played in prisons, in brothels, and in the bars or on the streets of the slums.[57]

Three Political Functions

INSTITUTIONAL SCAPEGOATING. Institutions that serve or control the poor also participate in the scapegoating of the undeserving poor, blaming them for the same phenomena as individual blamers. Institutional scapegoating takes some or all of the responsibility off the shoulders of elected and appointed officials who are supposed to deal with these problems. For example, to the extent that educational experts decide that the children of the poor cannot be taught, or that they are "learning disabled," or genetically inferior in intelligence, attempts to improve the schools can be put off or watered down.

Scapegoating by institutions also personalizes the shortcomings of various sectors of American society. As a result, the anger aimed at the alleged laziness of the jobless and beggars takes the heat off the failure of the economy; the derelictions of slum dwellers and the homeless goes some way to absolving the housing industry; and the existence of poor addicts, mentally ill, and others diverts attention from the destruction of the welfare state and its safety-net measures since the late 1970s. When the undeserving poor are blamed for poverty and poverty-related evils, they are also made responsible for the unwillingness of politicians and voters to do anything about these evils.

CONSERVATIVE POWER SHIFTING. Once poor people are declared undeserving, their already minimal political influence declines even further. Some cannot vote, for example, for lack of a stable address, and many do not choose to vote because politicians do not listen to them. Politicians would probably ignore them even if they did vote, because they cannot possibly satisfy their demands for economic and other kinds of aid. In addition, the undeserving poor make a dangerous constituency. Politicians who say kind words for them, or who act to represent their interests, are likely to be attacked. Jesse Jackson was hardly the first national politician to be criticized for being too favorable to the poor.

Due partly to its ability to ignore the stigmatized poor, the political system can pay greater attention to the white-collar and professional classes. These have enough economic security and political savvy so that their demands on government are not taken to be immoderate. Meanwhile, many people in the working class seem willing to play down demands for their own economic improvement and security as long as the undeserving poor are kept in their place, and out of their neighborhoods. Without accountability to the stigmatized poor and their economic needs, the polity as a whole can concentrate on economically more conservative issues and so shift to the right.

That shift is also ideological. Since the claims of the poor are part of the liberal and Left repertoires, the undeserving poor offer ample opportunity for conservatives to attack their liberal and Left enemies. If liberals can be accused of favoring "criminals" over "victims," their accusers can launch, and legitimate, incursions not only on the civil liberties and rights of the undeserving poor but also on the liberties and rights of those defending the poor.

Likewise, the undeserving poor can be used to justify attacks on the welfare state, which also makes them politically useful, directly and indirectly, to conservatives. Charles Murray understood the essence of this ideological function when he was able to argue for the abolition of welfare and related welfare-state legislation on the grounds that it only increased the number of poor people.[58]

SPATIAL STIGMATIZATION. Poor areas can be stigmatized as "underclass areas," making them eligible for other uses. They may be used as drug markets for middle-class customers for drugs, from the suburbs and elsewhere, who would not want to be seen buying drugs in their own areas or have such markets located there. City officials can decide that underclass areas will be used for facilities other neighborhoods reject, from homeless shelters and halfway houses for AIDS patients and rehabilitated drug abusers to toxic and other dumps. In fact, municipalities would have difficulties operating if they lacked stigmatized areas in which necessary but unwanted facilities can be located.

Two Macrosocial Functions

REPRODUCTION OF STIGMA AND THE STIGMATIZED. For centuries now, un-deservingness has enabled agencies that are established for helping the poor to evade their responsibilities. Indeed, these agencies—and the policies and programs they pursue—prevent many of the stigmatized from shedding their stigma, and also unwittingly manage to see to it that their children face the same hostility and thus grow up poor.[59] In some cases, this pattern works so fast that the offspring of the labeled face "anticipatory stigmatization"; for example, when the children of welfare recipients are expected, even before they have been weaned, to be unable to learn, to work, and to remain on the right side of the law.

If this outcome were engineered deliberately, one could argue that politically and culturally dominant groups are reluctant to give up a badly needed scapegoat.[60] Usually, however, the reproduction function is an unintended effect that follows from other intended and often popular practices. For example, the so-called war on drugs, which has unsuccessfully tried to keep cocaine and heroin from coming into the country but meanwhile offered very little effective drug treatment to addicts seeking it, has thereby aided the continuation of addiction, street crime, and prison building, as well as of the familial and other disasters that often visit the children of addicts. Similarly, discouraging and even preventing the poor from obtaining abortions has helped to increase the future number of poor youngsters. Schemes to eliminate welfare will make sure to increase that number even further, to worsen their poverty, and help see to it that more of them are forced into street crime when they are adolescents.

The other major source of the reproduction of stigma and the stigmatized is the routine activities of the organizations that exist to service welfare recipients, the homeless, and other stigmatized poor. These activities continue to take place partly because the organizations involved lack the funds or power to provide the resources that would help their clients to leave welfare or rejoin the housed population, or for that matter, to escape poverty altogether. One major reason they lack these funds and this power is because the clients are stigmatized, and thus not viewed as deserving of much help.[61]

The workings of this function can best be summarized by two insightful victims of the agencies that deal with the stigmatized poor. A homeless New York woman attempting to obtain welfare pointed out: "I don't get welfare. . . . I hate those people in there. They make you fuckin' sit and sit and ask you questions that don't make any sense. . . . You're homeless but you have to have an address. They want you to get so fuckin' upset that you get up and walk out. They test you. And if you do get up and walk out that means you don't really want it."[62] And a college junior at Grambling State University commented on the attacks on "midnight basketball" during the debate over the 1994 crime legislation: "If they don't fund these kinds of programs, it's like they are saying to us, 'Go out and sell drugs.' It's like they want to see us locked up."[63]

FORCING THE POOR OUT OF THE LABOR FORCE. Ultimately, perhaps the most important function of undeservingness is to push the poor completely out of the labor force. People who have been labeled as undeserving may first be banished from the formal labor market and forced into the informal economy and the criminal underworld. Banishing the undeserving poor from that labor market can also be used to reduce the official jobless rate, a useful political function for election campaign purposes. If the economy of the future requires fewer and fewer workers, however, the easiest and cheapest way of reducing the work force and saving the jobs for the deserving poor and the nonpoor population is to make the undeserving poor ineligible for as many jobs as possible in all labor markets.

This goal can be achieved through legislation—in the case of illegal immigrants, for example—or by labeling, as is the case with poor young males who are stereotyped as unable to learn the job skills and cultural requirements of the modern economy.[64] Once people are unable to find jobs, some will be encouraged directly or indirectly to enter criminal occupations, and can subsequently be kept out of the labor force as ex-convicts. Should labeling people as morally ineligible fail to force enough people out of the labor force, it appears possible to declare them genetically lacking in the intelligence to work. Whatever the methods, they will not be eligible for the jobs sought by the more fortunate population, and will thus reduce the competition in both the formal and informal labor markets if and when the erosion of jobs becomes more serious and permanent.[65]

In the longer run, extrusion from the labor force could even be followed by the gradual extermination of the surplus labor.

In earlier times, when the incomes of the poor regularly fell below subsistence levels, they frequently died at an earlier age than everyone else, thus performing the set of functions forever associated with Thomas

Malthus. Standards of living, even for the very poor, have risen considerably in the last century, but rates of morbidity and mortality due to hypertension, heart disease, tuberculosis and many other chronic illnesses, homicide, and now AIDS, remain much higher among the poor than among working-class and moderate-income people, not to mention the higher-income groups.[66]

Whether stereotyping and stigmatizing poor people as undeserving also exposes them to more illness and a shorter life expectancy is not yet known. But even displaced workers who lose their jobs when their firms close begin after a period of unsuccessful job hunting to think that their unemployment is their own fault—and thus to treat themselves as undeserving. Eventually many become depressed and begin to share in the illnesses of the stigmatized.[67]

If the present erosion of jobs continues indefinitely and more people have to be banished from the labor force, they too will suffer more of the chronic illnesses of the poor, more dangerous lives, and a shorter life expectancy. The original Malthusian hypothesis has probably been falsified forever, but advanced capitalism may be supplying data for a new one.[68] In the very long run, then, an even more drastic—and deadly—form of reducing competition for jobs might take place.[69]

FUNCTIONS AND THREATS, DISPLACEMENT AND SCAPEGOATS

The thirteen uses are at best ancillary to the threats that the nonpoor perceive to come from the undeserving poor, and if the actual and imagined threats could be abolished or reduced significantly, most of these functions would eventually wither away. Neither threats nor functions can be eliminated, however, without confronting the *displaced* threats that the better-off lay on the poor, and the corresponding functions that the poor play in this regard: to serve as scapegoats for the various problems and conflicts in the society. Only when Americans discover that labeling and blaming the poor only supply symptomatic temporary relief but solve nothing, can both undeservingness and poverty, as well as all the problems in their wake, be attacked.

CHAPTER 5

Policies Against Poverty and Undeservingness

If labeling the poor as undeserving is intended to drive them out of the labor force so that they do not compete for the existing jobs, then the future of antipoverty policy presently looks dim, at least until the economy returns to full health.

Meanwhile, American policy will continue to be the present *subsistence* policy, which seeks to keep the undeserving poor functioning at subsistence level, although that policy may start deteriorating to a *survival* mode, in which help to the poor is supplied only at a level that avoids politically embarrassing increases in extreme misery and death among them.[1] But the poor themselves, their political representatives, as well as pundits and policy-oriented social scientists, have to keep the idea of antipoverty policy alive and to discuss and debate future policies.[2]

This chapter is intended to contribute toward that discussion, and to suggest three basic components of such a policy. One is that the best way of removing the label of undeservingness is to give the poor the opportunity to be seen as deserving. This means a job-centered antipoverty policy for all those able to work. A second component is to try to reduce undeservingness itself by correcting the stereotypes with which the poor are stigmatized, and questioning the imagined and displaced threats that the undeserving poor constitute for the better-off population. The third component, which must probably be the first temporally, is to reduce street crime by the poor, and even more important, the fear of crime among the nonpoor.

The entire scheme is predicated on the possibility that if and when crime and the fear of crime decline, the poor may begin to be perceived as sufficiently deserving to create an opportunity for the other two components of the policy.[3] Since the future feasibility of any policy cannot be predicted, this chapter emphasizes what is needed by the poor, leaving the ifs and whens of feasibility for the end of the chapter.

ELIMINATING THREATS TO PERSONAL SAFETY

Policies to eliminate street crime and related threats to personal safety are as old as the hills, and in 1993 the Clinton administration set in motion a new spasm of increased punishments, longer prison sentences, and prison building. These may put away parts of the present cohort of violent street criminals for a yet unpredictable period, respond to popular anger and fear about crime, and satisfy desires for revenge. Whether they, or the yet more punitive policies in the Republican program, will actually reduce violent and other street crime is widely doubted by the experts. In fact, the new policies may only increase further the public's fear of crime.[4] And these policies will do nothing to stem the recruitment of jobless youngsters in poverty-stricken areas into street crime. Nonetheless, an effective crime prevention program that concurrently attacks crime and its poverty-related causes is at present probably politically unrealistic, although someday American politicians and voters may have to persuade themselves of its necessity, both to reduce crime and to prevent imprisoning an ever larger proportion of the country's poor males.[5]

The first step of a comprehensive crime policy has to remove people who are guilty of violent street and other major crimes from everyday life, but it must treat them in such a way that some or many can eventually be returned to that life and are not likely to become recidivists.[6] The preventive part of the program must aim once more to try to transform prisons and work camps into rehabilitative institutions or camps for all but the most chronic, violent, or otherwise disturbed lawbreakers. When a political and organizational opening for innovation and experimentation becomes available, such prisons and camps should be "workplace prisons" that would also offer schooling and job training oriented to the world outside.[7] Prison industries could be funded by government or franchised by private enterprise, with prisoners earning a proper wage, most of which they must be required to send home or to bank so they will have some funds to fall back on when released. Such prisons will obviously compete with the low-wage civilian economy, but that is one cost of reducing safety threats.

"Workplace prisons" will have to begin as experimental institutions, and even if they are perfected not all prisoners will be able to respond to a quasi-rehabilitative environment. Chronically violent and disturbed criminals, for example, and also those for whom street crime satisfies emotional needs that everyday life cannot offer, may not be able to benefit from such programs.[8] Moreover, these prisons are intended only for those who threaten public and personal safety. In order to reduce prison building, other methods for punishing and rehabilitating petty drug sellers and other petty offenders must be invented.[9]

Another policy to reduce street crime, also often suggested before, is to explore new ways of preventing recidivism among all types of criminals. Recidivism can only be reduced significantly if jobs for ex-convicts can be found or created.[10] Without such an effort, prisons will remain places for advanced training in street and other crimes, and thus breeding grounds for new threats to safety. Conversely, if the job commitments can be made and are accompanied by other antirecidivism programs, they may even bring about a decline in the fear of crime and in imagined threats.[11]

Even if a rehabilitative prison that sends its graduates into the employed labor force could finally be invented, it and the other programs suggested here need to become continuous and permanent. Since street crime is generated mainly by poverty, new recruits to street crime, particularly drug selling, and other poverty-related behavior that produces safety threats, are created all the time. As a result, additional cohorts stream into criminal activities as quickly as old ones are removed.[12]

While the creation of jobs targeted strictly and solely to crime reduction and prevention as well as ending the recruitment of new cohorts might be politically acceptable now, at least on a small scale, such a policy cannot stay targeted for long. The causal relation between street crime and poverty is complicated, but it is not a fantasy of knee-jerk liberals.[13] Whether poor youngsters will be drawn into drug selling, for example, may depend less on them than on the demand for hard drugs in their community, the opportunities available to them in the legal labor market, formal and informal, and the penalties imposed on adult drug sellers that make youngsters attractive to the industry.[14]

Ultimately, however, street crime can never be visibly reduced until enough Americans realize that blaming the poor does not reduce crime and that prison-building and other punitive measures are insufficient. The politicians and voters must also support measures to reduce poverty and hopelessness, and assure poor parents and their children that the steady and decent jobs that offer the best chance of escape from poverty are available to everyone. Even then, actual threats to safety will continue—for example, from poor youngsters not ready for upward mobility. And until the actual threats decline significantly, imagined and displaced safety threats are not likely to be reduced either.

The political, and tragic, reality is that mainstream America appears to be unwilling to give the poor a proper chance at decent full-time jobs until threats to safety decline. For the poor, however, the jobs have to be available first—and their availability has to be assured enough to encourage young people to stay in school so they can work. Otherwise the lure of the streets will be too strong, and the temptation to try criminal occupations too great.

The even more tragic reality is that as decent jobs become scarcer and poor people's access to them becomes harder, street crime could become even more attractive. In a more ideal world, the worst jobs could be improved by raising wages for them to a level at which they might compete with at least the economic attraction of street crime, and the people who then still turn to crime could be deprived of further help. Such a policy would be economically irrational for private enterprise, but it would be rational for the public as it reduces the economic and social costs of crime and crime control that society now pays.

TOWARD A COMPREHENSIVE ANTIPOVERTY POLICY

Probably the most effective way to end poverty and not merely poverty-related crime would be an explosion in the demand for American goods that would in turn create a massive labor shortage, especially for low-skilled or quickly trained workers. Full employment, or total unemployment that is less than 3 percent, remains the one best way to increase everyone's income *and* bring the poor into the mainstream.[15] If such full employment is no longer achievable, substitutes will have to be invented.

A comprehensive antipoverty policy should emphasize four principles. First and foremost is that the policy must be job-centered, on the assumption that this is the best way to integrate the poor into the mainstream economy. From there, most if not all of those who can work should be able to move into mainstream society on their own, where they can be eligible for the entitlements and subsidies for housing and other needs that the welfare state makes available for the mainstream population.

A job-centered policy requires job creation, and these days not just for the poor. Although the country's elections have recently revolved around the issue of whether or not the welfare state is still desirable, in the long run the political debate will have to address whether, how, and when the state is ready to act to create and save jobs, even at some cost to zero inflation and other economic priorities.[16]

In fact, this debate should have begun long ago, because job scarcity is not a new problem. In 1980, the prominent economist Lester Thurow wrote, "Lack of jobs has been endemic in peacetime during the past fifty years of American history.... We need to face the fact that our economy and our institutions will not provide jobs for everyone who wants to work."[17] Recent estimates of the lack of jobs indicate that the number of poor jobless workers outweighs the number of vacancies by a ratio of from six to ten to one.[18]

One reason that the job shortage is not noticeable is that the official unemployment rate consistently underestimates the actual jobless rate. Thus Lester Thurow pointed out in May 1994 that while the official rate was then 6.4 percent, the actual figure was 15 percent.[19] Moreover, even still fully employed Americans, most of whom are not even part of the working poor, worry about losing their jobs. A 1992 survey by the Families and Work Institute reported that 42 percent of a national sample had experienced downsizing or permanent cutbacks in their workplace. Another 37 percent said that a temporary layoff or permanent job loss was likely or very likely in the coming year, a figure since reported in other national polls.[20]

A job-centered policy that promises integration into the mainstream economy also means jobs that are decent and pay decently, in wages or salaries as well as benefits so one or two breadwinners can raise a family, and that are as secure as the jobs sought by everyone else. Poor young people may start with entry-level jobs like others their age, but limiting them to such jobs permanently will not only keep them in poverty but also run the risk of their continued stigmatization. Should the properly paid full-time job begin to become extinct, as some observers have predicted, job creation will eventually have to shift to creating decently paid and secure part-time work with the fringe benefits of full-time work.

A job-centered policy that seeks to integrate people into the mainstream economy is important not only economically but also socially. It supplies the economic base for integration into the mainstream society, and it gives people the economic and social wherewithal to become members of healthy communities.

In addition, once people are in the mainstream, and know that they are eligible for all the rights that come with being in the mainstream, then they are also more likely to accept the responsibilities that come with these rights, and to feel responsible for the society of which they are a part.

A second principle of a comprehensive antipoverty policy is that in an economy dominated by private enterprise, most if not all of the created jobs have to be with private firms for the predictable future. This flies in the face of the downsizing trends in the private economy that began in the 1980s, and all of the other job-destroying trends that started a generation earlier. Politically vocal Americans still expect such corporations to supply the new jobs, however, partly because they do not trust government to do so, and partly because in hard times the old American desire for minimal taxes, and thus minimal government activity, becomes even stronger. Besides, government services are often delivered by monopolies, and monopolistic bureaucracies tend to be even less user-friendly than oligopolistic ones.

A third principle is that wherever possible, programs must be *universalistic*, serving everyone, rather than *specific*—that is, targeted only to the poor. Universalistic programs addressed to large and powerful constituencies create political support that can help the powerless poor, provided the powerful constituencies do not manage to exclude them. Specific programs serve only the poor and thus are politically weak, often underfunded, and usually the first to be shrunk or eliminated when public funds become scarce. In addition, they require means-testing, which can easily lead to stigmatized programs and thus stigmatized clients who are treated punitively. Universalism is particularly necessary in the area of job creation since an increasingly large number of people have been displaced from the secure full-time jobs they once held. These workers may now be involuntarily employed in part-time or minimum-wage jobs or in temporary, "contingent" jobs, if they are not without jobs. Such people, some of whom are not yet poor and others who are increasingly thought of as the "new poor," probably have more political power than the long-term poor, and thus may be the first to benefit from whatever governmental job creation takes place.

Universalism works more smoothly in the textbooks, however, than in the real world, where invisible administrative ways of leaving out the poor and other politically weak constituents can be invented, the ostensibly universalistic programs of the New Deal, which excluded many blacks, being a good example.[21] The proper solution would be "generous universalism": for example, creating enough jobs to discourage the establishment of a job-rationing system that practically assures the joblessness of the poorest people. Specific programs targeted primarily to the poor are also needed, particularly for people whose entry or reentry into the labor market may require a variety of distinctive support programs. And some specific programs are even politically popular in Congress; in the past they included most programs for poor children.[22]

A fourth principle is that wherever possible, policies must focus on economic—or race-blind—criteria rather than racial criteria, race-blind programs having more political legitimacy and appeal than those appealing to one or another race. Since blacks are among the poorest Americans however poverty is measured, race-blind programs will include them automatically, without further polarizing whites.[23]

These principles suggest the programs that follow. These programs are not meant to constitute a comprehensive antipoverty policy. Nor are they original, but old ones need to be restated and updated to help revive the liberal approach to antipoverty policy, and with it the pursuit of effective programs to help the poor.[24]

Increase in Consumer Demand

Governments have traditionally sought to put more people to work by increasing consumer demand through lower interest rates and similar measures. What has not yet been tried, at least in the United States, is to increase consumer demand among the people who are most likely to buy—the poor—and thus help put jobless people to work. Further increases in the Earned Income Tax Credit would help, as would a sizeable increase in the minimum wage, at least that paid to adults, as well as higher welfare benefits and unemployment insurance. Even aid in kind or vouchers that would provide poor people with goods the production of which increases jobs would contribute to achieving this goal.

Industrial Policy

This term is used broadly here to suggest that the federal government, and also states, must begin to experiment with a number of policies to encourage industries to create jobs and also to save them from being exported to low-wage countries. In the narrow sense, industrial policy still means direct or indirect aid to specific industries with a promising future, but America has been one of the few countries that has been reluctant to try it. That reluctance has stemmed in part from very real political difficulties in deciding whom to help, but other governments have confronted these problems. The U.S. government will finally have to bite the bullet, instead of creating jobs through the politically safer method of increased defense spending. Some of the risk might be reduced by obligating recipients of help to assume special obligations later, such as paying higher taxes temporarily if the help has produced an above-average level of profit.

The political risk cannot be reduced so easily, but since the voters permit the Pentagon and even NASA a number of technological failures, they are going to have to learn to let the makers of industrial policy fail as well—as they probably will once the need for constant job creation is more widely appreciated. Since no one can predict which industries, manufacturing or service, will do best in a future global economy, governmental support should be limited to industries that are reasonably labor-intensive. Certainly, no government aid should go to industries that will build or use machines to put yet more people out of work.[25] In fact, government expenditures for industrial policy might be retrieved in part from special taxes on industries, old and new, that continue to install computers and other machines that will add significantly to the jobless rolls.[26]

Public Works

Except in societies that are preoccupied with eliminating deficits, public works remain a constructive solution both for dealing with joblessness and for making productive use of people who would otherwise be on the dole.[27] Despite America's bias against government and government employment, as well as some taxpayer opposition, public works remain popular in Congress, particularly the kind disparaged as "pork." Combining the political strengths behind pork-barrel public works with what communities need in the way of infrastructural innovations and improvements as wel' as employment might therefore be politically viable even today. For example, a Public Works Administration for the 1990s might begin with building or repairing the bridges, roads, parks, and other public facilities sought by the suburbs that now hold the political power in the Congress, thereby generating political support for at least some badly needed urban public works programs.

Public works as a strategy is usually only short-term. Whenever possible, however, projects that lead to permanent jobs, particularly in private industry, and which are structured to include opportunities for further training, should also be planned—with voters being reminded that the holders of such jobs will become instant taxpayers. Moreover, public works should be used to undertake experimentation and innovations in products, services, and work methods that can lead to further job creation if and when private enterprise is unable or unwilling to do so.

The previously mentioned generous universalism is particularly important in public works job creation, for jobs must be created in such large numbers to make sure that, in still unionized industries, they are not doled out only to union members and their friends, or only to whites. When there are enough jobs for everyone, the opposition to hiring poor people can be dealt with, for example, by promoting union members and other experienced or senior workers to the status of trainers and supervisors.

Public works jobs must be created for women as well as for men, and while women now work in many construction jobs, there are also data bases to be established and maintained that supply jobs that have traditionally gone to women not trained for manual labor. Another source of jobs is as assistant teachers and teacher-trainees, especially in conjunction with an educational program that would bring the classroom size down to ten or less wherever schools and students are not performing up to standard. Enough studies exist now to show that classrooms of that size can be a major aid to teaching and learning, which is why they are often found in private schools serving the rich. For cost reasons, small classes are rarely tried in poor neighborhoods, but this policy can be justified on the grounds of both job creation and educational quality—and it will help recruit future teachers as well.

All public works programs, and others that make work opportunities for previously discouraged workers and those already labeled as unemployable, automatically face not only the stigma associated with such workers but also the likely failures of some of them, and the occasional instances of crimes among the people they serve. Unless politicians and the general public are warned not to expect perfection, opponents of public works and of employing the poor will be sure to use such problems as political weapons. Easy solutions are not available, but if these problems are not expected and attacked, the economic integration of the jobless poor cannot be achieved.

Community Development

A small but essential part of any antipoverty policy is exploiting the opportunities for community development that bring jobs and money into poor neighborhoods. The 1960s faith that local communities could create large numbers of new jobs has long been shattered; however, they can control and manage local housing projects, shopping centers, and community facilities that employ local people. In the process, community development projects will also supply on-the-job training to local residents that some can then apply outside the neighborhood. An additional training opportunity is for community leadership; locally managed projects can help train a new generation of local managers, civic leaders, and politicians.

Work Sharing

America may well be the only modern industrial nation that still does not believe in the likelihood of a steadily increasing job shortage, but if and when reality finally overturns the country's skepticism, another and very different approach to jobs policy will be needed. That approach, usually called work sharing, is based on the principle that if individual work time is reduced, some of the available work can be spread among more people to save existing jobs and even create some new ones. The spreading of the work can take place through reductions in the work day, the work week, the work year, or through mandating parental leaves, sabbaticals, long vacations, and early retirement.[28]

American workers and union leaders began to press for reductions in the work day early in the nineteenth century, but today work sharing policy is virtually unknown here, although it is being implemented in bits and pieces in Western Europe, where the average industrial work week is gradually being driven down to thirty-five hours or less.[29]

A thirty-five-hour work week will probably make only a slight difference in jobless rates, because the number of jobs saved or created comes to only 40 to 50 percent at most of the hours shared.[30] A 20 percent work time reduction would, however, result in an 8 to 10 percent increase in workers, which is the case if the work week were to be reduced from forty to thirty-two hours.

Since work time reduction, at least without wage and salary reduction, results in higher labor costs, moving from the forty-hour to the thirty-two-hour week cannot be undertaken without concurrent increases in productivity and in demand for goods that would hold wage rates at their present levels.[31] Modest work time reductions can be handled without serious wage loss, and even a period of regular annual reductions of an hour per week may be feasible on that basis.[32] A less desirable alternative for reducing labor costs is wage reduction, not only because it hurts workers but because it would lead to intensive moonlighting to recoup the lost income.[33] In an economy in which wages are being reduced anyway, people might accept reductions in exchange for fewer working hours, but imaginative policy analysts and politicians who do not want to be voted out of office will have to figure out how to minimize or offset reductions in the standard of living; I will examine the possibilities more thoroughly in chapter 6.

The Upgrading of Part-Time Work

Actually, many Americans, like workers in other countries, have already experienced a negative form of work sharing: involuntary part-time work at lower wage rates and without fringe benefits. On the assumption that this work arrangement is unlikely to disappear even if and when economies become healthier again, government intervention and regulation to upgrade general working conditions will be needed. Upgrading means increased wage rates, access to health insurance, pension and other benefits, and conventional job security arrangements, as well as the right to full-time work if and when it becomes available. Unionization of part-time and other kinds of contingent work is also necessary, in part to persuade the federal government to require the provision of benefits most of which are already standard in Western Europe. Unions to serve part-time workers have yet to be invented, however.

Income Security Programs

Unless economic miracles can once more bring about full employment, increasing numbers of workers who are able to work will not find jobs. They need income grants in lieu of work and as a nonpunitive entitlement, at least until they obtain jobs once more or it becomes clear that they will never find jobs again.[34]

In addition, there are people who work full-time but at wages that are too low to enable them to escape poverty. They should be compensated decently, with an increase in the minimum wage large enough to bring them above the official poverty line. Until such an increase becomes politically viable, the Earned Income Tax Credit, which became politically acceptable in the 1990s, will have to serve the same purpose. It only needs to be made more widely accessible to all those eligible, and paid out monthly rather than in an annual lump sum.

For those who cannot work or cannot find work, the most sensible alternative is a single income grant to replace unemployment insurance and welfare payments. Eliminating unemployment insurance and welfare would not only end two punitive programs and the bureaucracies attached to each, but would also signify that the people who now obtain these payments are victims of the economy's inability to supply jobs.

In effect, all citizens should be protected by what the early builders of the American welfare state called social insurance, whether the citizens are retired, ill, or jobless. Social insurance would not only assume the essential equality of all jobless people, current welfare recipients included, but credit and reimburse them, as well as discouraged workers, for not competing for scarce jobs with the rest of the labor force. More important, the social insurance payment must be set high enough that its recipients could afford to continue to participate in mainstream society, as is the case in Western Europe.

Until the sharp economic decline that began at the end of the 1980s, most European welfare states tried hard to keep unemployment insurance and welfare up to 60 or 70 percent of the median income, partly so that recipients would remain participating members of their communities and could retain their self-respect.[35] Incidentally, 60 to 70 percent of the median is also the range of income Americans say they need to get along in their community.[36] Even though the Western European benefits have been reduced in the 1990s, they still remain far above American ones, where welfare and food stamps together come to only about 25 percent of the median American family income.[37] This is one reason American crime and addiction rates are far above European ones.

Forcing poor people to find work before they can eat, even when there are not enough jobs, is indirectly more expensive than higher welfare payments because eventually, larger expenditures for police, shelters for the homeless, and other poverty-related effects are required. Welfare is also cheaper than job creation, one reason why past welfare reform efforts have in the end not been approved by Congress. Still, as long as Americans expect the jobless poor to work, jobs may have to be created. Most of these are likely to be of the "community service" variety, an as yet undeveloped minimum-wage or below-minimum-wage tier of public works employment.[38]

While many poor mothers may be eager to take community service jobs, especially if they can lead to better jobs, those who ought to stay home should be allowed to do so, particularly if the children are very young, or if they lack relatives, friends, or a trusted day care facility to take care of them. In fact, if letting poor mothers stay home would also increase their ability to help older children escape poverty, for example, by keeping them in school and away from the "culture of the street," welfare (or social insurance) would be socially desirable as well as economically efficient. In any case, current welfare policy needs to remain in place until a more desirable alternative is found. Ending welfare before nonpunitive "welfare reform" can be achieved, or in the mere hope that it will be achieved, would be disastrous.

Special Services and Facilities

Enough consensus exists on what services and facilities should be part of an antipoverty program that there is no need to repeat the standard list here. Moreover, the quality of social services almost always reflects and reproduces the class structure and its pecking order, so that more services for the poor usually just means more inadequate services for them. Consequently, maximizing the income of the poor is probably also the most direct route to better services.

Education is still held out as the best escape route from poverty, but only if the class structure is *not* reproduced, so that poor children get the best schools, teachers, and equivalents for the preschool preparation more affluent parents can give their children.

Equally important, the willingness of youngsters to work at education is affected by occupational and other expectations for the future. At present, poor youngsters who must endure low-quality public schools sometimes stop trying when they become adolescents or earlier, because they doubt that they can obtain decent jobs even if they stay in school and study hard. Without eliminating that doubt and replacing it with hope for the future—and above all making the prior changes in the labor market that that hope requires—the peer pressure to eschew success in school will remain powerful. In addition, expecting academic talent and a strong school performance from everyone is not only unrealistic but unfair to the poor. Instead, job creation policy must provide for blue- and white-collar jobs for people who were not academic stars in school.

In fact, youngsters who did not study hard often realize as adults that they must catch up on the education they missed as children. They need help to go back to school, with money for tuition and living expenses, when they are older. Public works and other job programs for the poor could build in opportunities for additional education. The post–World War II G.I. Bill, which enabled war veterans to return to school, offers one model for the needed policy.[39]

What may turn out to be one of the most important challenges for education is helping poor people seek employment in the office-centered world of "service" jobs. Manufacturing work takes place in the working-class culture of the shop floor, but offices are run by the rules and social relations practices of middle-class and professional cultures. Many poor people who obtain jobs in offices learn these cultures on their own, but some may need a kind of schooling, not in punctuality and dress codes, but in the subtler cultural practices that are needed for success in the office world, and which the middle class learns almost automatically.[40]

Dealing with the Casualties of Poverty

Last but not least, every antipoverty policy must make provision for the casualties of poverty: the people who are too ill physically or mentally, or too depressed or angry, or too set in criminal ways to be able to respond to the standard incentives of antipoverty policy. Many jobless people will not need much more than a decent job to become able workers, and some will need time, patience, and cognitive or other support—and in varying amounts—to perform properly in the labor market.

But many of the problems of the casualties, which resemble those of the casualties of wartime combat, remain because no solution has yet been found for their disabilities or pathologies. This category includes not only work failures but also the chronically or sporadically violent: disturbed youngsters who act out continuously, seriously impaired alcoholics and drug addicts, adult psychotics, and others.

When they break the law they can be imprisoned, but when they are released, their problems still remain. The casualties who "act out" may not break any laws, but they nevertheless make life difficult for themselves and other people, or create political obstacles to helping other poor people when they act out. Indeed, many of the normative threats that the poor constitute for the more fortunate population are the results of acting out by a small minority. Residential projects, including halfway and rooming houses, are beginning to be developed to try to help the casualties of poverty, and may function as surrogates until the time permanent solutions are found.[41]

The permanently damaged may only be able to function in sheltered living and work situations, or in hospitals not unlike those the Veterans Administration provides for the casualties of war. If it is ever possible to invent prisons that rehabilitate, it should also be possible to invent mental hospitals, like those now sheltering the very rich, which are not punitive and may even be therapeutic.

Paying the Costs of Antipoverty Programs

The conventional way to end discussions of antipoverty policy proposals is to estimate their costs and ask who will pay them. Past experience has shown that welfare grants or their equivalents are cheap. Federal welfare expenditures have never exceeded one percent of the federal budget; the total cost of welfare and food stamps in 1992 came to $47 billion; and in 1991, the Census Bureau determined that it would have cost another $37 billion to raise the incomes of all poor families with children to the poverty line, then set at $13,900 for a family of four.[42] Job creation is expensive, usual estimates of the cost of creating jobs starting at $10,000 and up, but creating decent jobs will cost even more. Labor-intensive services to help the poor or the casualties of poverty will also be costly.

Antipoverty programs have rarely been costed out to determine their benefits, such as what people employed in newly created jobs return to the tax rolls, what job and income grant programs save in spending for controlling and reducing crime and the physical and mental illnesses associated with poverty.[43] If all the externalities, good and bad, associated with spending by and for (or against) the poor were added together, they would show that the country can afford far better antipoverty programs than it now provides. What the country can afford is not what it is now willing to afford, however, in part because the poor are needed—as scapegoats as well as for other uses. But in that case, the cost of antipoverty policy is irrelevant.

ENDING UNDESERVINGNESS

Since the poor may not get much help from their fellow citizens as long as these think that so many of the poor are not deserving of help, the last component of the three-step policy laid out here is a set of programs to attack the idea of undeservingness and the stereotyping of the poor as undeserving. For reasons of political feasibility, this step may have to be implemented before the job-centered policy just discussed, or at least concurrently with it.

The anticrime program may make a dent in fear of and hostility toward the undeserving poor, but in order to build sufficient popular support for an effective antipoverty policy, undeservingness per se will need to be attacked head-on. If and when street crime is reduced, the exaggerated and imagined safety threats should also decline, but ending the scapegoating of the poor—ceasing to blame them for social problems they have not created—requires other approaches. This may be the most difficult challenge of all, because it involves confronting the social problems now displaced onto the poor and beginning to make the social, economic, and political changes required to solve them.

Since no one has yet formulated a program to remove blame and to erase all it entails, the aim here is far more modest: to try to figure out how to debunk the stereotypes of the undeserving poor, to question the credibility and social desirability of such notions.[44] What follows is tentative, partly because so little is known about the social and psychological "needs" of the affluent for the undeserving poor, but at least it is a start on a task that has been strangely neglected in past attacks on poverty.[45]

The debunking proposals are based on the hope that some or many

Americans are willing to entertain a more descriptive and less judgmental view of the poor, of how they live and why some behave in ways that deviate from those of the mainstream. To describe or to explain is not to justify, but to point out that the world of the poor differs in many respects from that of the better-off, that the poor act on the basis of understandable reasons just like everyone else, and that knowing these is, at least in the long run, helpful to the reduction of poverty. For example, if Arline Geronimus is correct to argue that poor women bear healthier babies when they are young and can call on mothers and grandmothers to help raise them, then other Americans need to understand them, just as they have learned to understand the delay of childbirth among career women. And if enough people understand, then perhaps policymakers and politicians will act to make jobs available for the young mothers (and young men) who are willing and able to get married. Once more poor people have access to the prerequisites for following mainstream rules for bearing children, they will begin to do so.

Admittedly, debunking has its limits. Whatever people choose to believe privately is not easily changed unless they want that change, although it may be possible to sow doubts even in what people believe strongly. Debunking racism, together with providing information about racial issues, has helped to reduce racial prejudices as well as some, if not enough, discriminatory and segregating behavior on the part of whites, and perhaps questioning class prejudice, or "classism," can be helpful as well.

After generations of American poverty, informational programs should not really still be necessary, but they are. The country's public communication media rarely consider how poor people act and think, because there are no media by and for the poor, and because the poor cannot even afford to be customers for the mass media that serve the more affluent population. Although ultimately poor people have to be able to represent themselves, questioning the stereotypes about them can be initiated by others until the poor have an effective voice.[46]

Debunking Through Popular Ethnography

The first task is to encourage the country's public media to use what is currently known about poverty and the poor in "debunking stories" in both news and entertainment media that correct inaccuracies and try to puncture stereotypes about the poor, deserving as well as undeserving. For journalists, debunking is a conventional method; it is one of the angles for writing news stories. Likewise, some popular television series, once established, use their stories to inform their viewers even as they divert them, and debunking conventional wisdom or puncturing popular stereotypes is also one of their methods.[47]

A yet-to-be-invented method of media debunking might be called popular ethnography: stories that draw on this social science method to report how people live and why they live that way, which can debunk stereotypes in the process.[48] For the most part, popular media now use biographies— for example, of delinquent youngsters or welfare mothers who are going to college in their attempt to escape poverty. Biographies are often effective, and ethnographies can include biographical sketches, but reporting about larger groups is more useful for showing audiences the powers and processes that dominate the lives of various types of poor people.

For example, popular ethnography can help to demonstrate why poor people cannot always act like better-off people, and how much their life consists of coping with frequent crises and trying to obtain the security that are prerequisites to practicing the mainstream values.

Nonetheless, the most urgent ethnographies have to report about the various agencies that affect the lives of the poor, and that sometimes make their clients appear to be undeserving when they are trying hard to stay in the mainstream. News stories from police stations, welfare agencies, the courts, schools, emergency clinics, and the like usually cover the news that agency officials want covered, although journalists will also report gross injustices against the poor when they find out about them. In any event, ethnographic stories are needed to make the general public acquainted with the daily routines of these agencies and the way these can make life difficult for the poor and put obstacles in their way on a regular basis.

Identifying Harmful and Divergent Behavior

A more analytical complement to the ethnographies would require journalists, government officials, and others to encourage better-off Americans to look anew at what they judge to be the deviant behavior of the poor: to make the distinction between behavior that is *harmful* to the poor, the better-off, or society as a whole; and behavior that is merely *divergent* from mainstream ways but hurts no one.

The distinction between divergence and harmfulness is, at one level, easily made; only the latter leads to effects that actually hurt someone. Many people are morally and emotionally hurt at the culturally divergent behavior of others, however, especially when that behavior diverges sharply from values about which people feel deeply, but even so, there is a difference between individual moral hurt and social harmfulness. Furthermore, the morally hurt can be asked to think about whether, how, and why values that diverge from their own actually hurt them or anyone else. For example, however abhorrent illegitimacy may be, particularly to religiously observant Americans, questions must be raised about whether illegitimacy is actually harmful in a society that no longer brands illegitimate children, literally or figuratively.

Likewise, some Americans might be ready to think differently about when the single-parent family is divergent and when it is harmful once they understand why it exists in the first place, and learn to see how the scarcity of decent and secure jobs, especially among males, has led to single-parent families in many countries and eras. Better-off Americans might also look anew at the single-parent family if they understand that a properly and peacefully functioning single-parent family, particularly one that is supported by fathers, uncles, mothers, and grandmothers, may raise emotionally healthier children than a two-parent family in which the adults are fighting bitterly and continuously. And they might learn more about the destruction poverty can cause if journalists compared the lives of divorced but affluent single-parent families and their equivalents among the poor.

Furthermore, even the morally hurt need to think about whether their reactions justify punishing the divergent. After all, their own ostensibly mainstream values may also hurt others. In an increasingly diverse country, people also need to learn that fears of diversity are common and that they are often masked by judging that diversity as harmful. Above all, everyone has to realize that insisting on the harmfulness of divergent behavior is a way of asserting the cultural and political power of one's own values, and thus concurrently of blaming the diverse for asking for their place in the cultural sun.[49]

In this connection, so-called white ethnics might rethink some of their beliefs about the harmfulness of poor blacks, Hispanics, and illegal immigrants by realizing that less than a hundred years ago, their own ancestors were labeled morally and otherwise harmful by earlier arrivals to the

United States. This message might be even more impressive if the descendants of past immigrants knew that their alleged harmfulness was blamed on the same genetic inferiority that the neo-eugenicists of the mid-1990s have asserted to blame poor blacks. That the harmfulness of their ancestors was perceived as divergence once these ancestors were no longer poor, and that the divergence then turned into admiration of their ethnic distinctiveness after World War II, suggests that this history could also repeat itself for today's stigmatized poor once they were enabled to escape poverty.

The distinction between divergent and harmful behavior is crucial from a policy perspective, because in a diverse or multicultural society punishing divergent behavior cannot be tolerated. Indeed, the distinction may be useful for showing people that the limited facilities and resources available for punishment and therapy should be spent only on truly harmful behavior. America cannot long afford, financially or morally, to stigmatize or harass citizens whose only offense is that the mainstream population deems them culturally repugnant.

Exposing the Ineffectiveness of Blaming

Another component of a debunking program must point to the limited usefulness of blaming. Although the practitioners of blame do not realize it, blaming poor people for moral shortcomings, cultural divergence, or even harmful behavior cannot bring about the behavior and value changes sought by the blamers. The same could be said about blaming society instead of the poor. The ineffectiveness of blaming is underlined if and when other parts of the debunking program can indicate concurrently that blamers are aiming at inaccurate or nonexistent offenses. For example, blaming the poor for being too lazy to work can become an embarrassment once blamers and their friends have and accept information about the shortage of jobs available to the poor.

Blaming is only a form of name-calling, which may make blamers feel better for having expressed themselves and perhaps reassured themselves that they are not alone. Christopher Jencks puts it well when he writes, "Even in the world's most commercialized society, blame is still free. That means there is still plenty for everyone."[50] Name-calling also expresses anger at unnamed social conditions, but in the end, the larger displaced problems that often produce the anger and the blaming have to be confronted.

Attacking Class Prejudice and "Classism"

Another form of debunking would draw on the white acceptance of and experience with fighting racial prejudice and racist behavior to question *class* prejudice and "classism." The methods used to fight racism could be used to show the better-off how similar their prejudices against the poor are to racial prejudices—and how to be aware when both are reactions to imaginary threats.

Changing behavior is always more productive than changing attitudes, but when the law and the economy are not available to change behavior, debunkers must be satisfied with changing attitudes, and hope that these may have some impact on behavior. Although the long fight against racial prejudice cannot be said to have been won, and sometimes has actually driven antiblack and antiwhite attitudes underground, its net effect has been positive; the country is better off for that fight.

A successful attack on classism will not happen quickly. To complicate matters, reducing classism implies more economic equality, which may have less support than greater racial equality. Even so, one does not have to believe in economic equality in order to fight biases against the poor. In fact, a debunking program could begin merely by showing the many ways in which the poor are treated differently than the more affluent for similar behavior. A program to fight classism can also show the better-off population to what extent racism is infused with traditional fear of and hostility toward the poor, and how racial prejudice can be reduced by helping the black poor move into the middle class.

IMPLEMENTING A DEBUNKING PROGRAM

Debunking the conventional wisdom is like swimming against a strong tide. Although government is often expected to make sure everyone is correctly informed, elected officials are normally reluctant to debunk ideas that many voters believe to be true, or to supply information thought to be controversial. The courts must often be asked to give legal support to nonconforming ideas before government is willing to communicate them. Also, judges, like other government officials, themselves need to be persuaded to understand the validity of nonconforming views that they themselves may not share personally, as well as accurate information that they do not personally find credible. This is one reason why governmentally led attacks on racial prejudice were a long time in coming.

Still, governments have to be asked to debunk biased and inaccurate information about poverty and the poor, and they could be asked on two grounds. One is that if they participate in programs against racial prejudice, they should begin to fight what is, among other things, class prejudice. Even writing and trying to pass legislation against classism is itself an important informational program.

The second model is borrowed from public health. If government can support campaigns against smoking, it could be asked to sponsor campaigns against stigmatizing the poor, if necessary as an indirect way of improving the health of the poor. Again, much political debate must occur before such a model can be implemented, but this debate can itself be turned to informational uses.

Nonetheless, most of the support and energy for debunking programs must probably be found among institutions already concerned with antipoverty policy, and advocates for specific programs such as educating the poor or aiding welfare recipients. They will already be prepared to help debunk inaccurate fears about the specific issues on which they work.

The funding for both kinds of institutions will have to come mainly from foundations, especially at the start. The ostensibly nonideological foundations often described as liberal have funded a great deal of the research that has produced and is producing the needed information, but the truly liberal foundations ready to support programs directly opposite to those now supported lavishly by conservative foundations still need to be established. In the 1970s Irving Kristol was able, almost singlehandedly, to mobilize a handful of conservative foundations and corporations to fund the revival of right-wing thought and analysis that helped to bring Ronald Reagan and, in the mid-1990s, Newt Gingrich and his colleagues to power. Thus one would think that truly liberal foundations and corporations can be found to do the same for liberal thought and analysis.[51] Kristol was also able to initiate the recruitment of the necessary intellectuals and analysts, and a somewhat similar process, also well-funded, is required if liberal ideas are to be once more given a chance to seek adherents and persuade the country.

Even before then, however, debunking and informational stories and programs should be made attractive to the media, and as much as possible to the commercial media, especially those attracting the largest audiences.[52]

The news media always need newsworthy stories, and such stories emerge out of and deal with conflict. Conservative voices were able to get some of their ideas into the media because they were different or even dramatic, even before there was widespread support for some conservative positions. And at this writing, conservatives are using the outrageousness of such proposals as placing children from single-parent families into orphanages to get publicity. Getting into the news does not require money so much as newsworthy information, dramatic news stories, or extreme ideas.

True, the news media also feature conservatively inspired news stories about orphanages because they believe, sans evidence, that the country has gone conservative—and they will always prefer crime stories to information about the deservingness of the poor. To the extent that skillful newsmakers can transform debunking programs into news and features that will meet the standards of newsworthiness, they are likely to succeed, even if liberal ideas are not ideologically dominant in the country or popular with journalists at the time. Thus, news stories, documentaries, and even entertainment dramas that can show teenage mothers not to be immoral or immature youngsters are so original that they might appeal on that ground alone. A historical documentary that would demonstrate and illustrate the extent to which the labeling and stereotyping of the poor have remained nearly unchanged for the last two centuries might fit public television's proclivity for historical programming.

Above all, the dramatic conflict with conventional wisdom or stereotypes inherent in debunking stories should make them attractive to the media, or at least those that can overcome their felt need for "balance," which enables or requires them to give equal attention to facts and outrageous claims. While the poor are particularly subject to outrageous claims about their undeservingness, debates in which presenters of factual information can show up makers of outrageous but unsupportable claims could be dramatic media fare.

Responsibilities of Social Scientists and Journalists

The social scientists, journalists, and other writers who have helped to make and use labels that stigmatize the poor obviously have the right to do so. Still, they also have the right to debunk such labels.

Journalists have less autonomy in this respect than social scientists, for, being in an audience-maximizing profession, they will be unable to discourage the use of labels and other stereotypes that attract audiences. Journalists also have the right to indulge in "media criticism," however, and to question the use of stereotypes, and information about the poor, good or bad, that is not based on journalistically reliable and credible evidence. They could even begin to apply the journalistic norms of balance to complement stories about the undeserving poor with stories about similar members of better-off classes.

Even so, a major burden will fall on the social scientists. They should argue with journalists or other label-makers if and when social science concepts are improperly being turned into labels, and they should warn colleagues and funders if they are being used unwittingly to help legitimate upcoming new labels. Also, researchers need to be constantly careful that the concepts they develop do not lend themselves to becoming labels.[53] And they should be more energetic than they have been in criticizing labeling, debunking the conventional wisdom when it is wrong, and correcting inaccurate information. Social science organizations need to be enrolled in all these efforts as well.

In addition, social scientists should think about and debate further the intellectual and conceptual bases of poverty research. Today, most of the research on the poor concerns their personal characteristics, as if the neighborhood in which the poor are currently residing or how long they are on or off welfare were really major causes or even significant correlates of poverty. Basically, these studies measure, or analyze qualitatively, who has been selected or, in a few cases, self-selected to be poor, and how the losers are squeezed economically, socially, and psychologically. But the studies ignore the fact that if the economy and society create and tolerate poverty, some groups and individuals have to be selected to suffer it. Trying to determine how family or neighborhood influence poverty ignores how much both are themselves caught in and responding to the poverty that agents and forces in the larger society impose.

When the research paradigm is framed around characteristics, some researchers will inevitably blame the losers and the squeezed, in the way that poverty researchers and their predecessors have done since the inception of poverty research. The political and ideological reasons were not hard to find, as Michael Katz and others have shown in their historical studies. But it is time to ask how and why the basic paradigm persists, and why it should not be changed. Admittedly, governments and other major funders of research in a capitalistic society may be drawn to a paradigm that emphasizes the undeservingness of the poor rather than the faults of the economy that cause poverty. But independent foundations and researchers need not follow the current paradigm, and the philosophers of the social sciences can question it and propose the use of others.

The principal subject of poverty research, although not its sole subject, ought to be the forces, processes, agents, institutions, and so on that "decide" that a proportion of the population will end up poor. Thus, among the primary specific topics of poverty research are the larger economy and the kinds of workers it chooses and rejects, the labor market, employers and their behavior and biases; also the class hierarchy, and the various agencies that in one way or another create and maintain the economic and social inequality that helps to produce poverty.

Social scientists, whether government-funded or independent, should learn to fight against the ideological polarization of antipoverty research, not only for themselves but also for the sake of the writers and officials who write or make policy about poverty, as well as the general public.[54] The old dichotomy in which the Right blames the poor and the Left blames society is dubious even when it appears in more complicated guises, for whatever the role of society or the economy, which poor people are selected and self-selected to turn to street crime and other forms of violence may be to some extent an instance of individual dynamics and a matter of some kind of choice, if not a rational kind.

Also, more attention needs to be paid to the relation between ideology and empirical fact, and researchers can insist on empirical research for those questions that can be answered empirically. Either street crime *is* primarily caused by poverty and unemployment, directly or indirectly, or it is not; this need not be a matter of permanent empirical or other debate.[55] Likewise, either the high numbers of poor unmarried mothers can be traced principally to the Left political culture of the 1960s, as conservatives insist, or they cannot. Similarly, carefully designed empirical research could determine how many poor youngsters attempt to succeed in school, to find work, to put off pregnancy, and so on, with the researchers looking concurrently at the roles of personal choices and contextual social and economic factors that make these attempts succeed or fail.

To be sure, disagreement will continue because causal questions will be answered tentatively until all the data are available, and all the data never are. Disagreements will also continue because facts are always subservient to ideological and political needs, and even determinedly empirical researchers can unintentionally find facts to fit these needs. Nevertheless, social scientists and others can point out when ideology is presented in false empirical trappings, although this requires both more ideological training and more sophistication than social scientists now typically obtain, as well as *very* carefully designed research. Unfortunately, ideologically satisfactory answers are frequently easier and cheaper to find, for example, in already available statistics from which undeserving behavior and undesirable motives can be inferred. It is even cheaper and more satisfying to argue that personal beliefs are more accurate than data, or, as Representative William McCollum of Florida once pointed out in a discussion of the death penalty, "While statistics might not indicate that it deters crime, it's common sense that it does."[56]

ON THE FEASIBILITY OF THE THREE ELEMENTS OF THE POLICY

Although the policy proposals in this chapter have been framed so as not to depart too drastically from current cultural ideas and political arrangements, few are now feasible, and may not even be feasible should the economy achieve the kind of health that made the War on Poverty, small as it was, possible for a few years in the 1960s.

Almost every American now seems to worry about personal safety and to favor costly anticrime policies, but present policies are fueled as much by the expression of popular anger and the desire for revenge as by the attempt to find ways of actually reducing street crime and the fear of such crime. Perhaps someday people's fear of crime will outweigh the desire to express anger and obtain revenge, in which case policies that can reduce street crime may at least move onto the political agenda.

If that reduction takes place, and if the economy is healthy, the better-off population can perhaps be persuaded to support a more comprehensive antipoverty policy. It is equally conceivable, however, that if there is a significant decline in threats to safety, the voters could decide that little or nothing more need be done to help the poor. In that case, antipoverty policy can be revived only if enough constituencies are organized and mobilized in its favor.

The most logical constituency for an antipoverty policy should be the poor themselves, but they are either excluded or self-excluded from effective political participation, and thus do not seem to be useful coalition partners for anyone else. At present, the poor are not even a constituency, and they may too divided by racial and other differences ever to be a politically effective one. In the 1960s, organized protest and spontaneous uprisings produced some short-range changes in welfare and other antipoverty programs, but if the Los Angeles "riot" of 1992 is an example for the future, disrupting the public peace may not help the disrupters in the present era. Perhaps new methods by which the poor can make their voices heard can be found, and new organizers will be able to mobilize enough of the poor so that they can become a constituency for antipoverty policy, or at least for membership in a larger coalition. But this may be too much to ask from the poor.

A related albeit equally potential constituency includes the many people now losing their places in the mainstream economy, or the approximately 40 percent who have reported in various national polls that they are fearful about it. Some of the workers who have already lost their jobs or who have had to take low-wage ones already consider themselves poor, while those who are worrying about the future probably have not yet thought that they might someday be poor. Then, many workers would undoubtedly support government employment programs that would create jobs for *them*. They might be less supportive of jobs and other programs for the previously and persistently poor, however, and might even view them as competitors for limited jobs and public funds. These newly poor could easily think of themselves as deserving but feel that the previously poor are undeserving. The new poor might also be more easily mobilized politically than the previously poor.

Yet another potential constituency is the union movement, which needs not only additional paying members but more of the power that comes with numbers. Unions have not been particularly supportive of the jobless in recent years, and they are not influential these days, although they still make their weight felt in the Democratic party.[57] In theory unions might be able to bring the new jobless and the previously jobless together, but that would require more political creativity than they have shown for many years, if in fact such a coalition were even possible.

One further possible future constituency is made up of the American corporations that earn their profits by making and selling consumer goods and services. They cannot afford to see too many of their present customers lose their incomes and their purchasing power. Sheer economic necessity might persuade these corporations to support antipoverty efforts.

The last potential constituency is the large population of better-off Americans who still tell pollsters they want the poor to be helped, even if they oppose welfare. They may not want to pay the real costs of reducing poverty, however, particularly if they feel insecure about their own economic position.

A large number of poll respondents also continue to complain about the inequality of the tax system, and appear to favor some "soaking" of the rich. Admittedly, the rich, supported by the immense number of Americans who feel that they are being overtaxed, have so far been able to scotch any really progressive tax on income and especially on wealth. Nonetheless, under the right conditions, someday a "poverty tax" on the incomes and wealth of the very rich should be politically feasible. This would pay at least a portion of the costs of a new antipoverty policy. Sufficient political support for soaking the rich would also begin to reduce the immense inequality between the very rich and the very poor that contributes to the existence of and rationalization for the idea of the undeserving poor.

The various debunking and informational programs that seek to attack the notion of undeservingness may be easiest to implement, since most cost little enough that private foundations could at least initiate them. Religious organizations that oppose poverty might help too, but support for programs against undeservingness also has to come from liberal thinkers, writers, educators, and others ready to counteract the conservative ideological movement and its supporters. If liberals are a sufficiently large and active political and cultural force, private funders will rally to their side, and even government may be ready to support educational and related efforts if Congress sees that a viable intellectual constituency has resurfaced.

But if liberalism is truly dying, or if liberal thinkers continue to be intimidated by the influence and audacity of conservative activists, then even debunking programs cannot be established. And even if they are established, there can be no guarantee that they will have any effect. Perhaps the general public's fear of crime and its hatred of the stigmatized poor have become strong enough that there are other obstacles to a revival of liberal strength.

Further obstacles to the return of liberal influence are current political arrangements, including an electoral process that forces candidates to pursue ever larger funds for television, and then encourages them to push hot-button issues that will attract viewers to the ballot box. Undeservingness is such a hot-button issue, and the poor are dramatic villains with which to attract viewer attention. Once the election is over, many of the ideological organizations, corporations, and wealthy individuals who pay the campaign funds want the elected candidates to pursue policies that save tax money and thus increase poverty as well as the poverty-related behavior that spells "undeservingness." Thus electoral reform, public financing of campaigns, and legislation for free or inexpensive television campaigning for candidates are essential to the future of antipoverty efforts.

DISPLACEMENT, SCAPEGOATING, AND PUBLIC POLICY

The prognosis that a job-centered antipoverty program would eventually be politically feasible does not seem hopeful at present, but the political future is even less predictable than some others. Nevertheless, the biggest obstacle to the feasibility of the proposed antipoverty policies may be the utility of the undeserving poor as scapegoats onto whom the better-off population can displace the larger problems and conflicts in American society.

The displacement and scapegoating processes cannot be successfully attacked, however, until more is known about why they exist, how they work, and how they could be eliminated. The first step has to be research and public discussion, which should be connected with the consideration of policies to deal with the conflicts producing the public anger and to eliminate the sources of that anger.

Although displacement seems to be a largely unconscious or unselfconscious process, getting people to talk about whether, how, and why they are angry at the scapegoats of the moment should not be difficult. Further talking to identify other dimensions of their anger should make it possible to begin to trace that anger to its more general, and actual, causes.

While people could talk about all this to researchers, talking with each other in public institutions that foster public discussion would be preferable. The available political institutions have not been very hospitable to such discussion, which may be one reason for the fantastic growth of "talk radio" and the rise of computer networking in the 1990s.[58] Still, the conventional forms of public discussion also need to be used, including public debates, the news media, and election campaigns, as well as all the other informal and formal channels that now make up the public communication process.

Many questions need to be raised in what becomes essentially a process of societal self-knowledge and self-awareness that should have been undertaken long ago.[59] For example, are such scapegoats particularly prevalent in unequal societies, in which the majority of the population need power-less scapegoats on which to blame problems for which they dare not accuse the powerful (or even themselves, that is, majority opinion)? Are there any societies that have functioned without the use of scapegoats, especially poor scapegoats, and if so, how and why?[60]

Does America, or any other society, really need scapegoats? If so, why? If the answer to this is yes, could, and should, the scapegoats then be peo-ple who can bear the burdens of displacement more easily than the poor?[61] And how could the members of a society, and through them its decision-makers, be made to face the problems and conflicts it needs to solve instead of blaming innocent others—or even guilty others? What changes can be made in the polity and economy so that difficult problems can be resolved?

Scapegoating and displacement are presumably invoked to shield politi-cians and citizens from having to deal with difficult social problems. If this is generally true, then societies and their polities have to figure out how to overcome the evasions that lie behind displacement. For example, if it is true that poor young unwed mothers are used to displace unhappiness with the various forms of sexual liberalization that have taken place among adults and young people since the 1960s, is there any way to lift the dis-placement burden off these mothers and to start debating the issues?

Perhaps the most difficult task is ending the displacement of seemingly insoluble problems—for example, those arising from the emergence of the global economy. What if poor people are labeled as lazy because the better-off population does not then have to think about replacing eliminated jobs? Or what if welfare recipients are blamed for being dependent so that the more fortunate classes do not have to confront the fact that America may no longer be able to afford costly forms of middle-class, upper-class, and corporate "welfare"? And would confronting these examples of displace-ment help to begin debating needed national and even international solu-tions?

Once questions such as these have been raised in informal public discus-sions, they should also enter the political process, eventually being placed on the formal political agenda. Unless this happens, the poor could be harassed as undeserving far into the future.

CHAPTER 6

Joblessness and Antipoverty Policy in the Twenty-first Century

This book has been concerned mainly with today's poor, many of whom are the victims of the "deindustrialization" that began in the 1960s. Further changes in the world economy and thus the domestic economy, however, are already creating new victims. Although official figures still mask the new realities, the further decline of well-paying manufacturing jobs and increased job losses to the computer, to other countries, and to corporate downsizing suggest that new cohorts can be expected to enter the ranks of the jobless, the temporary workers, and involuntary part-timers.[1]

Suppose the new downward trends that are associated with the 1980s and 1990s continue or even increase. Perhaps further advances in computerization or in other technologies will eliminate more jobs. For example, robotization is today still an infant industry, but it is likely to be perfected one of these years. Additional foreign low-wage labor markets might open, including the yet untapped but immense one in the rural hinterlands of the People's Republic of China, resulting in the departure of other American jobs.[2]

What if, moreover, managements find yet other techniques to reduce low-wage workers? Or consumer demand becomes saturated, except for population growth? Should all these trends come together, the *actual* jobless rate, which was estimated at 15 percent in May 1994, could begin to head toward 25 percent or more.

It is even possible that sometime in the twenty-first century, private firms may conclude that many can function, and best compete, with a minimum number of decently and poorly paid full-time workers, supported by a set of permanent and temporary part-timers as well as other kinds of contingent workers whose numbers would rise and fall depending on the state of the economy. Since public and nonprofit agencies tend eventually to follow the employment patterns of private enterprise, they too might shift to a work force that consists primarily of contingent workers.

If current trends become permanent, it is even conceivable that sometime in the new century, full-time workers, in good or bad jobs, would no longer be today's overwhelming majority. When the change would come and what the new proportions might be cannot even be guessed at now. Even so, a labor force could someday consist, in an average year, of 40 to 50 percent more or less securely employed full-time workers; another 25 to 35 percent who may work at a mixture of temporary full-time jobs and part-time ones, or who are fully and involuntarily part-time workers; and the rest who are jobless for all or significant parts of the year—or longer. Some of these proportions might be altered by possible expansion of the informal economy, which appears currently to be a better creator of jobs than the formal economy. Still, most of its jobs pay low wages, and many are also part-time and temporary.[3]

In the late nineteenth century, utopian writers such as Edward Bellamy extrapolated possibilities like these into a glorious future in which people would only have to work a few hours a day, spending the rest of their time in educational and constructive leisure activities. Bellamy not only assumed a new technology that adapted harmoniously to people's needs and demands but also unlimited resources and a benevolent dictatorial government that brought about economic equality, and made sure that everyone would live comfortably.[4]

Today, other authors have developed quasi-utopian models in which the machines do most of the work, and their ownership, as well as the profits therefrom, are somehow distributed to the population.[5] Utopian speculations are often useful, but in real life, resources are not unlimited, machines cannot do all the work, and even if they could, their owners and managers are not going to give up their capital or profits for the general welfare. Instead, the political economy will continue to reflect new versions of old forms of stratification—of power as well as resources. Under such conditions, a massive reduction of work could become dystopian. As long as people must live from what they earn, poverty would not only be at least as widespread and severe as during the Great Depression, but it might also become permanent.[6]

The preceding observations could also be totally wrong. New sources of peaceful economic growth in manufacturing and in services could require so many new workers that joblessness would become a minor problem, and an antipoverty program would not even be necessary in the years to come. In that case, much of chapters 5 and 6 of this book would be irrelevant, and I could not be more pleased.

WHAT WILL HAPPEN TO AMERICA'S JOBS AND SOCIETY?

But what if these fears turn out to be accurate? In the 1930s, the Great Depression produced the New Deal, but partly because of fear on the part of economic and political elites that socialism would replace capitalism if nothing was done. No one can predict what would happen this time, but in the last generation or so, the American economy has not found new sources of economic growth, and the polity has not developed mechanisms either to invent public methods of growth or to help the victims of economic change.

Downward mobility is always socially and individually destructive, and even the mild forms that most affected Americans have experienced since post–World War II affluence ended have wrought considerable personal and social damage.[7] Drastic downward mobility would most likely have effects similar to those long felt by poor blacks who were first driven out of their rural communities and then rebuffed time and again from their efforts to become part of the economic and social mainstream.

Today's middle-class and working-class whites may not be able to imagine it, but only a generation of severe and persistent downward mobility is enough to produce children and grandchildren who could develop the same poverty-related behavior patterns found among today's poor. Some will become school dropouts, unmarried mothers, and street criminals reacting with the same despair and anger, and many others will be accused of departing from mainstream ways even if they have not done so.

Given the ease with which new labels can be constructed or old ones extended to new populations when their jobs have disappeared, the new poor of the twenty-first century will probably be subjected to the same kind of stereotyping and labeling described in previous chapters of this book. If most of these new poor are whites, undeservingness would no longer be considered a predominantly racial failing.[8] But because they have fallen from greater socioeconomic heights, the reactions of the newly labeled poor could be more intense than those of people who have been stigmatized for generations.

Whether the better-off population of the twenty-first century can imitate its ancestors and escape from the poor is hard to predict. Land for moving ever farther away from the poor is still available in most metropolitan areas and beyond, thanks to the immense amount of vacant land on the American continent. Should the economy be weak, however, the various private and public funds needed for escaping the poor may no longer be so plentiful.

There is no way to predict how much poverty and misery, crime and violence, higher risk and lower expectations Americans, both better-off and poor, can get used to if joblessness worsens.[9] In many parts of the world, the fortunate classes have lived under highly guarded conditions amidst oppressed and powerless poor populations for centuries. The overt social peace is interrupted from time to time by bloody uprisings as well as by preventive or retaliatory police and military violence, so that no one can ever feel completely safe. Under such conditions, democracy disappears even if formal elections survive, and the institutions that are armed to control the poor also hold sway over the general polity.

This describes life in many Third World countries, including, until recently, South Africa. America is not a Third World country, even if some of its poor urban neighborhoods and their informal economies have developed Third World characteristics. Nonetheless, if joblessness and poverty rise in the future, and no more is done about them than has been the last quarter century, living in America would become a grimmer experience for most people, including even those who can hide in the protected parts of the economy or escape to sheltered parts of the country.[10]

WHAT COULD BE DONE?

Instead of trying to guess what the future might bring, it is far more useful to consider what might be done if the erosion of full-time jobs and of work generally continues. Even if the economic future turns out to be bleak, it is still far enough away to allow analysts time to investigate all possible scenarios for it. Meanwhile, planners can start to consider solutions for the political and social problems that could lie in its wake.

Actually, right now the time is ripe to set out on the thinking, speculating, and data-gathering that is preliminary to the making of long-term economic and social policy. A special opportunity awaits scholars who are interested in undertaking necessary studies because otherwise they may not be done. Most of the major think tanks and private economic research firms devote themselves to short-range policy studies that supply immediate answers for questions of the moment.

European and American social scientists began to think about job-related long-term economic and social policy during the automation scare of the 1960s, but most Americans, with the exception of scattered futurists and social scientists, stopped shortly after the scare ended. The Europeans have continued to work on this topic.[11] Thus some ideas and proposals are already available, and part of the task is to improve and update them as better estimates of the economy of the future become available.

This chapter's task is more limited: to extend some of the policy ideas proposed in the last chapter, and to add some others that seem necessary to counteract what may loom ahead in the next century.

Massive Job Creation and the Labor-Intensive Economy

If the decline in jobs and in full-time jobs becomes serious, more massive job creation and preservation policies than those described in the last chapter would be required. Government will have to intervene in the economy to a much greater degree, and public works would need to turn into a permanent institution, often trying desperately to create productive opportunities for new employment, private and public. Even if private enterprise remains nominally dominant, it could maintain its political dominance only by giving a higher priority to the maximization of jobs than it does now, and by paying less attention to the maximization of profit. The result would be a very different kind of capitalism than exists today.

One possible government role could be to help to reinvent a more labor-intensive economy, which might not only prevent the further proliferation of job-destroying technology, particularly by private enterprise, but could also consider when, where, and how human beings could replace some existing machines that have eliminated a sizeable number of good jobs.

America, like all other industrial and postindustrial economies, has for at least two centuries defined virtually all technological innovation as progress. In the process, the powerful victims of new technology have been paid off but the rest have been disregarded, or pacified with promises that they too would eventually benefit from the growth produced by new technology. If creating and saving jobs became the highest public policy priority, the benefits of reclaiming jobs from the machines and the costs of doing so would have to be analyzed closely, and the conception of technological progress, as well as the definitions of benefits and costs, rethought radically.

The technological innovations that have ended the most dangerous and dirty physical labor, added to the quality of work life, and improved the quality of goods and services have to be preserved. Also worth saving are the technologies that have increased the intellectual level of work, the quality of health care, and the like, and many of the machines that have increased the comforts of everyday life. Luddite nostalgia is out of place, and giving up the computer is senseless, but a case could be made for returning to the labor-intensive and thus costlier manufacture of, say, cars, particularly if environmental considerations and the virtues of mass transit could justify more expensive cars.[12]

The policy and political planning for a more labor-intensive economy require decisions involving not only the voters but the corporations who have to maintain the private economy, and the private and public agencies concerned with global economic considerations. Moreover, the policy issue is probably never a choice between labor-intensive and capital-intensive production, but of using tax policies and other sanctions to reduce some capital-intensive work, as well as financial and social incentives to preserve and create as many jobs as possible through labor-intensive production. Some such incentives already exist, handmade pottery and furniture being more prestigious than machine-made.

Since modern economies became capital-intensive largely as a way of cutting costs, especially labor costs, the more labor-intensive economy, like other transformations to be discussed below, would require a less competitive global economy. This is clearly impossible in the short run, particularly as long as the Third World continues to industrialize, but in the very long run all economies will probably experience the same mass unemployment. In that case, many if not all would eventually be driven toward the same need to create and save jobs.

At the same time, opportunities for competition in the race to develop innovations and searches for new markets, which could include wars, warlike acts, and other socially destructive processes, will remain. Countries that are not democratic and can ignore the niceties of international competition would be advantaged, including totalitarian countries that can use war-making to stimulate their economies. Societies able to invent new economic products and services that can temporarily gain in or sidestep the global competition would be at a great political and cultural advantage as well.[13] Ultimately, however, sectors of the American economy that have become labor-intensive would have to determine whether it is possible to compete successfully with similar sectors in other countries that have remained more capital-intensive.

Workplace Democratization

A related if more indirect policy for saving and creating jobs is the democratic reorganization of workplaces, in which America also lags behind other countries. If increasing worker autonomy on the job and worker control over the job can increase productivity and lead to lower prices that spur demand, some jobs may be saved or created.

Other forms of improved working conditions may have similar results. For example, worker profit-sharing schemes may increase productivity, but also enable workers to take wage cuts to save their jobs if economic conditions make such cuts unavoidable.[14]

Workplace democratization is not likely to spread widely without a revival of unionization or other employee organization, particularly in the white-collar class. Most likely little can be accomplished without the invention of unions of part-time and contingent workers. Also, the worker organizations of the future must be more democratic, and more responsive to unorganized workers. They will otherwise be too weak to resist corporate and governmental enemies only too eager to eliminate them.

Drastic Work Sharing

The other major policy to deal with sharply rising unemployment and involuntary part-time work is upgrading work sharing from a modest to a drastic level. This could eventually mean the virtual abolition of full-time work. Alternative ways of achieving this are available, from a work week that would likely shrink to twenty-four hours or even less, to a shorter work year or work life that retains the present work week. The drastic spreading of work would presumably save and create enough jobs to do away with unemployment—but everyone would then be working part-time by twentieth-century standards.

If drastic work sharing were to coincide with already changing work time trends, as well as with the present temporal organization of modern society, one possible solution would be the twenty-four-hour work week. That solution would, however, be very different from today's involuntary part-time or other forms of contingent work. For one thing, all workers would be in the same boat. More important, the jobs would need to become secure, and to carry all the rights and benefits now connected to secure, well-paying full-time work. Drastic work sharing would thus universalize part-time employment, redefine it as full-time work, and restore the temporal equality that existed during the periods of full-time full employment.

Drastic work time reduction is accompanied by a variety of problems, although only a few can be touched on here.[15] Work sharing would only apply to people and not to machines, which could run twenty-four hours a day and seven days a week if demand for their output exists. True, putting the machines to work longer hours negates the job-creating aim of the labor-intensive economy discussed previously, and might become a weapon in the global competition as well, but entrepreneurs, firm owners, cost analysts, elected officials, unions and other employee organizations, as well as workers and voters could determine whether the benefits of running the machines on this basis outweigh the social as well as economic costs.

One of the effects of drastic work sharing is its possible impact on people's work incentives, particularly for badly needed highly skilled work that requires years of training. Many people engaged in such work enjoy it enough that they might not want to do it for only twenty-four hours a week.[16] In some cases they might be able to work longer but at only twenty-four hours' pay. Others, however, might decide not to undergo the needed lengthy training or choose a less arduous profession.[17] Should any profession then wind up in short supply, brain surgeons being the usually mentioned example, temporary or permanent exceptions can be made to the work-sharing rules.[18]

Perhaps a more realistic problem is whether a firm or public agency, particularly a large one, can be headed by a single executive working only twenty-four hours a week, or whether effective two-person executive heads can be invented. But many firms may not even need to remain so large in an economy of part-time work.

Drastic work sharing would also require concerted attention to the effect on labor costs, particularly when such costs may constitute a problem in global competition. Actually, the twenty-four-hour week would work best if it were globally instituted, and it may well be so instituted some day if all national or other economies are driven by the same forces. The short work week might function even more effectively if comparative labor costs were similar, but such equality might not be achievable for centuries.

Nonetheless, unless a sizeable increase in national resources occurs, drastic work sharing would probably require some wage, salary, and profit reduction, with national politics determining who bears a larger share of the costs. Whether and how much reduction in all three will be needed cannot be decided now, and it is true that in the past, modest and gradual work time reduction has so far taken place without parallel decreases in pay.[19]

Even so, pay decreases of some kind will probably be needed under drastic work reduction, if only because a twenty-four-hour work week cannot produce the same take-home pay as a forty-hour or even a thirty-two-hour work week. Moreover, the American standard of living has long been supported artificially by paying many workers minimum wages, particularly in sweatshop industries, that would have to be raised if people could only work twenty-four hours a week.

These low minimum wages are not paid in other modern countries, and they keep American prices lower than elsewhere. They thus boost the standard of living for moderate- and middle-income people, since low prices for necessities leave them disposable income for some luxuries, but they also subsidize the rich, who benefit from lower-priced luxuries. The victims are the workers who receive wages too low to buy either the necessities or the luxuries, as well as the people who never get jobs because prices can be kept low only by keeping the work force to a minimum.[20]

A second subsidy keeping prices low has been the American tax system. Perhaps it can be sustained even with a twenty-four-hour work week, but most likely America is going to have to adopt the European value-added tax (V.A.T.) sales tax system, as well as the other taxes needed to supply public services, especially once part-time workers can no longer pay for private services. For example, people who work twenty-four hours a week cannot afford private health insurance, but neither can their government supply public health insurance if tax receipts are not increased beyond today's levels.

Maintaining the American Standard of Living

Americans have rarely objected when private enterprise raised prices, but they frequently object to governmental tax increases, and effectively so. As a result, they have taken reductions in their standard of living out on government even when the causes lay more with the private economy. Assuming these political reactions will not change, it is also fair to assume that if pay reductions are needed, imaginative policy-making will have to find ways of *offsetting* these reductions to maintain as much of the country's standard, or standards, of living as possible. As in the case of modest work sharing, many people will take offsetting into their own hands, and immediately resort to moonlighting. Since there are only so many opportunities for moonlighters, and their successes could endanger other jobs, government will have to undertake public offsetting.

One possible offset, which would currently be unlikely to obtain much American sympathy but might receive a different response in the future, is to have government offer more of those goods and services that it can truly supply more cheaply than private enterprise. In that case, the benefits of economies of scale could be fed back into maintaining the standard of living.

A second offset, which is also not likely to be received positively in late-twentieth-century America but may turn out to be necessary and therefore politically feasible when jobs become really scarce, is to cut the tie between work and income by establishing a basic minimum income grant for all Americans. A basic income grant, when added to the pay for twenty-four hours of work, should enable two, or one-and-a-half, breadwinners to support a family. Equally important, a basic income would enable people to afford more of the goods and services being produced by the economy.[21]

Basic income schemes were first discussed in America and western Europe during the automation scare of the 1960s, but they have not been publicly discussed in America since the 1970s, perhaps because of the icy political reception given the "demogrant," presidential candidate George McGovern's basic income proposal from 1972.[22] In Europe, policy-oriented thinkers have discussed the basic income grant not only as a replacement for pay lost from work but as an income for which all people are eligible as citizens rather than workers: "to distribute to everyone the wealth created by society's productive forces *as a whole*."[23]

Political economists would have to analyze how much income from these productive forces would be available for general distribution, and under what conditions, in good times and in bad. Unless American attitudes about self-reliance and "dependency" vanish completely, however, it seems prudent to propose the separation of work and income by initially treating the basic minimum income as a replacement for lost work income.

Under such conditions, a basic minimum income would function like a universal version of today's Earned Income Tax Credit, which would be taxed away from high-income workers. The more universal and generous the basic income grant, however, the less some will want to hold jobs. On the one hand, dirty and undesirable jobs might not find takers until wages and salaries for them were raised, which seems only fair. On the other hand, some people might be willing to give up their jobs and live on the basic minimum, "donating" their jobs to the general job pool so that work can be spread around further.[24] Whether twenty-first-century Americans would permit government to pay people for not working and would refrain from stigmatizing them need not be determined now.

A third offset to pay reduction from work sharing would be a vastly extended "community service" job program. Instead of using it as a punishment for white-collar and other criminals and as a job of last resort for welfare recipients, community service work would be turned into a regular and sizeable second-tier, lower-wage labor market. It would be used not so much to increase people's incomes, but to find a way of supplying those goods and services significant for the country's standard of living that can no longer be afforded in the regular twenty-four-hour-a-week labor market. Community service work would also help to occupy people who do not want additional leisure time.

Some community service work would be expected from everyone in exchange for the basic income grant—or, putting it in European terms, the service jobs would be a citizen's responsibility in return for the citizen's grant. To maximize both the citizens' and the economy's flexibility, people would have the right to reduce their community service work in exchange for a reduction in their basic income grant, or to increase it somewhat if they want to add to their income. Hours and pay rates (or the portion of the basic income grant) for community service work would probably have to be varied to make sure that the needed work is carried out. Workaholics who would be rationed to twenty-four hours in the regular labor market should be allowed to work as long as they want to in a community service job, except if and when their long hours deprive others of the opportunity to earn regular or community service pay.

Perhaps the most difficult question that policy analysts, politicians, and citizens have to decide is which jobs fall into the regular and community service tiers. A number of criteria for deciding are available, but in the end, public and private functions that serve only a minority, like some of the arts, are likely candidates for community service work.

A fourth but supplementary offset solution is typically American: the already widespread practice of people volunteering for tasks for which religious, charitable, and other nonprofit organizations cannot afford to pay. Such volunteering would perhaps continue and even expand under drastic work sharing, since it could exist as a third tier alongside community service jobs. Thus organizations, including perhaps even commercial firms that do not obtain community service positions, would recruit volunteers if they could offer them something in return—skills training, for example. People who do not want all of their basic income grant might choose to volunteer instead of doing community service work. So would retired people and others who seek to fill up some of their spare time or want company. However it is organized, increased volunteering is also another way to minimize reductions in the standard of living, allowing the continuation of activities that cannot be afforded even as community service work.[25]

Drastic work sharing creates many other problems, material and otherwise, which can be studied and discussed before the need for such a policy becomes apparent. For example, a twenty-four-hour work week raises questions about the social and emotional functions of work. Most likely, people can obtain the same feelings of social usefulness, respect, and self-respect from a short work week, or from community service work, that they can from today's full-time work week, as long as everyone is roughly in the same boat. The establishment and nurture of careers probably needs to be reorganized under drastic work sharing, assuming careers remain a viable goal, and the allocation of occupational prestige will no doubt change as well. The jobs downgraded to community service work would probably lose some of their prestige.

Traditionally, work time reduction schemes aroused fears among the elite that the "masses" could not find enough to do to fill their additional spare time and would spend it drinking and fighting. Since World War II, the main elite fear has been a mass lapsing into passivity in front of the television set. Such concerns are likely to be raised again even if only the moderate work sharing discussed in chapter 5 has to be instituted, but a nation of home owners, many of whom have also become world travelers, should have enough to do to keep busy. By the next century, cultural innovators may find ways to make more people want to interact with interactive television or its computerized equivalents and successors, just in case people do not invent enough of their own new pursuits to keep them busy.

Actually, the availability of more leisure time will encourage some people to grow some of their own food, manufacture some of their own goods, and engage in nonmonetary barter with friends and neighbors.[26] In fact, barter, and present institutions that foster cooperation, could be developed, should they not develop spontaneously, to function as yet another way to offset possible reductions in the standard of living.[27]

The Limits of Futuristic Planning

Futuristic economic and social plans are easier to write than to implement. None of these policies—massive job creation, the encouragement of a labor-intensive economy, taxing the machines and their owners, the separation of work from income, drastic work sharing, as well as the offsets to reductions in the standard of living—could be made to work effectively and fairly without extended technical and popular discussion. Indeed, policies like those proposed here all need a more pervasive and intensive level of public support than any of today's public policies or private practices.

Also, those proposed here may not be the right policies, or ones that will be politically acceptable in the twenty-first century. Perhaps policies requiring no significant involuntary reduction in work or any other untried innovations in economic policy will solve the erosion of work that is currently being forecast.

Then too, futuristic planning inevitably suffers from the tendency to assume too much perfection. For one thing, it is easy to forget that class and racial divides do not disappear by themselves, and in fact generally turn worse when the economy becomes more troubled. As a result, all of the programs I have sketched could be manipulated along class and racial lines so as to provide minimally for the poor, and especially the nonwhite poor. Proposing full employment by inventing twenty-four-hour-a-week jobs does not thereby eliminate the possibility that these can be denied to the descendants of today's jobless.

While manifest racial sabotaging may remain unconstitutional in the twenty-first century, the legislation for most programs can set eligibility limits, excluding people who have been poor or jobless for a long time.[28]

After the Los Angeles earthquake of 1993, the homeless were denied the various kinds of housing aid available to residents whose homes had been damaged or destroyed, on the grounds that, being homeless, they lacked housing that could have been affected by the earthquake.

Furthermore, even if all the policies suggested here were race- and class-blind, and even if they should somehow work as intended, they probably cannot do away completely with joblessness, and they will certainly not eliminate all poverty. Every social arrangement creates casualties as well as those who find loopholes to obtain more resources for themselves, thus leaving fewer for others. And all societies have people who are unable or unwilling to participate. Even so, polities that are oriented to dealing with joblessness and poverty are going to be very different from those that treat these evils as natural. This difference includes plans that at least prepare their members to get ready for expected economic change and for the possible end of full-time work.

The Egalitarian Implications of Future Jobs Policies

Perhaps the greatest limit of futuristic planning is that planners can insert their goals without concurrently planning for drastic political change. For example, most of the policies described in the previous sections are to some extent economically egalitarian, seeking to eliminate or minimize differences between full-time, part-time, and jobless workers, and at the least save further workers from becoming jobless and thus poor. Although more equality may not be a planner's goal as much as a necessity in the twenty-first century if the grim costs of widespread joblessness, poverty, and dramatic inequality are to be avoided, egalitarian policies still involve political change and economic redistribution. Even if the country deems more equality necessary, those who would have to give up some income and wealth as well as autonomy and political influence would fight it, as they have all through history. Such a fate might beset drastic work sharing, which is, among other things, an egalitarian full-employment policy in which everyone works the same number of hours so that no one is jobless.

Still, work sharing need not end the inequality of income and particularly of wealth, for wages and salaries need be no more equal for a twenty-four-hour work week than they are for a 40-hour work week. Even the basic income grant is not inherently egalitarian, although it, like the American demogrant, has been so conceived by social thinkers, who assume it to supply a proportionally larger addition to the income of poor people than to that of rich ones.

Even so, the economy and society envisaged in these pages cannot function on the same inegalitarian basis as twentieth-century America. If the work week is reduced to twenty-four hours—that is, by 40 percent from the forty-hour week, wages cannot be cut by the same proportion. Thus drastic work sharing would be more egalitarian almost by definition. In addition, a progressive tax system may be needed to pay for the costs of the basic income grant, as well as to assure that owners of capital and those entrepreneurs and self-employed individuals who can evade the twenty-four-hour-a-week work schedule will pay their share of the cost of running the economy.

An economy in which the government intervenes actively to foster drastic job creation, administers work sharing, and supplies a basic minimum income, among other activities, is assumed to be more egalitarian because government is often (if unwisely) assumed to be automatically more egalitarian than private enterprise. In fact, an egalitarian government requires an egalitarian polity, but such a polity cannot be planned, or legislated by decree. Scholarly research and public discussions about the shape of the future will have to supply ideas about how twentieth-century structures of economic and political inequality, as well as traditional American individualism, could be nudged in a more egalitarian direction. These discussions might also help to make people realize that if the era of full-time jobs is going to end, a livable economy and society can most likely exist only with more equality of all kinds for everyone.

Notes

INTRODUCTION

1. In addition, the label became the title of a recent and widely read book, the subtitle of which helped to inspire the title of this book: Michael Katz's *The Undeserving Poor: From the War on Poverty to the War on Welfare* (New York: Pantheon, 1989).

2. In fact, the popularity of "underclass" as an economic and sociological concept helped to revive antipoverty research in the 1980s.

3. In 1990, fewer than 12 percent of poor white, black, and Latino unmarried mothers of children under two were under the age of eighteen (Lee Rainwater, "A Primer on American Poverty: 1949–1992," Working Paper 53 [New York: Russell Sage Foundation, May 1994], p. 18).

4. See, for example, Frank Furstenberg, Jr., et al., *Adolescent Mothers in Later Life* (New York: Cambridge University Press, 1987).

5. Indeed, the language of choice is sometimes ill-suited for the poor, since we know from history, sociology, and psychology, not to mention common sense, that in desperate situations the people with the fewest resources are most likely to resort to desperate solutions.

6. My favorite response to the call for such self-improvement remains that of R. H. Tawney, the British economist. In 1913, he wrote, "Improve the character of all individuals by all means—if you feel competent to do so, especially of those whose excessive incomes expose them to peculiar temptations." R. H. Tawney, *Poverty as an Industrial Problem* (London: London School of Economics, 1913), pp. 11–12.

7. In fact, poor people also apply the label to their neighbors and often define undeservingness in the same way as the more fortunate classes. They do so in part because they share the values of these classes, and sometimes hold such values more intensely. They almost have to, because for the poor, these values signify a set of aspirations that supply hope in an otherwise depressing life, protection against cynicism and despair, and self-respect in a society that often has little respect for the poor.

In addition, the poor need more than anyone else to protect themselves against crime and exploitation. They must distinguish constantly between people they can trust and those they cannot; between responsible neighbors and the irresponsible, often dangerously troubled ones who constitute threats to safety. Better-off Americans may occasionally have reason to fear street crime, but the poor must be on guard all the time, since they live in the middle of it.

CHAPTER 1: LABELING THE POOR

1. Even well-trained researchers who feel themselves to be fully objective will make judgments that reflect their own biases, in the process unquestionably accepting unreliable evidence without a second thought. Like other professional people, they may judge welfare recipients as undeserving, even as they offer different explanations for their undeservingness than their lay neighbors.

2. This formulation departs somewhat from prevailing sociological practice, which generally considers labeling to be the process by which one set of people declare another set of people, or some of the behavior of the latter, as deviant; the prevailing practice is less interested than I am in the knowledge used for labeling and the labels themselves. I treat deviance itself in the now conventional sociological fashion, however: a claim by one set of people (or institutions) that some actions of another set of people or institutions deviate from those of the rest of society, or at least its mainstream.

Mainstream values are those claimed as such by a dominant numerical or cultural population, although no one knows which of these values are practiced by most, many, or even some people who think of themselves as mainstream, are preached but not practiced, or are only preached ritually, as during election campaigns. Moreover, values people adhere to publicly may not be practiced privately. Thus whoever has power over the public definition of mainstream values also has control over the determination of deviance.

3. Extrapolating from Georg Simmel, the deviant or undeserving poor are determined not by their behavior but by their receipt of disapproval from others (Georg Simmel, "The Poor," *Social Problems* 13 [Fall 1965]: 118–40, esp. 140).

4. Terms base their description on actual knowledge, whether personal or public, popular or scientific, while labels are, as already noted, based on imagined knowledge that seeks to stigmatize. An assertion that most poor men are muggers, or that most stockbrokers are crooked, is an example of labeling. Labels can also derive from what appears to be actual knowledge, which is, however, based on assumptions that incorporate imagined knowledge. A good example is the tortured "scientific" research of the turn-of-the-century eugenicists who argued that the poor people they had studied in hovels or in jails had to be feebleminded because they violated so many of the researchers' mainstream values.

My application of the term/label distinction will be conservative, insofar as "term" is used unless I am reasonably sure that a word is based on imagined knowledge or used for labeling, as in the brief survey of past and present words for the undeserving poor in the next section of this chapter. Also, since labeling involves intent or outcome, when knowledge of either is unavailable "term" rather than "label" is used, even when it appears as if the words are really used for labeling. Thus much of the analysis of the history of the underclass in chap. 2 is framed as the history of a behavioral term.

5. As soon as poor people are judged to be undeserving, terms used to describe them almost immediately become labels, because undeservingness is a moral label that cannot meet the requirements of a term.

6. Karen R. Wilkinson, "The Broken Family and Juvenile Delinquency," *Social Problems* 21 (June 1974): 726–39. Other examples are cited at the end of chap. 3.

7. Professionally used terms and labels have usually been invented by professionals. Incidentally, the currently preferred term for communication is "discourse," but I am not sure there is enough empirical evidence for the existence of a public *discourse*, not to mention a public sphere, or for that matter, even a marketplace of ideas. These all suggest more back-and-forth communication than I believe exists.

8. Actually, all labels appear to be hard to study sociologically, since no one seems ever to have conducted surveys or interview studies to determine what kinds of people use various kinds of labels. Until such studies are done, one must infer such uses from the kinds of news media that use different labels, a risky procedure that I have not tried because it assumes, without evidence, that specific media correctly represent the vocabulary preferences of their audiences.

9. Privately used labels or terms are not often volunteered to survey researchers studying attitudes toward the poor. Lexicographers collect them for dictionaries. Irving Lewis Allen has compiled a list of such labels and terms, and found 223 for blacks, far more than for any other racial or ethnic group (Irving Lewis Allen, *The Language of Ethnic Conflict: Social Organization and Lexical Culture* [New York: Columbia University Press, 1983], pp. 80–81).

10. Jonathan Rieder, *Canarsie: The Jews and Italians of Brooklyn Against Liberalism* (Cambridge, Mass.: Harvard University Press, 1985). Ethnographers have access to such words because they are with the people they study long enough to be allowed to share all kinds of private conversations.

11. The publicly used labels can appear to be more polite than they are, for they can be embedded in a punitive rhetoric that suggests or implies other failings of the labeled. Newspaper stories and television news items about unmarried mothers and street criminals sometimes describe them or their actual or imagined misbehaviors, in words or pictures, to make them seem more sinful or vicious than they are. The classic analysis of this rhetorical method is Chandler Davidson's "On 'the Culture of Shiftlessness,'" *Dissent* (Fall 1976): 349–56.

12. When technical or analytic terms are systematically thought out and thought through, and when they are usable for systematic empirical and theoretical analyses, they *are* concepts—and this is so even if they are inspired by metaphors, as is often the case. Myrdal's underclass was a concept that could even be operationalized, but chap. 2 tells the story of how it later also became a label.

13. The social sciences are full of labels that are wrongly described as concepts, and that are so full of biases and imagined knowledge that they cannot be used as such. For example, concepts that make empirically unjustifiable extrapolations, such as treating a single parent as a proxy for promiscuity, are labels, but so is a class analysis that celebrates working-class people as heroic proletarians.

14. In this section, I shall not distinguish between terms and labels, although all of those discussed have been used to stereotype poor people. Greeks were already known to be concerned about whether the poor were deserving of help or not. See Robert Morris, *Rethinking Social Welfare* (New York: Longmans, 1986), pp. 88–90. Cicero thought of the needy as near-criminals (P. A. Brunt, *Social Conflict in the Roman Republic* [New York: Norton, 1971], p. 138). His view of Rome may have been influenced by his position as a "slumlord."

15. In fact, an informal survey of continental western European dictionaries found no translations for the phrase "undeserving poor." These countries appear to have used other types of labels to stigmatize their deviant poor. Distinctive features of the Anglo-American Protestant religious tradition may also be responsible for the notion of undeservingness.

16. Sidney and Beatrice Webb, *English Poor Law History* (Hamden, Conn.: Shoe String Press, 1963 [1927]), pt. I, p. 7 ff. Before then, the medieval church believed, at least officially, that all poor people were eligible for charity (pp. 3–6).

17. England may not been first, however, for an 1827 Philadelphia Board of Guardians already separated "the more deserving from the abandoned and worthless" (David Rothman, ed., *The Almshouse Experience: Collected Reports* [New York: Arno Press, 1971], p. 8).

18. For one of the few analyses of the deserving poor as a label, see Donileen R. Loseke and Kirsten Fawcett, "Appealing Appeals: Constructing Moral Worthiness, 1912–1917," *Sociological Quarterly* 36 (Winter 1995): 61–77, which analyzes case histories from the *New York Times*'s annual charity for its "Hundred Neediest Cases."

I should add that the poor may consider those of their economic peers that are celebrated by the American mainstream culture as upwardly mobile traitors and prospective deserters of the community, just as poor black youngsters sometimes consider their academically successful fellow students to be behaving like "whitey."

19. No one has yet conducted a comprehensive historical study, but the most thoughtful analyses of American labels can be found in the various works on poverty by Michael B. Katz, notably his *Poverty and Policy in American History* (New York: Academic Press, 1983). For a good history of American terms and labels for the poor, including those used in popular culture, see Robert H. Bremner, *From the Depths: The Discovery of Poverty in the United States* (New York: New York University Press, 1956). For English labels, see Gertrude Himmelfarb's classic *The Idea of Poverty: England in the Early Industrial Age* (New York: Random House, 1983).

20. Bryan S. Green, *Knowing the Poor: A Case Study in Textual Reality Construction* (London: Routledge and Kegan Paul, 1983), p. 81.

21. Mark H. Haller, *Eugenics: Hereditarian Attitudes in American Thought* (New Brunswick, N.J.: Rutgers University Press, 1963), p. 202, n. 6.

22. Michael Katz credits it to Frederick H. Wines, a minister, prison reformer, and organizer, who also called himself a "scientific" reformer. As Katz points out in a systematic exposé of Wines's "scientific" thinking and empirical work, some of it, like that of his colleagues who also wore "scientific" mantles, was doctored

or made up, all in the cause of justifying new forms of reforming or punishing the poor (Katz, *Poverty and Policy*, pp. 134–56).

23. "Culturally deprived" is one of a subclass of academic labels, and seems to have been invented by psychologists (Lee Rainwater, Frank Riessman, personal communications). For a critique of the label and its redefinition as a largely economic term, see Frank Riessman, *The Culturally Deprived Child* (New York: Harper and Row, 1962), chap. 1.

24. These were all initially western European terms used mainly to describe people who might join or help revolutionary movements, or who might upset the social and/or public order without being explicitly political in their actions. Marx's German translation of the English "ragged poor" described people who were unfit to be mobilized for the revolution, although they might serve as scabs and mercenaries for the *ancien régime*. However, Marx's definition was broad and bourgeois enough to include also poor people he considered morally unfit. See Lydia Morris, *Dangerous Class: The Underclass and Social Citizenship* (London: Routledge, 1994), p. 15.

25. Charles Loring Brace, *The Dangerous Classes of New York and Twenty Years of Work Among Them* (New York: Wynkoop and Hallenbeck, 1872). Brace may have used the term because he was responding to American fears following the Paris Commune. Most of his work among this class was devoted to shipping the children west where they were thought to have been used as cheap farm labor.

26. At this writing, however, no one has yet revived "bastard."

27. Tinkers and Gypsies belong on the list as well, despite their racial connotations.

28. For good historical analyses, see, for example, Paul T. Ringenbach, *Tramps and Reformers, 1873–1916: The Discovery of Unemployment in New York* (Westport, Conn.: Greenwood Press, 1973); and Kim Hopper, "A Poor Apart: The Distancing of Homeless Men in New York's History," *Social Research* 58 (Spring 1981): 107–32.

29. Lee Rainwater, drawing on the work of Bernard Beck, also refers to them as people who "play the role of the roleless and are in the structural position of being outside the structure." Lee Rainwater, "Neutralizing the Disinherited: Some Psychological Aspects of Understanding the Poor," in Vernon L. Allen, ed., *Psychological Factors in Poverty* (Chicago: Markham, 1970), pp. 9–27, quote at p. 11.

30. An entirely different category of pejorative labels has been invented by conservatives to criticize political and professional people who seek to aid or empower the poor. Because conservatives are especially active in inventing labels, the list is long, one of the more graphic ones of the 1990s being "paleoliberal"— which was borrowed from the liberal label "paleoconservative."

31. Brace, writing about the dangerous classes in 1872, was as appalled about the unmarried mothers he found among the German immigrants as today's critics are about poor black or Latino mothers.

32. Bernard A. Weinberger, "A Nation of Immigrants," *American Heritage* 45 (Feb.–Mar. 1994): 72–91, quote at p. 84 (emphasis added).

33. I draw here on an unpublished review essay by Linda Gordon, "Remarks on the History of the Underclass" (New York: Social Science Research Council, Apr. 27, 1992).

34. One of the few exceptions that thereby helps to prove the rule was a 1986 CBS News documentary, "Crisis in Black America," anchored by Bill Moyers, which interviewed several "studs," but it was never followed up by other journalists (Howard Husock, "Moynihan to Moyers: The Black Family and the Political Agenda" [Washington, D.C.: Woodrow Wilson International Center for Scholars, Media Studies Project No. 5, n.d.]). Charles Murray, who has become a popular media debater for his proposal to end welfare, does not seem to have suffered in popularity for assigning no responsibility to the men who impregnate young women.

35. William Kornblum describes them more graphically as "lumping terms" (William Kornblum, "Lumping the Poor: What *Is* the Underclass?" *Dissent* [Sept. 1984]: 295–302).

36. Social umbrella terms function similarly. For example, popular stratification terms like lower, middle, and upper class, or, for that matter, "the poor"—which is both a major label and a term—complicate the lives of stratification researchers because the empirical reality is so much more complex. See Richard P. Coleman and Lee Rainwater, with Kent A. McClelland, *Social Standing in America: New Dimensions of Class* (New York: Basic Books, 1978).

37. The process described here is a general picture, almost an ideal type, based on my reading of the histories of past labels and the history so far of the underclass.

38. Stafford and Ladner call them "active members of the labeling professions" (Walter W. Stafford and Joyce Ladner, "Political Dimensions of the Underclass Concept," in Herbert J. Gans, ed., *Sociology in America* [Newbury Park, Calif.: Sage, 1990], pp. 138–46, quote at p. 141).

39. I mean this term to be descriptive, and do not mean to be critical of alarmists, who are a particular kind of what sociologists call "claims-makers."

40. Teachers and researchers are sometimes also good storytellers, as are people in religious work and, in our day, in advertising.

41. Label-making is thus like other manufacturing for a fickle consumer market, and the history of successful labels for the undeserving poor is not entirely dissimilar to the history of popular advertising slogans. Both are marked by the inability to predict in advance what the market will accept, but the concurrent ability to discover, with hindsight, a usually considerable similarity in the kinds of labels and slogans the market did accept.

42. If the tryouts seem successful, the sorting process operates in some respects like a relay race, a new label being used alongside an older one with the newcomer eventually supplanting the other, sometimes just because it grabs better than the old one. In the sorting process to find a term for an allegedly new wave of suburban development in the 1980s, "edge city" finally drove out a number of others, including "technoburb" and "pizza-with-pepperoni cities."

43. Journalists also look up old stories in the Nexis data base, the successor to the "morgue," or respond to definitions they have heard among colleagues.

44. By and large, these are print media, since the electronic media have so little

time to communicate to a large diverse audience that they must use common terms that neither need definition nor antagonize anyone. But willing media presuppose events and "pegs" for which labels are relevant.

45. Legitimators may offer label credibility intentionally, but they may also be quoted or misquoted without their consent.

46. Although researchers may not intend to contribute to the legitimation of a label, if they write carelessly or allow themselves to be misquoted, they function as direct legitimators, whatever their personal intention.

47. Gareth S. Jones, *Outcast London* (Oxford: Clarendon Press, 1971).

48. David Matza has suggested in passing that the credibility of labels is terminated because they are themselves stigmatized, but he did not indicate who does the stigmatizing, how it works, and under what conditions it fails to work (David Matza, "Poverty and Disrepute," in Robert K. Merton and Robert Nisbet, eds., *Contemporary Social Problems*, 3d ed. [New York: Harcourt Brace & World, 1971], pp. 601–56, at p. 625).

49. On the Bushmen, see Robert J. Gordon, *The Bushman Myth: The Making of a Namibian Underclass* (Boulder, Colo.: Westview, 1992).

50. Only an immense archival study could recreate the long formation process for "feeblemindedness," and the shorter one for "the culture of poverty," but this account will only reconstruct the bare bones of the process that created the two umbrella labels that preceded "the underclass."

51. Galton coined the term "eugenic," but eugenicist ideas were already held by others, including Darwin. I rely here mainly on Haller, *Eugenics*, and Stephen J. Gould, *The Mismeasure of Man* (New York: Norton, 1981).

52. Rafter argues that the Americans were mostly concerned with demonstrating the arrival of the new professional class of reformers and scientists, and its ability to exercise social control (Nicole H. Rafter, *White Trash: The Eugenic Family Studies, 1877–1919* [Boston: Northeastern University Press, 1988], chap. 1). The professionals were funded by rich individuals and organizations that represented the upper-class WASP elite, as did the professionals themselves.

53. R. L. Dugdale, *"The Jukes": A Study in Crime, Pauperism, Disease and Heredity* (New York: Putnam's, 1875). Dugdale was also, like many of those who preceded and followed him, concerned with the expenditure of public funds, that is, taxes. Consequently, he worked out the exact cost of the "social damage" caused by the Jukes, which he estimated at $1.3 million over 75 years (pp. 69–70).

54. Dugdale, *The Jukes*, p. 65. He even noted the poverty of the Jukes, but his policy emphasis was training the poor, especially in "esthetic tastes" and "the habits of reasoning" (p. 66). These quotes are taken from Robert J. Karp, *Malnourished Children in the United States* (New York: Springer, 1993), pp. xx–xxi. I am also indebted to Dr. Karp for a wealth of other information gained from his recent restudy of the data about the Jukes and the Kallikaks collected by their researcher-inventors. On Dugdale's environmentalist thinking, see also Carl N. Degler, *In Search of Human Nature: The Decline and Revival of Darwinism in American Thought* (New York: Oxford University Press, 1991), pp. 37–39.

55. Goddard did invent "moron" as a technical term, but it did not become a popular label till after his death.

56. Henry H. Goddard, *The Kallikak Family* (New York: Macmillan, 1912); and Henry H. Goddard, *Feeblemindedness* (New York: Macmillan, 1914).

57. Although most of the "family" studies were conducted among the rural WASP proletariat, some of the earlier ones had already reported on the hereditary defects of people their authors described as foreign and dark-skinned (Rafter, *White Trash*, pp. 7–8).

58. Haller, *Eugenics*, p. 120 and p. 227, n. 31. Goddard is reported as having "trained" his fieldworkers, but either did not know or did not supervise her field methods. According to Rafter, the writers of the earlier family studies operated on a less scientific basis than even Goddard and his colleagues, but all of them, trained or untrained, found what they wanted to find (Rafter, *White Trash*, pp. 17–31). In addition, research or governmental agencies to hold researchers accountable were not created until later in the twentieth century.

59. Gould, *Mismeasure of Man*, pp. 172–74. Goddard was not only an expert alarmist, but he was also an active counter.

60. In fact, the 1925 legislation included virtually all the labels and concepts used by the eugenicists beginning with Dugdale, for it called for the exclusion of, among others, "idiots, imbeciles, feebleminded, epileptics, insane persons . . . [and those] affected by constitutional psychopathic inferiority . . . paupers, vagrants . . . beggars . . . prostitutes [and] mentally or physically defective . . . [such as to] affect the ability of the alien to earn a living." Paul Popenoe and Roswell H. Johnson, *Applied Eugenics* (New York: Macmillan, 1920), pp. 302–3.

61. Troy Duster, *Backdoor to Eugenics* (New York: Routledge, 1990).

62. See, for instance, Richard J. Herrnstein and Charles Murray, *The Bell Curve: Intelligence and Class Structure in American Life* (New York: Free Press, 1994) and Seymour Itzkoff, *The Decline of Intelligence in America: A Strategy for National Renewal* (Westport, Conn.: Praeger, 1994).

63. Oscar Lewis, "The Culture of Poverty," in Daniel P. Moynihan, ed., *On Understanding Poverty* (New York: Basic Books, 1968), pp. 187–200, quote at p. 188 (emphasis added).

64. According to Rigdon's fine and unfairly neglected "biography" of the culture of poverty, Lewis first used it in 1958 (Susan Rigdon, *The Culture Facade: Art, Science and Politics in the Work of Oscar Lewis* [Urbana: University of Illinois Press, 1988], pp. 51 ff). Lewis first published the phrase in his *Five Families: Mexican Case Studies in the Culture of Poverty* (New York: Basic Books, 1959).

65. Of the 35 articles Lewis published between 1960, when he first used "culture of poverty" in the title of one of his articles, until 1970, when he published his last paper, nine articles featured the concept in their titles. Computed from Rigdon, *Culture Facade*, pp. 302–4.

66. Rigdon, *Culture Facade*, pp. 173–80. I should note that Rigdon was writing as a family friend, and not as a critic of Lewis.

67. Lewis, "Culture of Poverty," p. 191.

68. In fact, he probably hastened his death by doing research in Cuba under extremely stressful conditions in order to test his hypothesis. Lewis also did not shrink from moral judgments, however, and never took back any of the negative judgments he made about the people he studied.

69. To complicate matters further, Lewis resembled other anthropologists of his

time in envying some elements of the fatalism of the poor people he studied, and their more relaxed attitudes about sexual and other pleasures.

70. Michael Harrington, *The Other America: Poverty in the United States* (New York: Macmillan, 1962), for instance, pp. 15 ff, 168 ff.

71. Rigdon, *Culture Facade*, p. 90.

CHAPTER 2: THE INVENTION OF THE UNDERCLASS LABEL

1. The story of the label-formation process that follows is by necessity historical. It was reconstructed from available literature, from the sometimes spotty memory of the participants whom I was able to interview, and in a couple of cases, my best guesses as to what happened in between periods covered by available sources. The first complete history of the underclass term and its various uses, to which I am indebted, is Robert Aponte, "Definitions of the Underclass: A Critical Analysis," in Herbert J. Gans, *Sociology in America* (Newbury Park, Calif.: Sage, 1990), chap. 8.

2. Gunnar Myrdal, *Challenge to Affluence* (New York: Pantheon, 1963).

3. Ibid., p. 10. Myrdal's under-class concept was not a research tool, for he did not try to explain how one would measure how the population was set apart, or its inability to share in American life, although he suggested a kind of national isolation that in retrospect bears some resemblance to William Julius Wilson's later concept of local social isolation.

4. Myrdal never used its companion term, *overklass*, and he never explained how and why he chose to use "under-class," although his daughter, Sisela Bok, to whom I am grateful for extended personal correspondence on this topic, thought that he had learned about it from his reading in Swedish literature. Stellan Anderson, of the Workers' Archive in Stockholm, thought Myrdal may have also heard about the word from a mentor, the economist Knut Wicksell. Myrdal probably did not know about the English word's earliest recorded use, for according to the Oxford English Dictionary, the Scottish socialist John MacLean used it in 1918 as a synonym for a revolutionary working class.

5. Strindberg's most frequent use of the term occurred in his first autobiography, *Son of a Servant* (Gloucester, Mass.: Peter Smith, 1975 [1886]).

6. I owe this translation to the late Vernon Boggs (personal communication). Its source is from the entry on *underklass* in Olof Oestergren, *Nusvensk Ordbok* (Stockholm: Wahlstrom and Widstrand, n.d), vol. 5, p. 86.

7. Myrdal had written little about America since his *American Dilemma* (New York: Pantheon), which was published in 1944 but had become a virtually forgotten classic in the early 1960s, except in the black community.

8. Since Myrdal remained in Sweden the last few years of his life, and was ill, he may never have known what happened to his term.

9. Tom Kahn, "The Economics of Equality" (pamphlet) (New York: League for Industrial Democracy, 1964).

10. In addition, this author followed Myrdal's pessimistic predictive mode, testifying in 1966 to a U.S. Senate committee investigating the ghetto civil disorders that "a pathology-ridden and hostile 'underclass'" could develop if the federal

government did not move to ameliorate urban poverty (Herbert J. Gans, *People and Plans: Essays on Urban Problems and Solutions* [New York: Basic Books, 1968], p. 301).

11. Actually, "Underclass" was the title of a special section, and the only other reference to the term was in the lead article by Lee Rainwater. He later wrote me that he used it instead of "poor" or "lower class" "because it seemed more catchy." For references to the term's use in the 1960s, see Aponte, "Definitions of the Underclass."

12. The Moynihan Report mentioned two other causes of the problems of the black family: rising male black unemployment and America's overall economic inequality. Unfortunately, both were forgotten in the heat of the attack on him in 1965, and then in later years often by Moynihan himself.

13. Frazier's biographer, Adam Platt, later claimed that Moynihan had read selectively. Both Frazier and, earlier, W. E. B. Du Bois were members of the black bourgeoisie, and although they were also socialists, they nevertheless could not refrain from occasional conventional upper-middle-class stereotyping of the black poor as undeserving (Anthony M. Platt, *E. Franklin Frazier Reconsidered* [New Brunswick, N.J.: Rutgers University Press, 1991]).

14. It appeared in James Q. Wilson, ed., *The Metropolitan Enigma* (Cambridge, Mass.: Harvard University Press, 1966), and in Edward Banfield, *The Unheavenly City* (Boston: Little, Brown, 1968), chap. 9.

15. Banfield took the term from Lee Rainwater, this author, and other Chicago and Harvard students and colleagues of the Chicago anthropologist W. Lloyd Warner, who had used the term as a neutral descriptive one, but Banfield gave it a pejorative spin even as he acknowledged his debts to his sources. Warner had also written about a lower-lower class, of which he was somewhat more critical (W. Lloyd Warner and Paul S. Lunt, *Social Life of a Modern Community* [New Haven, Conn.: Yale University Press, 1941], chap. 22 and *passim*). Subsequently, however, "lower-lower class" was sometimes used as a pejorative term. See, for example, Martin B. Loeb, "Social Class and the American Social System," *Social Work* 6 (April 1961): 12–18, at 16.

16. See, for instance, Gareth S. Jones, *Outcast London* (Oxford: Clarendon Press, 1971), pp. 262–64.

17. However, Banfield's book, and its sequel, *Unheavenly City Revisited* (Boston: Little, Brown, 1974), became academic best-sellers.

18. Winston Moore et al. "Woodlawn: The Zone of Destruction," *Public Interest* 30 (Winter 1973): 41–59.

19. Except when otherwise indicated, all quotes from Moore et al., "Woodlawn: The Zone of Destruction," are from p. 42.

20. The Blackstone Rangers began as a boys' club, but later turned into a delinquent gang and organizer of such gangs, which received government funds, a lot of publicity, and radical chic support before it came out that the gangs were or had become well-organized violent criminal organizations.

21. The analysis of the gangs was supplemented by a more general comparison of the area population as consisting on the one hand of "large families headed by dependent mothers" and "disorganized families" (p. 48) and on the other hand, "the victims . . . black and white working people . . . the 'respectable' poor, the

elderly, the abandoned, traditional poor, the residue of hard-working ethnic communities that have yet to make it into the professional and white collar classes" (p. 54). The terminology alone suggests that the authors were writing about the undeserving poor and their victims, the deserving poor, although they supplied no empirical data about either group.

22. The professionals who had earlier participated in making and communicating the label "feebleminded" had also been psychologists, social workers, and prison officials.

23. Moore was also a well-known leader of Chicago's black community. It took me several years to trace the three authors, but I was able to interview them by phone in 1994.

24. Although other people in Woodlawn were characterized negatively by the article—for example, "disorganized families" and "dependent mothers"—Livermore did not consider them members of the underclass.

25. In addition, the article offered a backhanded defense of private enterprise, at least insofar as its extended discussion of the arson of abandoned buildings ended by debunking the possibility of a "real estate developers' conspiracy" (p. 51).

26. The box appeared on pp. 26 and 27 of the June 17, 1994, issue of *Time*, but offered no explanation about what troubled this underclass.

27. In fact, none of the major participants in producing the cover story had seen the *Public Interest* article.

28. "The American Underclass: Destitute and Desperate in the Land of Plenty," *Time*, Aug. 29, 1977, pp. 14–27, quotes from 14.

29. Until the 1980s, *Time* and *Newsweek* stories were put together in several stages. Reporters gathered the information, writers analyzed it and wrote the story from the former's files, after which their work was edited by several editors. Sometimes it was rewritten several times, often at the last minute, at which point illustrations were also chosen, and occasionally all the pieces did not fit together. The underclass cover story was not, however, heavily edited or often rewritten.

30. Also, of the fifteen people quoted in the main body of the story, nine were critical of one or another part of American society, as compared to six who criticized the behavior of the poor—and three of these were other poor blacks.

31. "The American Underclass," p. 15.

32. Ibid., p. 16.

33. I interviewed all the participants in the cover story I could find, but in 1990, when these interviews took place, Hedley Donovan was no longer alive. I was told that he had been opposed to a show business story replacing a major domestic story on the cover, even in summer, although by then the underclass cover, which was first written in June 1977 and had been pegged to a looting spree in several New York ghetto areas, had already been postponed a few times. Newsmagazines then as now often "killed" covers that are perceived to have become stale news. Another consideration for the editor's decision could have been *Time*'s longterm policy of trying to catch up with *Newsweek*, its principal rival, in the coverage of American poverty.

34. He was not even sure where the term had come from. As Chicago bureau chief, and the chief reporter for the underclass cover story, he had heard the term

mentioned by University of Chicago social scientists and by others at Harvard, where he conducted additional reporting.

In 1990 he could not recall who, if anyone, had used the term in 1977, including William Julius Wilson, with whom he said he had become close in Chicago. By 1977, Wilson had finished but not yet published *The Declining Significance of Race* (Chicago: University of Chicago Press, 1978), in which he first used "underclass," but as a sociological term, not a behavioral one. Wilson was not quoted in *Time's* underclass cover story.

The bureau chief was also aware that some black activists and intellectuals were already critical of the term in 1977, but he did not feel that this should have affected the magazine's choice of words. Journalists often keep their distance from ideological and terminological disputes in the activist and intellectual communities.

35. Writing the cover story sparked his interest in the topic and term, and he later reported on the underclass in Latin America.

36. In 1990 he was no longer sure whether he had invented the word or whether he had read it somewhere. Incidentally, a number of the other early users of "underclass" thought they had perhaps invented the term when I first started talking with them.

37. The 1977 cover article incorrectly described "underclass" as a term long used in "class-ridden" Europe, implying that *Time* did not favor using terms that would help turn America into a class-ridden country.

Time's collective memory was short enough that some of the journalists involved in the 1977 cover seemed to have participated in an attempt to reinvent it once more, in an abortive underclass cover project in the mid-1980s. The story is reported by a young and disenchanted black participant, Jake Lamar, in his *Bourgeois Blues: An American Memoir* (New York: Summit, 1991), pp. 139–51.

38. Ken Auletta, *The Underclass* (New York: Random House, 1982).

39. He also told me that no particular event set him off: "It was just curiosity."

40. Auletta, *Underclass*, p. xiii.

41. Ibid., pp. 27–30.

42. Ibid., p. xiii, emphasis his. Unlike most other writers on the underclass, Auletta viewed it as including both blacks and whites.

43. Much of the book is devoted to reporting on a project of the Manpower Demonstration Research Corporation.

44. Auletta, *Underclass*, p. 26. His flexible term is close to what I call an umbrella term.

45. I interviewed Ken Auletta in January 1990.

46. Conversely, Auletta may have also devoted so much time and energy to the topic that no books devoted to establishing the underclass as a label were needed.

47. One scholar subjected to journalistic questioning was Robert B. Hill, a sociologist who was then research director of the Urban League—the organization then by far the most important source of data about black America. A thoroughly empirical researcher, Hill tried to persuade journalists that behavioral terms, whether "lower class" or "underclass," could not be properly supported by credible sociological evidence. Reflecting later on his contacts with journalists, Hill thought he had been able to persuade few journalists in search of a behavioral

term to write about chronic joblessness, or to use his preferred term, the "acute poor," instead. Consequently, he wrote about them himself, debunking behavioral analyses in the process (Robert B. Hill, *Illusion of Black Progress* [Washington, D.C.: National Urban League Research Department, 1978], p. 234). Hill had debunked behavioral analyses of the poor long before journalists even became curious about the underclass, in his *Strengths of Black Families* (New York: National Urban League, 1972).

48. The dearth of terms may be signified by Susan Sheehan's 1975 *New Yorker* series and subsequent book, *A Welfare Mother* (Boston: Houghton Mifflin, 1976). It dealt with a poor Puerto Rican unmarried mother and her family, all of them children by different fathers, who fit all the stereotypes possible considering it was based on a sample of one. However, while the book was thus ostensibly a prototypical subject for a variety of behavioral terms, Sheehan made only one reference (positive) to Oscar Lewis and the culture of poverty.

49. Between 1975 and 1980, when Nexis tracked only *Newsweek* and *U.S. News & World Report*, "lower class" was used no more often than later, and only slightly more often than "underclass": 30 and 27 instances respectively for both magazines combined during this period. In fact, "lower class" has always served as an all-purpose term for people placed low or lower in a variety of hierarchies, at least since Nexis started its data base in the mid-1970s, which may explain why it is the only term displayed in table 2.1 that has never peaked and declined, with the years of highest use varying sharply between the newspapers and magazines studied.

Perhaps "lower class" was a behavioral term or label during the 1960s period of ghetto uprisings, but if this had been the case, Banfield's behavioral definition should not have evoked as much attention as it did.

50. Reasons for the success of the term and label "underclass" are discussed later in this chapter.

51. Actually, in the late 1970s and early 1980s, "underclass" was used frequently for immigrants, especially illegal ones, but then they were characterized as politically vulnerable and/or economically exploited, and their behavior, whether deserving or undeserving, was not considered newsworthy.

52. Tamar Jacoby, "Thinking About the Homeless," *Dissent* (Spring 1991): 249–53, quote at 250.

53. Gwen Ifill, "Clinton's Tightrope," *New York Times,* Nov. 14, 1993, p. B8.

54. This must be distinguished from most references to the black underclass, which treat it as simply a dark-skinned subset of the poor, or of the undeserving poor.

55. Surprisingly enough, some writers, and not just in sports publications, still write about the underclass with a meaning that predates Myrdal: to describe the third-year cohort in a four-year school.

56. Jacqueline Jones has written a powerful study that describes the bitterly oppressed and exploited poor, black and white, of the nineteenth and twentieth centuries as members of the underclass (Jacqueline Jones, *The Dispossessed: America's Underclasses from the Civil War to the Present* [New York: Basic Books, 1992]).

57. This, like the more general cross-national analysis of stigmatization and

labeling, and of the export and import of social science concepts, are fruitful topics for another study. See, for example, Hilary Silver, "National Conceptions of the New Urban Poverty," *International Journal of Urban and Regional Research* 17 (Sept. 1993): 337–54. In perhaps the most intricate import-export activity to date, Charles Murray exported the U.S. behavioral underclass label to Great Britain via a well-publicized article in the *London Times Sunday Magazine* in 1989, which was then reprinted in *Public Interest* in 1990, after which Murray began to use the label in the United States, but mainly to announce the arrival of a white underclass. Murray may not have known that Anthony Giddens had already imported the American term in 1973, or that an English debate about whether the underclass was an economically deprived or an undeserving poor population had already taken place in the 1970s. For a comparison of American and English writings and debates on the underclass term, see Lydia Morris, *The Dangerous Class: The Underclass and Social Citizenship* (London: Routledge, 1994), especially chap. 4.

58. Malcolm W. Browne, "For Iguanas, Place in Sun May Be Too Bright," *New York Times,* Oct. 28, 1989, p. C1.

59. Even though this chapter is partly about the diffusion of the underclass label, I have abstained from the use of diffusion terminology because the data are not sufficient for any particular sociological theory of diffusion.

60. My frequent, but not random, viewing of local and network television news programs turned up so few references to "underclass"—or to other terms that take too much precious time to define—that I chose not to study television, or for that matter, radio.

61. Between 1975 and 1980, the Nexis data base included only the three national newsmagazines, as well as the *Wall Street Journal.* Other daily newspapers were not added until the 1980s.

62. What these figures do not tell, and what deserves to be studied, is that some publications use the term infrequently. Among those in the Nexis data base, they include, among others, the *Denver Post, San Francisco Chronicle, USA Today,* surprisingly, the *Wall Street Journal,* and unsurprisingly, *People.*

Nexis also does not yet track the weekly "journals of opinion" and the general monthly magazines written largely for the educated reader, but a separate analysis of the DIALOG data base from 1983 to 1989 indicated that these publications used the term "underclass" mainly when reviewing books about it, notably those by Ken Auletta and William Julius Wilson. Insofar as journalists read these reviews, they also learned in more detail about the underclass than they might have in the daily papers and weekly magazines to which they had access.

63. The three papers were chosen as major elite newspapers from three regions of the country, and although I wish I could have included popular newspapers as well, Nexis, which serves mainly the national commercial community, was only just beginning to add them to its data base in the mid-1990s.

64. In the *New York Times,* "lower class" was used in 44.2 stories per year on the average between 1981 and 1993, with a low of 31 in 1988 and a high of 48 just two years later.

65. Regional media, which I did not study, might be different, particularly in regions like Appalachia, which has a large number of extremely poor whites.

66. Many news organizations discourage their employees from referring to the work of other journalists, whether these are direct competitors or not. When the *Chicago Tribune* published its 40-story series on the behavioral underclass in 1985, Auletta was never even mentioned.

67. In fact, between 1975 and 1980, *Newsweek* did not use the term behaviorally at all, while *U.S. News & World Report* did so once.

68. Most of these immigrants were not black but they were not described as a white underclass. Perhaps the term was then too new for journalists to decide that the underclass could come in various colors.

69. A fifth use referred to the "so-called underclass," allowing journalists to question its meaning, validity, or existence. Some of these undefined uses of "underclass" were simply transferred from similar kinds of uses of "lower class."

70. From the start, *Newsweek* used the undefined term more than any other, and so did *Newsday* most of the years I analyzed its usage of the term.

71. In the 1970s, *Newsweek's* book reviewers and theater critics used the term before reporters and front-of-the-book writers; *U.S. News & World Report*, which does no reviewing, chose to quote experts before journalists began to use the term.

72. These were people writing letters to *Newsday*; newsmagazine letter writers were not captured by my Nexis tabulations.

73. This is probably also why radio and TV talk show hosts are so often conservative. Liberals do not seem to use their telephones, or their pens and computers, to complain about the state of the world.

74. They include, for example, Patrick Buchanan, David Duke, and William Bennett, rather than the political spokespersons for Wall Street or the U.S. Chamber of Commerce. In fact, business publications in general have not used the word "underclass" very much, including the *Wall Street Journal*, even though it also caters to social conservatives.

75. That politicians and government officials used "underclass" comparatively more often in *Newsday* than in the national newsweeklies also suggests that "underclass" may be a big-city word that is heard less often in the rural and small-town parts of America. Another clue is that big-city papers like the *Chicago Tribune* and the *Los Angeles Times* have employed the term more often than the papers of smaller cities, such as the *Denver Post* or the *Tulsa World*. Perhaps the term is also more likely to be found in cities with large racial minority populations, or with anxious white ones.

76. The annual average rate was about half that of the media reported in table 2.1, but then the *Record* is not a daily paper, and Congress is not in session year round. The highest number of speeches or text insertions using the term was 61, in 1989; the lowest, 33, in 1993, but otherwise there were fewer fluctuations than among the news media.

77. Curiously enough, the year a Democratic president entered the White House the economic and behavioral uses occurred equally often, a third of the time. My analysis focused on definitions of the term, however, not on the ideological thrust of the uses. Occasionally a liberal elected official used a behavioral term and a conservative official the economic one.

78. The trend began in 1988. Over the whole period, 25 percent of the uses of

the term were undefined, although in 1992, the proportion climbed to 42 percent.

79. Of the references to the underclass, 14 percent either discussed an educational underclass, a phrase never heard among the journalists, or education as a solution to the problems of the underclass. Incidentally, nearly every speaker talked about a permanent or growing underclass, but then their purpose in speaking was often alarmist.

80. Outsiders were referred to infrequently, most of them being either columnists, or social scientists quoted in the media.

81. *Plyler v. Doe*, 72 L. Ed. 2nd 786, 800 (1982). In 1988, the court referred to this case again, *Kadrmas v. Dickinson Public Schools et al.*, 101 L. Ed. 2nd 399 (1988), Thurgood Marshall writing about an underclass in a dissenting opinion (p. 417). In both instances, the court defined "underclass" as an economically and politically exploited population, although by 1988, journalists had begun to view illegal immigrants as a behavioral underclass. I am indebted to David Gans for alerting me to the court's reference to the underclass.

82. Sidney and Beatrice Webb, *English Poor Law History* (Hamden, Conn.: Shoe String Press, 1963 [1927]) pt. I, pp. 31–32.

83. Michael B. Katz has written extensively on the movement and the quality of its "science," for instance, his *In the Shadow of the Poorhouse: A Social History of Welfare in America* (New York: Basic Books, 1986), chap. 3.

84. For example, E. A. Ross, one of the founders of American sociology, was a tireless spokesman for the eugenicist cause (Mark H. Haller, *Eugenics: Hereditarian Attitudes in American Thought* [New Brunswick, N.J.: Rutgers University Press, 1963], p. 146). See also Carl N. Degler, *In Search of Human Nature: The Decline and Revival of Darwinism in American Social Thought* (New York: Oxford University Press, 1991), p. 44.

85. I should note that experts can only propose legitimacy, since their readers and other users of the term must ultimately decide whether they consider it to be legitimate or credible. How much they rely on experts, foundations, governments, and all the other participants in the legitimation process described in this section remains to be fully studied, although the mere attempt by powerful or prestigious agencies to use or support a term or label legitimates it for organizations or people who are beholden to such an agency or for people who respect power, prestige, and authority.

86. However, the two magazines also employ "fact-checkers" who are employed to supply accuracy as the legitimation for the "facts" they publish, even if they do not fact-check terms or analyses.

87. In addition, Wilson's definition was sometimes used, not always correctly, without reference to him. For example, Wilson's analysis in *The Truly Disadvantaged* of the underclass as socially isolated has sometimes been transformed into voluntary, and morally faulty, choices of the poor rather than the consequences of persistent poverty to which Wilson had pointed. See William Julius Wilson, *The Truly Disadvantaged: The Inner City, the Underclass and Public Policy* (Chicago: University of Chicago Press, 1987).

88. Isabel V. Sawhill, "The Underclass: An Overview," *Public Interest* 96 (Summer 1989): 3–15, quote at 4–5. The norm violations—dropping out of school, being a member of a female-headed family, being a welfare dependent, and being

a jobless or irregularly employed male—were used to place people in the under-class. Sawhill's subsequent article with Ricketts operationalized these four norm violations. That article and its operational definition will be discussed in chap. 3.

The four criteria for the underclass based on these norms have also been picked up in news stories and columns, often without attribution.

89. In the early 1980s, when journalists were still getting used to the behavioral definition of the underclass, academic definitional debates and the ideological debates that followed were reported in the national news media once or twice.

90. Frank Levy, "How Big Is the American Underclass?" (Unpublished paper, 0090–1 [Washington, D.C.: Urban Institute, Sept. 1977]). Robert Hill of the Urban League, like other research directors of the League before and after him, have supplied numbers intended to alarm people about the extent of black poverty, although inquiring journalists sometimes used these in alarmist articles about the underclass.

91. As a result, some have counted the persistently poor, while others have tab-ulated welfare recipients or high school dropouts. For example, in 1986 alone, four counting projects resulted in estimates ranging from less than one million to eight million. To this day, everyone has adjusted definitions to the available data, and no one has yet, as far as I know, developed a definition of "underclass" and then undertaken his or her own data-gathering.

92. Henry Goddard's work was partly funded by the Philadelphia philan-thropist Samuel Fels; by Mrs. E. C. Harriman, who gave half a million dollars to eugenic research institutes, including Goddard's; and by the cereal manufacturer John H. Kellogg, who established the Race Betterment Foundation (J. David Smith, *Minds Made Feeble: The Myth and Legacy of the Kallikaks* [Rockville, Md.: Aspen System Corporation, 1985], pp. 42–45). Students of the eugenics movement are still unsure to what extent the various funders shared the move-ment's aims, and how many thought they were funding important new advances in science.

The revival of eugenicist research, starting in the 1970s, has been mainly funded by the Pioneer Fund, a small foundation set up in the 1930s by survivors of the previous eugenicist movement, including Frederick Osborn, the money coming from "textile tycoon" Wyckliffe Draper (Michael Lind, "Brave New Right," *The New Republic*, Oct. 31, 1994, p. 24).

93. The last-named supported Charles Murray's writing of *Losing Ground*, which has spearheaded the attack on welfare and welfare recipients.

94. Their staffs are generally politically more liberal than their boards, but this is true of many foundations.

95. Some Rockefeller staff considered the foundation's role to be experimental, trying out antipoverty policy ideas and activities that, if successful, might some-day be taken up by public agencies. My observation of the foundation's activities suggests, however, that the staff generally chose to further develop already rea-sonably conventional ideas, if only because these were most likely to be accept-able to the board.

96. Most of my observations about the foundation's, and the Social Science Research Council's, underclass programs stem from some formal and informal interviews conducted with various staff members, mainly in 1989 and 1990 but

also, subsequently, at meetings and conferences on the underclass that involved the two organizations.

97. Judging by her published writings at the time, Ms. Norton was mainly concerned with economic and other policy to help the black working class and with fighting what she called "the predatory ghetto subculture" and "an American version of a *lumpenproletariat* (the so-called underclass)," although her definition of that underclass was strongly influenced by the ideas of Gunnar Myrdal and William Julius Wilson. (Eleanor Holmes Norton, "Restoring the Traditional Black Family," *New York Times Magazine,* June 2, 1985, p. 43.)

98. The powderkeg concerns resemble the "things are getting worse" comments made by journalistic label-makers nearly a decade earlier, but none of the foundation's underclass-related work ever expressed the urgency reflected in the powderkeg metaphor.

99. Academics are generally unenthusiastic about, or even critical of, the popular terminology of the media. The SSRC memo writer pointed out, however, that eschewing the term "underclass" would mean that "the research will not be engaged with contemporary public discourse on this subject." In addition, the SSRC's board of directors, also all academics, did not want to launch a new research program on poverty.

100. For the SSRC's description of its underclass research and policy activities, see David Featherman, "Annual Report of the President," *Social Science Research Council: Annual Report 1992–1993* (New York: Social Science Research Council, 1994), pp. 19–26.

101. In fact, the foundation had funded Ricketts and Sawhill to develop the definition, which helped to inaugurate the foundation's underclass program. Ricketts's own formulation of and advocacy for a behavioral approach to the underclass appears in his "The Nature and Dimensions of the Underclass," and "The Underclass: Causes and Responses," in George C. Galster and Edward W. Hill, eds., *The Metropolis in Black and White: Place, Power and Polarization* (New Brunswick, N.J.: Rutgers Center for Urban Policy Research, 1992), chaps. 3, 12.

Another example of the foundation's interest in a behavioral definition of the underclass was a *New York Times* interview with foundation president Peter Goldmark, in which he practically equated the underclass with hustlers (Kathleen Teltsch, "Charity to Focus on Underclass," *New York Times,* Jan. 22, 1989, sec. 1, p. 24). Goldmark's remarks were not treated as foundation policy, however, and Equal Opportunities Division staff distanced itself from them, at least to this author.

102. Moreover, "underclass" was used in part as a tribute to William Julius Wilson, who had pioneered the revival of poverty research under that rubric, and was taking leadership roles in both the Rockefeller Foundation's and the Social Science Research Council's underclass activities. Wilson's ideas and theories were centered on the processes that make people poor, rather than on their characteristics or their poverty-related behavior.

103. Perhaps the SSRC's major contribution to data on the characteristics of the poor was the funding of John Kasarda's massive data base on the underclass, which provided raw material and perhaps legitimation of the alarmist head-counting reflecting the behavioral definition of the underclass.

104. Paul E. Peterson, "The Urban Underclass and the Poverty Paradox," in Christopher Jencks and Paul E. Peterson, eds., *The Urban Underclass* (Washington, D.C.: Brookings Institution, 1991), p. 3.

105. This was probably unfair, since the SSRC had never undertaken domestic policy research before, and could not have been expected to make original contributions on such short notice even if any original contributions to antipoverty policy research could still be made.

106. So actually did the SSRC, for its final public conference, held in November 1993, was conducted by a new entity called the Program on Persistent Poverty. The SSRC staff in charge of the conference engineered the name change on its own, but without objection from any of its superiors at SSRC or at Rockefeller. And the next year, the section of the SSRC president's annual report on the underclass research was titled "Persistent Urban Poverty."

107. For example, the Department of Health and Human Services funded a research program on the underclass that resulted in a 1990 conference dominated by conservative economists, many of whom faulted the poor for their behavior. Neither the department nor the rest of the government ever exploited the research papers politically, however, or used them to legitimate the Republican war against the poor.

108. Robert Pear, "White House Spurns Expansion of Nation's Anti-Poverty Efforts," *New York Times,* July 6, 1990, A1, A12, quote at A12. This was also the meeting at which the Bush administration decided not to launch new antipoverty programs, but instead to "polish the old toys."

109. The other two classes were an "overclass" in the safety of elite suburbs, and a new "anxious class," trapped in "the frenzy of effort it takes to preserve their standards" (Catherine S. Manegold, "Reich Urges Executives to Aid Labor: Secretary Will Push for More Training," *New York Times,* Sept. 25, 1994, p. 25). Reich blamed the violence on the surroundings rather than the people, thus avoiding suggesting that the poor were now a behavioral underclass. His introduction of "overclass" into governmental terminology evoked little reaction and no imitation.

110. "The American Underclass," p. 14. Neither he nor *Time* indicated who was meant by "we."

111. Time's cover story made it appear as if it were quoting Vernon Jordan, then executive director of the League, about the dangers of the underclass, but his name was outside the quotation marks. "The American Underclass," p. 15. A Nexis analysis of Jordan's speeches and interviews in the *New York Times* indicated no use of the term by him during the 1980s.

112. Philip Gleason writes that the popularization of a less dramatic academic term, "minorities," took a quarter of a century (Philip Gleason, "Minorities [Almost All]: The Minority Concept in American Social Thought," *American Quarterly* 43 [Sept. 1991]: 392–424).

113. When Richard Coleman and Lee Rainwater studied Boston and Kansas City, two cities without major racial disturbances, the people they interviewed told them that the "welfare class" was generally the lowest class (Richard Coleman and Lee Rainwater, *Social Standing in America: New Dimensions of Class* [New York: Basic Books, 1978], pp. 191–99).

114. Besides, what happens in New York City is not only bigger news but also more alarming. However, the city's function as a national Sodom and Gomorrah is duplicated by the cultural capitals of many other countries.

115. I borrow this intriguing hypothesis from Mark Haller, who argues that at the turn of the century, feeblemindedness was popularized as a "biological" case to shift the blame from the professionals and officials supposed to "control" the mass of incoming poor immigrants to the immigrants themselves (Haller, *Eugenics,* p. 24). If Haller is right, the possibility cannot be discounted that the underclass will eventually be viewed as a permanent biological stratum, at least by the most alarmed and insecure white Americans.

116. I have often wondered what Myrdal would have written could he have had any inkling of the subsequent transformation of his concept.

117. Since journalists do not often cite social scientists, the extent to which they played both roles would require a study of textbooks and classrooms, as well as many other forms of public communication—a study that badly needs doing.

118. "Defense" agencies to investigate prejudice against the poor would have helped, but if the poor could afford such agencies, they would probably no longer be poor.

119. See, for example, Mickey Kaus, "Bastards: The Right Abandons Workfare," *The New Republic,* Feb. 21, 1994, pp. 16–19. Kaus's earlier writings demonizing welfare recipients and the underclass helped to produce the effect he deplores in this article.

120. Perhaps the stigmatization of labels takes longer, or needs to be pushed by powerful interests.

CHAPTER 3: THE DANGERS OF "UNDERCLASS" AND OTHER LABELS

1. This chapter is a drastically revised version of my "Deconstructing the Underclass: The Term's Dangers as a Planning Concept," *Journal of the American Planning Association* 52 (Summer 1990): 271–77; and chapter 21 of my *People, Plans and Policies* (New York: Columbia University Press, 1991, 1994). I am indebted to Michael B. Katz and Sharon Zukin for comments on these versions, and to the long list of scholars who wrote about the dangers of the term "underclass" before I did, among them Robert B. Hill, Richard McGahey, Jewelle T. Gibbs, and Michael B. Katz.

2. They deserve to be called official labels because the criteria by which federal government described slums and blight had as much to do with the undesirability of their poor inhabitants as with the condition of the housing in which they lived.

3. This is of course one of the virtues of labels for cultural and political conservatives who prefer not to acknowledge the existence of poverty.

4. Irving Lewis Allen distinguishes between euphemisms, which are innocently substituted for labels, and code words, which are intentional substitutes, but empirical researchers will have to discover whether people are willing to discuss the intent involved in Allen's distinction (Irving Lewis Allen, *Unkind Words:*

Ethnic Languages from Redskin to WASP [New York: Bergin and Garvey, 1990], chap. 8).

5. European analysts have developed the phrase "social exclusion" to describe both economically excluded native-born people and immigrants who are excluded on ethnic, racial, or citizenship grounds. For a comprehensive analysis, see Hilary Silver, "Social Exclusion and Social Solidarity: Three Paradigms" (Geneva: International Institute for Labour Studies, DP/69, 1994).

While the European phrase is a scholarly concept used for studies concerned with ending exclusion, it is possible to imagine redefinitions, particularly in America, in which the phrase becomes a popular label to condemn the excluded.

6. The prefix "under-" has often been pejorative in America, as in "underhanded," "underworld," and even the untranslated but occasionally used *Untermensch.*

7. Blaming poor people may help lead to their imprisonment, since prisons exist in part to isolate the blamed, but imprisonment does not seem to be an effective policy against street crime either.

8. Erol R. Ricketts and Isabel V. Sawhill, "Defining and Measuring the Underclass," *Journal of Policy Analysis and Management* 7, no. 2 (1988): 316–22.

9. Welfare recipients are a "proxy for women who are not married and not working," while female heads are a proxy for "early child-bearing, risk of dependency, and the possible long-term adverse consequences of children being raised by only one parent." This and all other quotes are from Ricketts and Sawhill, "Defining and Measuring the Underclass," p. 321.

10. Ibid., p. 318. Actually, their quartet of underclass populations consists of people they deem to vary from the mainstream who have also been studied already by the U.S. government. The two authors pointed out that their definition was "heavily influenced by the availability of data," indicating that they would have added street crime and drug use if data had been available (pp. 317, 321).

11. Ibid., p. 318. Isabel Sawhill's "The Underclass: An Overview," *Public Interest* 96 (Summer 1989): 3–15, referred to in chap. 2, suggests that she was not agnostic about causes in a later publication.

12. Ricketts and Sawhill, "Defining and Measuring the Underclass," p. 320. The authors sometimes seem to shift ground from mainstream behavior to mainstream expectations, arguing that "in American society, it is *expected* that children will attend school and delay parenthood until at least age 18 . . . work at a regular job . . . females will either work or marry . . . and that everyone will be law abiding" (p. 319–20, emphasis added). The meaning of this statement depends in part on the definition of "expectations," but if the authors mean aspirations, then the people they call underclass generally share them, as many studies have shown.

13. See, for example, Michelle Fine, *Framing Dropouts: Notes on the Politics of an Urban High School* (Albany: State University of New York Press, 1988), esp. chap. 3.

14. These are all explanations from the current poverty literature, and most can be found in William Julius Wilson's previously mentioned *Truly Disadvantaged* (William Julius Wilson, *The Truly Disadvantaged: The Inner City, the Underclass, and Public Policy* [Chicago: University of Chicago Press, 1987]).

15. The similarity of the authors' analysis to labeling is exemplified by generalizations for which they present no data. They suggest, for example, that an unemployed prime-age male in an underclass area is likely to be engaged in "hustling." Ricketts and Sawhill, "Defining and Measuring the Underclass," p. 320.

16. For more detailed and somewhat different critiques of the Ricketts-Sawhill definition, see Mark A. Hughes, "Concentrated Deviance and the 'Underclass' Hypothesis," *Journal of Policy Analysis and Management* 8, no. 2 (1989): 274–82; and Robert Aponte, "Definitions of the Underclass: A Critical Analysis," and Walter W. Stafford and Joyce Ladner, "Political Dimensions of the Underclass Concept," in Herbert J. Gans, ed., *Sociology in America* (Newbury Park, Calif.: Sage, 1990), chaps. 8, 9.

17. For the argument on the utility of attitude studies, see Kathleen J. Pottick, "Testing the Underclass Concept by Surveying Attitudes and Behavior," *Journal of Sociology and Social Welfare* 17 (Dec. 1990): 117–25.

18. The census does not, however, identify "extreme wealth areas," since the privacy of the rich is politically and otherwise privileged.

19. Ricketts and Sawhill, "Defining and Measuring the Underclass," p. 321 (emphasis added).

20. William Julius Wilson provides an illustration of this process in writing about the fate of his analysis of the concentration of the poor, pointing out that "arguments in the popular media tended to emphasize a crystallization of a ghetto culture of poverty once black middle-class self-consciously imposed cultural constraints on lower-class culture were removed." Wilson, *The Truly Disadvantaged,* p. 55.

21. Camilo J. Vergara, *The New American Slum* (New Brunswick, N.J.: Rutgers University Press, 1995), forthcoming.

22. William Kornblum, "Lumping the Poor: What *Is* the Underclass?" *Dissent* (Sept. 1984): 295–302.

23. Christopher Jencks, *Rethinking Social Policy: Race, Poverty and the Underclass* (Cambridge, Mass.: Harvard University Press, 1992), p. 202.

24. Henry H. Goddard, *The Kallikak Family* (New York: Macmillan, 1912), pp. 105–9, quotes at pp. 105, 107.

25. Such labeling is class-blind; it can hurt rich or poor, and it need not even be pejorative in intent. See, for instance, "A Disabilities Program that Got Out of Hand," *New York Times,* Apr. 8, 1994, pp. Al, B6, which describes the effects of special education experts labeling preschool children at one of New York City's most prestigious private schools.

26. Dirk Johnson, "Two of Three Young Black Men in Denver Listed by Police as Suspected Gangsters," *New York Times,* Dec. 11, 1993, p. B8. This procedure is akin to the one many police department "red squads" once used to list alleged communists.

27. Bruce Link, "Understanding Labeling Effects in the Area of Mental Disorders: An Assessment of the Effects of Expectations of Rejection," *American Sociological Review* 52 (Feb. 1987): 96–112.

28. Nan M. Astone and Sarah McLanahan, "Family Structure and High School

Completion" (Madison, Wisconsin: Institute for Research on Poverty, discussion paper 905–9, 1989).

29. John Hagan and Alberto Palloni, "The Social Reproduction of a Criminal Class in Working-Class London," *American Journal of Sociology* 96 (Sept. 1990): 265–99.

30. John Irwin, *The Jail: Managing the Underclass in American Society* (Berkeley: University of California Press, 1985), p. 84. The book, which refers to the underclass only in the title, is full of examples of the role of labeling in creating jail populations and repeaters.

31. Hagan and Palloni, "Social Reproduction," p. 293.

32. For an incisive and data-filled analysis of staff-client interactions, see Elliot Liebow, *Tell Them Who I Am: The Lives of Homeless Women* (New York: Free Press, 1993), chap. 4.

33. Ibid., pp. 139–40.

34. William K. Stevens, "Scattered Low Cost Housing Offers Renewed Hope to Poor and Minorities," *New York Times,* Sept. 18, 1988, p. B6.

35. The demanded goods and services the underclass supplies to the better-off are described in my discussion of the functions of the undeserving poor in chap. 4.

36. Committee on Ways and Means, U.S. House of Representatives, *1993 Green Book* (Washington, D.C.: U.S. Government Printing Office, 1993), p. 716. At any given time, however, the majority on AFDC are long-term recipients who also take up most of the resources.

37. *1993 Green Book*, p. 706, and Jencks, *Rethinking Social Policy*, p. 208. Most worked part-time, and only prostitutes earned a high income.

38. See, for instance, Linda Burton, "Teenage Children as an Alternative Life Course Strategy in Multigeneration Black Families," *Human Nature* 1, no. 2 (1990): 123–43.

39. See, for instance, Helen J. and Vernon J. Raschke, "Family Conflict and Children's Self-Concepts: A Comparison of Intact and Single-Parent Families," *Journal of Marriage and the Family* 41 (1979): 367–74; and James Peterson and Nicholas Zill, "Marital Disruption, Parent-Child Relationships and Behavior Problems in Children," *Journal of Marriage and the Family* 48 (1986): 295–307.

40. See, for instance, P. R. Amato and B. Keith, "Parental Divorce and the Well-Being of Children: A Meta-Analysis," *Psychological Bulletin* 110, no. 1 (1991): 26–46.

41. *1993 Green Book*, pp. 726 and 696. Also, I suggested in the introduction that most adolescent mothers are eighteen or nineteen, which used to be an accepted age of childbearing in poor and working-class families.

42. Burton, "Teenage Childbearing"; and Arline T. Geronimus, "Clashes of Common Sense: On the Previous Child Care Experience of Teenage Mothers-To-Be," *Human Organization* 51, no. 4 (Winter 1992): 318–29.

43. Arline T. Geronimus, "The Weathering Hypothesis and the Health of African-American Women and Infants: Evidence and Speculations," *Ethnicity and Disease* 2 (Summer 1992): 207–21. For a critique of this hypothesis, see Frank F. Furstenberg, Jr., "Teenage Childbearing and Cultural Rationality: A

Thesis in Search of Evidence," and the response by Arline Geronimus, "Teenage Childbearing and Social Disadvantage: Unprotected Discourse," *Family Relations* 41 (Apr. 1992): 239–43 and 244–48, respectively.

44. Christopher Jencks, *The Homeless* (Cambridge, Mass.: Harvard University Press, 1994).

CHAPTER 4: THE UNDESERVINGNESS OF THE POOR

1. Indeed, at that point, appropriate labels are at once attached, such as "Huns" in World War I or "gooks" in the Viet Nam war.

2. Concurrently, the conception of which poor are deserving has remained equally stable.

3. Of course, the poor who are labeled undeserving in turn feel angry at and fearful of the better-off, but that topic has not yet generated any visible interest among scholars or policymakers.

4. Most of the analysis of threats, as of functions, concentrates on the perspective of the nonpoor classes because they ultimately help to determine who and what are to be stigmatized as undeserving.

5. White equivalents are false rumors of black killings of white youngsters that are followed by murderous attacks on blacks.

6. Policy analysts, intellectuals, pundits, and others who are not standing for election are therefore needed to call attention to the facts and to rational argument.

7. English sociologists use the metaphor of moral panic to understand exaggerated and imaginary threats, but the panic is more than moral. Moral panic is a dramatic metaphor but it is also an umbrella term that may draw analytic attention away from the specific threats that excite people. On the concept itself, see Philip Jenkins, *Intimate Enemies: Moral Panics in Contemporary Great Britain* (New York: Aldine de Gruyter, 1992).

8. The poor are the major victims not only of street crime but also of the violence of "the streets," and of the street culture that sets its rules. That violence is also more unpredictable than conventional street crime, and results more often in death, especially among young people. For a particularly insightful analysis of this culture, see Elijah Anderson, "The Code of the Streets," *Atlantic Monthly* (May 1994): 81–94.

9. Researchers have long argued that the emphasis on crime news is connected to the publicity needs of police departments, especially at budget times, but news organizations also respond to perceived audience interest in crime news, and no one knows whether any reduction of it would reduce the fear of crime, or increase crime rumors.

10. Dan A. Lewis and Greta Salem, *Fear of Crime, Incivility and the Production of a Social Problem* (New Brunswick, N.J.: Transaction Books, 1986).

11. Richard L. Berke, "Fears of Crime Rival Concern Over Economy," *New York Times*, Jan. 23, 1994, sec. 1, pp. 1, 16. Seventy-three percent thought crime had increased in the country and 58 percent thought it had in their community, although the interpretation of the polls is hampered by their lack of specificity about "crime."

12. For the definitive ethnographic analysis of this phenomenon, see Elijah Anderson, *Streetwise: Race, Class and Change in an Urban Community* (Chicago: University of Chicago Press, 1990), chap. 6.

13. Brace was an upper-class civic reformer, but similar fears were expressed by professionals. See, for example, Regina Kunzel, *Fallen Women, Problem Girls: Unmarried Mothers and the Professionalization of Social Work* (New Haven, Conn.: Yale University Press, 1993).

14. Again, there are historical parallels, because at the turn of the century, innocent immigrants from groups with high arrest rates for the street crimes of the day were also viewed as cultural threats to safety. Legal immigrants have so far generally been treated with more tolerance, but this may end when and where their jobless youngsters turn to street crime or join criminal gangs.

15. "Oppositional culture" has other meanings, including as a term for the often violent culture of the streets, although in that case, the culture really expresses not only what Elijah Anderson calls the code of the streets, but the anger and desperation of poor young blacks who are rejected by white America, and therefore reject its values less in opposition than in revenge (Elijah Anderson, "The Code of the Streets").

16. The figure comes from Pierre Thomas, "Getting to the Bottom Line on Crime," *Washington Post Weekly Edition,* July 8–24, 1994, pp. 31–32.

17. Welfare cost $22 billion in 1992, and a further $25 billion was spent on food stamps, but nearly $6 billion was spent to administer the two programs, which did not go to the poor. Medicaid cost an estimated $120 billion in 1992, but these monies did not go to the poor either. Committee on Ways and Means, U.S. House of Representatives, *1993 Green Book* (Washington, D.C.: U.S. Government Printing Office, 1993), pp. 616, 1609, 1646.

An estimate of total subsidies and tax breaks to corporations, based on the very different conceptions of "corporate pork" held by the liberal Progressive Policy Institute and the conservative Cato Institute, came altogether to $238 billion. See Robert D. Hershey, Jr., "A Hard Look at Corporate Welfare," *New York Times,* Mar. 7, 1995, pp. D1, D2.

18. The often tested sociological theory that people change their values after they have had to change their behavior thus turns popular ideology upside down, but has never had much currency outside the discipline.

19. Larry C. Backer, "Of Handouts and Worthless Promises: Understanding the Conceptual Limits of American Systems of Poor Relief, *Boston College Law Review* 34 (Sept. 1993): 997–1085, quote at 1016.

20. Jason deParle, "House G.O.P. Proposes 'Tough Love' Welfare Requiring Recipients to Work," *New York Times,* Nov. 11, 1993, p. B19 (emphasis added).

21. "Poverty and Family Composition," in Michael B. Katz, ed., *The "Underclass" Debate* (Princeton, N.J.: Princeton University Press, 1993), p. 253.

22. On the scapegoating of the poor for what he calls the increasing elusiveness of the American Dream, see Stuart A. Scheingold, *Politics of Street Crime: Criminal Process and Cultural Obsession* (Philadelphia: Temple University Press, 1991), pp. 174–75.

23. Louis Uchitelle, "The Rise of the Losing Class," *New York Times,* Nov. 20, 1994, sec. 4, pp. 1, 5.

24. George Chauncey combines economic with sexual and cultural displacement when he traces the wiping out of gay culture in the 1930s to "the Depression-era condemnation of the cultural experimentation of the 1920s," suggesting that "with millions of male breadwinners losing their jobs, people were fearful of any additional threats to traditional family hierarchies." George Chauncey, "A Gay World, Vibrant and Forgotten," *New York Times,* June 26, 1994, p. E17.

25. It is not clear, however, whether the poor are role models for more affluent consumers, or whether they serve as inspiration for the manufacturers serving those affluent consumers.

26. The harshness of that culture is graphically depicted in Anderson's "The Code of the Streets," pp. 81–94.

27. The irony is that historically, the poor were labeled as lazy when they resisted the inhuman working conditions of slavery, or mine and factory levels of discipline that punished them like animals. For many examples, see, for instance, Jacqueline Jones, *The Dispossessed: America's Underclasses from the Civil War to the Present* (New York: Basic Books, 1992).

28. Interviews with better-off people who are threatened by or angry with the undeserving poor in places in which there are no poor people, or who are fearful of street crime where it does not exist, may be especially useful. Unless such people have escaped from the poor or from street crime, they may express more clearly than others when and how the undeserving poor are treated as proxies for other problems.

Studies comparing America with societies that do not stigmatize their poor as undeserving might be especially revealing of the extent to which America displaces its problems on the poor.

29. Bruce Link et al., "Attitudes Toward the Homeless," unpublished tabulation (May 8, 1992), p. 6. The "definitely true" answer rose to 13 percent in response to a statement that "It's only natural to be afraid of a person who lives on the street." For a fuller analysis of these data, see Bruce Link et al., "Public Knowledge, Attitudes and Beliefs about Homeless People: Evidence for Compassion Fatigue?" Unpublished paper presented at the 1992 American Public Health Association meetings (New York: School of Public Health, Columbia University, 1992).

30. Link et al., "Attitudes Toward the Homeless," p. 17.

31. Their income ranged from $0 to $19,999. These data come from a tabulation graciously run for me by Professor Link and his colleagues.

32. Whether actual amount of contact with the poor and homeless makes a difference is not clear. A small study among low-income whites in Baltimore indirectly offered a positive answer, finding that those more often panhandled viewed poverty as more of a behavioral than a structural problem. See George Wilson, "Exposure to Panhandling and Beliefs About Poverty Causation," *Social Science Research* 76 (Oct. 1991): 14–19.

33. Link et al., "Attitudes Toward the Homeless," pp. 6–7.

34. What follows is based particularly on James R. Kluegel and Eleanor Smith, *Beliefs about Inequality* (New York: Aldine de Gruyter, 1986) esp. chap. 4; Barrett E. Lee et al., "Public Beliefs about Homelessness," *Social Forces* 69 (Sept. 1990): 253–65; and two CBS–New York Times surveys in 1989 and 1990, for which I am indebted to Dr. Kathleen Frankovic of CBS News.

35. In addition, less affluent respondents generally criticize economic inequality and favor a larger welfare state, whatever the topic of the study, just as the more affluent respondents prefer to keep taxes low. Consequently, people's responses to these questions may have less to do with specific feelings about the poor than with their general ideological stance.

36. Link and his colleagues assembled 36 national and state polls conducted between 1978 and 1992, all of which reported sizeable majorities willing to help the homeless, and smaller ones ready to pay more taxes. Link et al., "Public Knowledge, Attitudes and Beliefs about Homeless People," appendix 1.

37. Another 18 percent said they would pay $100 or more, and 4 percent, $500 or more. Ibid., table 7.

38. Also, respondents might answer differently depending on whether they have recently had negative, positive, or no encounters with the homeless, panhandlers, and other very poor people, or with government, at the time they are being interviewed. Surveys often treat attitudes as timeless and unaffected by varying conditions.

There is no reason why a foundation or federal agency cannot undertake a sufficiently detailed study to find out who blames the poor, who blames the government, and who blames both, under varying conditions. Indeed, elected and appointed officials might find it somewhat easier to make policy choices with the help of a good study.

39. This part of the chapter is a revised version of my article "The Positive Functions of the Undeserving Poor: Uses of the Underclass in America," *Politics and Society* 22 (Sept. 1994): 269–83. It is in turn an updated version of my "Über die positiven Funktionen der unwürdigen Armen: Zur Bedeutung der 'Underclass' in den USA," *Kölner Zeitschrift für Soziologie und Sozialpsychologie* (Sonderheft 32, 1992): 48–62, which was published by the Westdeutscher Verlag, Opladen, Germany. The pages that follow can also be read as a sequel to my article "The Positive Functions of Poverty," *American Journal of Sociology* 78 (Sept. 1972): 275–89, which dealt with the poor generally. For earlier functional analyses of the poor, see Arland D. Weeks, "A Conservative's View of Poverty," *American Journal of Sociology* 22 (1917): 779–800; and Frances Fox Piven and Richard A. Cloward, *Regulating the Poor: The Functions of Public Welfare* (New York: Pantheon, 1971; 2d ed. 1993).

What follows is a straightforward functional analysis based mostly on Robert K. Merton's classic model, which is illustrated with a variety of data. I write it as an empirical analysis, despite its occasionally ironic tone, which is unavoidable given the sometime debunking connotation of the analysis of the functions Robert Merton called latent. Robert K. Merton, "Manifest and Latent Functions," in Robert K. Merton, *Social Theory and Social Structure: Toward the Codification of Social Research* (Glencoe, Ill.: Free Press, 1949), chap. 1.

40. Functions are not immediately apparent *sui generis*, because there is no easy systematic method for identifying them, but many consequences of labeling are apparent even to lay eyes. Some negative functions or dysfunctions of labeling were identified in chap. 3.

41. A good example is the expenditure of large sums to house the homeless in slum hotels instead of cheaper vacant, and decent, dwellings in standard

neighborhoods, in order to satisfy the political demands of working- and middle-class people to keep the homeless out of their neighborhoods.

42. Functions are not, however, causes of undeservingness or of poverty. Being consequences, these uses almost always develop after these causes have done their misdeeds, and except in unusual circumstances cannot enable any form of undeservingness to survive once the causes that brought it into being have disappeared. One set of consequences can, however, cause yet other, or secondary, consequences to develop. Thus if the fear of street crime by the poor results in an increase in the police force, that increase can itself have beneficial consequences for the police: for example, increasing its political power in the community, and its ability thereby to lobby for increased budgets in the future.

43. The sets themselves are arbitrary too; they are an appropriate device for grouping the thirteen functions.

44. The quote is from Andrew Hacker (paraphrasing Baldwin) in *Two Nations: Black and White, Separate, Hostile, Unequal* (New York: Scribner's, 1992), p. 61. Whites have invented so many other pejoratives intended solely for blacks that today terms other than "nigger" can be substituted without altering Baldwin's point.

45. Oscar Lewis, "The Culture of Poverty," in Daniel P. Moynihan, ed., *On Understanding Poverty* (New York: Basic Books, 1968), pp. 190, 192, 193.

46. Susan M. Rigdon, *The Culture Facade: Art, Science and Politics in the Work of Oscar Lewis* (Urbana: University of Illinois Press, 1988), p. 91.

47. More suspicious observers even believe that creating jobs for these classes is a major manifest function of all programs to deal with the poor, from prison building, which hires construction workers and then prison guards, to the nearly continuous investigations of welfare recipients, which supply jobs to college graduates and professional social workers.

48. Ron Harris, "Blacks Feel Brunt of Drug War," *Los Angeles Times,* April 22, 1990, p. 1.

49. For the strongest argument that welfare recipients are already a permanent part of the reserve army, see Piven and Cloward, *Regulating the Poor.*

50. Ralf Dahrendorf has suggested the revival of the reserve army implied in Marx's *Lumpenproletariat.* According to Dahrendorf, when Europe's very poor are excluded from full citizenship, they can become "a reserve army for demonstrations and manifestations, including soccer violence, race riots and running battles with the police." Ralf Dahrendorf, *Law and Order* (London: Stevens, 1985), p. 107.

51. "Normative" is used here as a synonym for "value," but "normative functions" sounds better than "value functions."

52. Since political legitimacy is involved, this function could also be listed among the political ones below.

53. Although Marxists might have been expected to complain that the notion of the undeserving poor enables the higher classes to create a split in the lower ones, Marxist theory copied the mainstream pattern. While declaring capitalists, and sometimes the entire bourgeoisie, undeserving, and ennobling the working class, Marx still found it necessary to construct the *Lumpenproletariat*, although some

of its behavior was for Marx, if less so for some of his successors, undeserving mainly in relation to Marxist political goals.

54. For a contrary view, in which the behavior of the undeserving poor is seen as becoming normatively acceptable for the mainstream, see Daniel P. Moynihan, "Defining Deviancy Down," *American Scholar* 62 (Winter 1993): 17–30.

55. Nonetheless, finding a "welfare queen" who defrauds the system is always a very newsworthy, even front-page, story, while cheating by businessmen and -women is almost always restricted to the business pages.

56. Mark R. Rank, *Living on the Edge: The Realities of Welfare in America* (New York: Columbia University Press, 1994), chap. 6 and *passim*.

57. It may be no coincidence that as far back as the eighteenth century, English "actors, fencers, jugglers, minstrels and in fact all purveyors of amusements to common folk" were thought undeserving by the higher classes (Sidney and Beatrice Webb, *English Poor Law History* [Hamden, Conn.: Shoe String Press, 1963 (1927)], p. 354).

58. Charles Murray, *Losing Ground: American Social Policy 1950–1980* (New York: Basic Books, 1984).

59. Many policies and agencies—notably the schools—reproduce the positions and statuses of the people whom they are asked to improve.

60. For an analysis that argues that the lobby of gun manufacturers and private prison operators, as well as political conservatives, have established a "criminal-industrial complex" with an interest in the persistence of crime, see Joe Conason, "Why Conservatives are Tough on Criminals but Soft on Crime," *New York Observer* (Aug. 29–Sept. 5, 1994): 2.

61. See also the discussion in Piven and Cloward, *Regulating the Poor*, 2d ed., pp. 445–49.

62. Reported by Gwendolyn Dordick, "Friends among Strangers: Personal Relations among New York City's Homeless," (Ph.D. diss., Department of Sociology, Columbia University, 1994), p. 47.

63. Don Terry, "Basketball at Midnight: 'Hope' on a Summer Eve," *New York Times,* Aug. 19, 1994, A18.

64. Kathryn M. Neckerman and Joleen Kirschenman, "Hiring Strategies, Racial Bias, and Inner-City Workers," *Social Problems* 38 (Nov. 1991): 433–47.

65. At present, this is only a prediction. It is also an extension of Gunnar Myrdal's 1963 analysis of the American economy, in which he introduced the underclass into America's dictionary for the poor (see chap. 2).

66. These rates are almost always higher for substance abusers, street criminals, participants in the drug trade, and the poor black youngsters caught in the violent culture of the streets.

67. See, for example, M. Harvey Brenner, *Mental Illness and the Economy* (Cambridge, Mass.: Harvard University Press, 1973).

68. For an early analysis along this line that focuses on blacks rather than the poor, see Sidney Wilhelm, *Who Needs the Negro?* (New York: Doubleday Anchor, 1971).

69. Killing off the undeserving poor may conflict with the prior function of reproducing them, but the consequences described by functional analysis do not

have to be logically consistent. Moreover, since reproducing undeservingness and turning poor people into undeserving ones can be a first step toward eliminating them, functions twelve and thirteen may even be logically consistent.

CHAPTER 5: POLICIES AGAINST POVERTY AND UNDESERVINGNESS

1. Since neither Roosevelt's New Deal nor the Skirmish on Poverty of the 1960s departed very far from the subsistence policy mode, the political and economic prerequisites for a reasonably popular but effective American antipoverty program still need to be determined.

2. Antipoverty policy must also continue to be justified on moral grounds, to reflect the immorality of poverty in a still affluent society, even if such an argument is currently unpersuasive.

3. Policy to eliminate the uses or functions of undeservingness will not be discussed here, on the assumptions that if other programs are effective in reducing poverty, the functions will disappear by themselves, or be transferred to another sector of the population.

4. See, for example, Jerome Skolnick, "Wild Pitch: 'Three Strikes, You're Out' and Other Bad Calls on Crime," *The American Prospect* 17 (Spring 1994): 30–37.

5. If schemes to end welfare are implemented, the number of imprisoned poor young women would also increase. If the orphanages that conservative Republican politicians proposed during the 1994 elections are built, a large number will be de facto prisons for poor children.

6. The prerequisite initial step would be to maximize the removal of threats to safety, particularly from poor neighborhoods, by guaranteeing their victims enough security so that they will cooperate with the police to catch them.

7. Among other things, these prisons would require larger and professionally trained staffs working under conditions where the incentive to be punitive is much reduced. The prisons could thus not be used to create low-skilled guard jobs in depressed rural areas—but then the prisons should not be located there for other reasons.

8. These are the subjects of Jack Katz, *Seductions of Crime* (New York: Basic Books, 1988). I am not convinced yet, however, that some of the various seductions Katz analyzes could not be replaced by the leisure time excitements and organizational roles affordable by and available to people who work for a living.

9. After the new 1994 prison-building legislation, some elected officials began to suggest moving petty offenders out of prison to save money. These offenders might be useful guinea pigs for testing rehabilitation and job programs, which if successful could then be adapted to the prevention of recidivism among more serious and violent criminals.

10. I need not detail the political complications that would develop if ex-convicts were given preference over the noncriminal jobless.

11. On the need for help for families of returning prisoners, see Jonathan

Simon, *Poor Discipline: Parole and Social Control of the Underclass, 1890–1990* (Chicago: University of Chicago Press, 1993), p. 264.

12. For simplicity's sake I assume here a dichotomy between work and crime that does not really exist, since workers can commit crime during or after work, and sometimes on the job itself. Wall Street is one example. For examples of this phenomenon among low-skilled workers, see Mercer L. Sullivan, *"Getting Paid": Youth Crime and Work in the Inner City* (Ithaca, N.Y.: Cornell University Press, 1989).

13. One of the research vacuums that a proper crime prevention program needs urgently to fill is to understand which poor people turn to crime under what conditions and why. Since only a minority do so, other causes are also at work, but these may themselves be poverty-related—connected, for example, to the destruction poverty wreaks on some families, particularly those unable to overcome its combatlike stresses.

Purely noneconomic causes exist as well, which, being unrelated to poverty, may not be very different from those bringing about crime among the affluent classes. Disturbed youngsters who later become criminals can be found in all strata, as can people who are consumed by such intense need for money that affluent people commit financial crimes in prestigious institutions if their need cannot be satisfied legally, just as their poor peers satisfy their greed in the underworld.

14. The more punitive the laws against drug selling by adults, the larger the number of jobs that the drug industry offers to younger people.

15. In the world of economists, the definition of full employment is constantly changing to meet the threshold of actual unemployment; that is, it writes off displaced, discouraged, and other jobless workers who are no longer counted as members of the official labor force. In late 1994, for example, the "natural" rate of unemployment was set at 6 percent. In effect, these economists, many of them with lifetime academic tenure, were using their definitions to legitimate forcing jobless people out of the economy.

16. Since the start of the 1990s, American politicians have celebrated America's low unemployment rate as compared with that of Western Europe, but this kind of rhetoric is not entirely convincing. One reason for America's seeming success at lower unemployment is that its minimum wage is set so low that people who would be eligible for welfare in Europe instead work as hamburger flippers and lavatory cleaners. Which is the better policy deserves discussion, for while working is preferable to welfare, America's minimum wage jobs pay less than Western Europe's welfare benefits. To keep the comparison in this hemisphere, Rebecca Blank and Maria Hanratty estimate that if America's single-parent families were receiving Canadian welfare payments, the poverty rate among them would decline from 45 percent to about 16 percent. David Card and Richard B. Freeman, "Small Differences That Matter: Canada vs. the United States," in Richard B. Freeman, ed., *Working Under Different Rules* (New York: Russell Sage Foundation, 1994), p. 214.

17. Lester C. Thurow, *The Zero-Sum Society: Distribution and the Possibilities for Economic Change* (New York: Basic Books, 1980), p. 203.

18. Gordon Lafer, "The Politics of Job Training: Urban Poverty and the False

Promise of JTPA," *Politics & Society* 22 (Sept. 1994): 353. For an analysis that insists that there are enough jobs, and that unemployment is the fault of the jobless, see Lawrence Mead, *Beyond Entitlement: The Social Obligations of Citizenship* (New York: Free Press, 1986).

19. Lester C. Thurow, "The Fed Goes Ghostbusting," *New York Times,* May 6, 1994, p. A29. To the officially jobless, Thurow, like others who have made the same computation in past decades, added government figures for discouraged workers and involuntary part-time workers looking for full-time work. In addition to the discouraged workers who are counted by the government, there are others who are not counted, because they have been out of work long enough not to be considered part of the labor force any more. Also, there are poor people who have been jobless and discouraged for so long that, like many of the people not counted by the decennial U.S. Census, they cannot be reached by governmental data gatherers.

20. Ellen Galinsky et al., *The Changing Workforce: Highlights of the National Study* (New York: Families and Work Institute, 1993), tables 2, 3. A 1994 *New York Times* poll reported that 39 percent of those interviewed expressed either a lot or some worry that they might be laid off, required to work reduced hours, or forced to take pay cuts. Michael Kagay, "From Coast to Coast, from Affluent to Poor, Poll Shows Anxiety over Jobs." *New York Times,* Mar. 11, 1994, p. A14. Several 1992 and 1993 *New York Times*–CBS News polls have reported similar results.

21. See, for example, Cheryl L. Greenberg, *"Or Does It Explode?": Black Harlem in the Depression* (New York: Oxford University Press, 1991).

22. Robert Greenstein, "Universal and Targeted Approaches to Relieving Poverty: An Alternative View," in Christopher Jencks and Paul E. Peterson, eds., *The Urban Underclass* (Washington, D.C.: Brookings Institution, 1991), pp. 437–59.

23. An important corollary of this principle is the need to reduce the socioeconomic gap between the poor and the other classes, without, however, eliminating it altogether. If any of today's working-class and moderate-income population, whatever their races, fear that the poor will become their equals, they may become opponents of antipoverty schemes. They might also quietly favor the persistence of poverty, and even of the undeservingness of the poor, as a way of maintaining their own status superiority over the poor. One reason for the demise of the antipoverty programs of the 1960s was a belief in some white working-class populations that antipoverty policy sought to make the black poor equal to them in income and overall class position.

24. For some other, and more complete, discussions of antipoverty policy, see, for example, Sheila Collins, Helen L. Ginsburg, and Gertrude S. Goldberg, *Jobs for All: A Plan for the Revitalization of America* (New York: APEX Press, 1994); and Alvin Schorr, *Common Decency: Domestic Policies after Reagan* (New Haven, Conn.: Yale University Press, 1986).

25. An exception might be made for industries that could assure the government that profits from the machines would go directly to the saving or creation of decent jobs.

26. If such a policy achieves its goal without serious side-effects, it might be

enlarged eventually to apply to all machines that destroy a large number of decent jobs.

27. See Philip Harvey, *Securing the Right to Employment: Social Welfare and the Unemployed in the U.S.* (Princeton, N.J.: Princeton University Press, 1989).

28. For an introduction, see Fred Best, *Worksharing: Issues, Policy Options, and Prospects* (Kalamazoo, Mich.: Upjohn Institute for Employment Research, 1981).

29. In fact, average American working hours for full-time workers have been increasing instead, partly because firms find it cheaper to require more overtime work from already employed full-time workers than to hire new workers. This practice would cease if Congress updated the 1938 law on overtime pay and set it at double or triple regular pay, thus making overtime less viable economically and encouraging more work sharing.

30. Additional jobs could be created if American workers started taking the 4–6 week vacations that have long been standard in Europe.

31. For an analysis showing that work sharing is economically workable, see Gilbert Cette and Dominique Taddei, "The Economic Effects of Reducing and Reorganizing Working Time," *Futures* 25 (June 1993): 561–77.

32. In some European industries using assembly lines, twenty-four- and thirty-hour weeks without wage loss have been achieved by letting employers set up a third shift on the weekend, in which workers are paid for working long daily hours, the extra cost being recouped by the fact that the machines can be kept running on a permanent basis.

For an analysis of this and other features of the Western European experimentation with work sharing during the boom years of the 1980s, see Herbert J. Gans, "Planning for Work Sharing: The Promise and Problems of Egalitarian Work Time Reduction," in Kai Erikson and Steven P. Vallas, eds., *The Nature of Work: Sociological Perspectives* (New Haven, Conn.: Yale University Press, 1990), pp. 258–76.

33. Some increases in moonlighting can be expected anyway, including in the off-the-books economy, though the moonlighters could also force out some present occupants of jobs in that economy.

34. Surely some jobless workers, like welfare recipients, will remain jobless because they are depressed, or because they are lazy—as are some coupon-clipping rich people and employed workers. Subsidizing laziness has its downside, but laziness may be preferable to encouraging jobless people to work energetically at drug selling and street crime.

35. American policymakers and voters have not yet adopted a poverty line that defines poverty relative to what others have so that they can remain community members—a concept usually operationalized at half the median income. Instead, American poverty is still measured on an absolute basis, which views people as physiological organisms who need only a minimal income to stay alive. Even that poverty line has not been updated since 1964.

36. See, for example, Lee Rainwater, "A Primer on American Poverty: 1949–1992," Russell Sage Foundation Working Paper 53 (New York: Russell Sage Foundation, May 1994).

37. The national average of AFDC and food stamps income for an otherwise penniless mother was $7,479 in 1992. Committee on Ways and Means, U.S. House of Representatives, *1993 Green Book* (Washington, D.C.: U.S. Government Printing Office, 1993), p. 1253. In 1992, the median family income was about $31,500.

38. At best it could be entry-level work for better-paid public employment, but at worst, it could turn into make-work jobs without work to satisfy welfare reform requirements.

39. Ongoing research projects by Kathryn Edin and by Katherine Newman among welfare recipients and "hamburger flippers," respectively, also suggest educational grants or vouchers that will help poor people obtain part-time technical training while raising children or working.

40. See, for instance, Philippe Bourgois, "In Search of Respect: The New Service Economy and the Crack Alternative in Spanish Harlem." Russell Sage Foundation Working Paper 21 (New York: Russell Sage Foundation, May 1991).

41. The danger is the concurrent creation of "therapeutic prisons" that disregard their constitutional rights, and will therefore be avoided by the very people who need therapy the most.

42. See chap. 4, n. 17. The total does not include public housing expenditures, which benefit only a small number of all poor people. Only Medicaid is expensive, although the monies actually go to doctors and hospitals. The amount to bring poor children and their families up to the poverty line is from the U.S. Bureau of the Census, *Poverty in the United States in 1991*, Current Population Reports, Series P 60 No. 181 (Washington, D.C.: U.S. Government Printing Office, 1992), table 22.

43. A proper cost-benefit analysis would also have to include the taxes returned to the Treasury by those working to police, control, and isolate the poor.

44. An alternative approach would be to extend the notion of undeservingness to all classes, but little is gained by adding further to the number of negative stereotypes.

45. The proposals that follow are primitive and overly rationalistic; they also ignore the obstacles some people and institutions will erect to maintain the credibility of undeservingness. Also omitted are needed programs to weaken the structural supports for undeservingness, many of which were mentioned in the functional analysis of chap. 4 and will reappear in somewhat different form at the close of this chapter.

46. The best person to initiate the questioning process would be the president of the United States. See William Julius Wilson, "The Crisis and Challenge of Race and the New Urban Poverty," The 1994 Ryerson Lecture, University of Chicago, April 8, 1994, pp. 31–33.

47. In the 1950s, a popular TV western series, *Bonanza*, used its historical context to attack racism; in the 1980s, *L.A. Law* regularly questioned conventional wisdom and stereotypes about a variety of matters.

48. Although ethnographic studies are conducted by anthropologists and sociologists, the method is not unknown to journalists, for a simpler version is sometimes used by investigative reporters.

49. People with strongly held ideological views often declare divergent behavior or thinking that they oppose to be harmful without even considering whether any evidence of harmfulness exists. Intellectuals who are supposedly trained to take evidence into account in reaching conclusions resort to this practice as easily as political leaders and leaders of ideological movements.

50. Christopher Jencks, "The Truth About the Homeless," *New York Review of Books* (Apr. 21, 1994): 20–27, quote at 27.

51. Perhaps a better term would be "left-liberal," to demarcate those sectors of liberal thought and action concerned with economic change, and to separate them from people who call themselves social or cultural liberals but are economic conservatives.

52. Some debunking news lends itself more to the print media than the electronic ones, but appropriate formats can be found for both, and the latter will most likely continue to have the largest audiences most of the time.

53. This is one instance in which a touch of jargon in the concepts is desirable.

54. The general public sometimes refuses to make either-or ideological choices, or indicates that both the poor and the society are guilty, as indicated by the survey results on attitudes toward the poor and the homeless that were summarized in chap. 4.

55. It is, however, a matter of obtaining pertinent and accurate measures of poverty, a topic to which almost no one pays any attention. Too often, it is easier and faster to construct "proxies" that permit the use of whatever data are already available, even if they may be neither pertinent nor accurate.

56. Katherine Q. Seelye, "House Talks Tough on Capital Punishment as It Begins Debate on Crime Bill," *New York Times,* Apr. 15, 1994, p. A23. Energetic argument with such defenders of "common sense" is another element in a debunking program.

57. In all fairness, the union movement was a loyal supporter of the antipoverty programs of the 1960s.

58. In the past, some advocates of public discussion put their faith in "interactive television," but so far it appears as if most people use their set for entertainment and information, and do not want to interact with it.

59. Only a few such questions follow below, and some of these may be left to researchers.

60. This question is particularly relevant to the Western European societies that after World War II virtually eliminated poverty.

61. Communist parties have usually scapegoated a ruling class, but it has always managed to defend itself, except in the countries taken over by the Communists, where it was killed and replaced by a Communist ruling class.

In America, politicians have been used as scapegoats for a long time, which helped to produce the widespread cynicism about politics and the lack of faith in government's ability to solve problems that are manifesting themselves particularly strongly in the 1990s. Europeans are often cynical about their politicians too, but they retain faith in the structure in which they operate, partly because it seems to exist more independently of the politicians than it does in the United States.

CHAPTER 6: JOBLESSNESS AND ANTIPOVERTY POLICY
IN THE TWENTY-FIRST CENTURY

1. When Gunnar Myrdal formulated the term "underclass," he meant it to apply to people being excluded from the economy, and if his meaning of the term had triumphed, it would today be more relevant than it was in 1963, even though the diversity of the excluded has increased since then.

2. There are many other countries in the world that have not yet begun to industrialize, and thus to compete for low-wage work. Moreover, the long-term effects of GATT cannot now be predicted.

3. All of the numbers in this paragraph are purely guesstimates, but they guess at actual work status, not at the sometimes peculiar definition of full-time and part-time that the U.S. government, like all other governments, uses to minimize bad news. As far as I know, no one has yet worked out the impact of informal economy employment on national labor force rates, and it may be empirically very difficult to get people to admit they hold an off-the-books job. For another estimate of future joblessness, see David Macarov, "Quitting Time," *International Journal of Sociology and Social Policy* 8, special iss. nos. 2, 3, 4 (1988): 141.

4. Edward Bellamy, *Looking Backward, 2000–1887* (Boston: Houghton Mifflin, 1888). Bellamy facilitated his social planning task by assuming the benevolent dictatorship to be a technocratic elite, which ran the economy as a quasi-military but entirely peaceful organization. He also imagined a homogeneous society in which conformity to a cosmopolitan life-style developed automatically, more or less as a result of what might today be called rational choice.

5. See, for example, Andre Gorz, *Paths to Paradise: On the Liberation from Work* (Boston: South End Press, 1985). For a more thoughtful analysis of the utopian position, see Macarov, "Quitting Time."

6. In addition, work continues to be people's major source of prestige, social usefulness, and self-respect, and that too cannot change overnight.

7. See, for instance, Katherine Newman, *Falling from Grace: The Experience of Downward Mobility in the American Middle Class* (New York: Free Press, 1988).

8. Once race can no longer be used as a popular explanation of undeservingness, class consciousness might finally develop in America, although perhaps not in forms ever conceived of by Karl Marx.

9. Generalizations about the quality of life are dangerous because many people may not care about those qualities that are most often discussed publicly, or even those that are most reduced.

10. In 1970, the sociologist Sidney Wilhelm wrote that "the day will eventually arrive, following perhaps a period of racial wars, when the surviving blacks become resigned to their fate as state wards on the borderline of existence." Sidney Wilhelm, *Who Needs the Negro?* (New York: Doubleday Anchor, 1971), p. 310. Sometime in the twenty-first century, these words could apply to surplus workers of all colors.

11. Among the American writers, see, for example, Stanley Aronowitz and

William DiFazio, *The Jobless Future: Sci-Tech and the Dogma of Work* (Minneapolis: University of Minnesota Press, 1994), chap. 10; Arthur B. Shostak, "The Nature of Work in the Twenty-first Century: Certain Uncertainties," *Business Horizons* (Nov.–Dec. 1993): 30–34; Shoshana Zuboff, *In the Age of the Smart Machine: The Future of Work and Power* (New York: Basic Books, 1988); and Macarov, "Quitting Time."

12. In some respects, circumscribing the role of the computer is tempting, for much of the labor-intensive work, other than key-punching, is white-collar and professional, and more pleasant work than manufacturing a labor-intensive automobile.

13. It would be pleasant to imagine a noncompetitive world economy, and even more pleasant to invent one that might be guided by an updated United Nations, but such changes would require now quite unimaginable elimination of, or functional alternatives for, the nation-state and other competitive institutions.

14. Worker stock ownership can have the same consequences, but workers have to be protected against losing all of their equity if the firm runs into serious difficulties, and workers must therefore be able to diversify stock holdings like all other shareholders.

15. The scenario for a twenty-four-hour-a-week economy requires its own book, but it probably cannot be written until experience with and research on more modest forms of work sharing are available.

16. Actually, there is no reason why parts of the economy could run on a twenty-four-hour-a-week basis while others make different arrangements as long as both end up with the same work year.

17. For the argument that all jobs can be shared, see Gorz, *Paths to Paradise*, p. 55.

18. A variety of other solutions suggest themselves, at least in theory. Brain surgeons could be paid so much that they can be persuaded to work only twenty-four hours; alternatively, enough could be trained so as to exceed demand, in which case the twenty-four-hour work week would be economically feasible, all other conditions being equal. Or nonmonetary social rewards could be provided in lieu of income, but these are easier to propose than to put into practice.

19. Gorz has argued that automation will be so profitable that pay reductions will not be needed, but I do not find it persuasive for the long run. See *Paths to Paradise*, chap. 4.

20. Among the byproducts of such low prices and the joblessness that accompanies it are high rates of crime among the jobless, the high costs of incarcerating them, the increased insurance rates, and so on. For a thoughtful analysis, see Edward Luttwak, "America's Insecurity Blanket: Why can't the politicians see how fearful people are about their economic futures?" *Washington Post National Weekly Edition,* Dec. 5–11, 1994, pp. 23–24.

21. In the long run, basic income schemes would probably encourage the development of multibreadwinner, multifamily households, which would use economy of scale to reduce the dysfunctions of lower wages and salaries, and other income and pay reductions. But these might also further encourage the increase in one-person households and childless families.

22. See, for example, Robert Theobald, *Free Men and Free Markets* (New York:

Clarkson & Potter, 1963); and David Macarov, *Incentives to Work* (San Francisco: Jossey Bass, 1970).

23. Gorz, *Paths to Paradise*, p. 42, emphasis his. See also Philippe van Parijs, ed., *Arguing for Basic Income: Ethical Foundations for a Radical Reform* (London: Verso, 1992); and Claus Offe, "Full Employment: Asking the Wrong Questions," *Dissent* (Winter 1995): 77–81.

24. These are most likely to be artists, filmmakers, and writers, as well as the people whom a Dutch study of the unemployed called the "autonomous." Godfried Engbersen, *Cultures of Unemployment: Long Term Unemployment in Dutch Inner Cities* (Boulder, Colo.: Westview, 1992).

25. For an ingenious scheme to use volunteering as a partial replacement for paid work, see Edgar S. Cahn, "Service Credits: A New Currency for the Welfare State," Discussion Paper 8 (London: London School of Economics, July 1986). I am grateful to Alvin Schorr for making Cahn's paper available to me.

26. Among hardier people, the twenty-four-hour work week might even spur a return to family farming. For more realistic but still relevant accounts of how people spend time without work, see Walli F. Leff and Marilyn G. Haft, *Time Without Work* (Boston: South End Press, 1983).

27. For a discussion of "cooperation circles" and other forms of moneyless markets, see Claus Offe and Rolf G. Heinze, *Beyond Employment: Time, Work and the Informal Economy* (Philadelphia: Temple University Press, 1994).

28. Such maneuvers could be reduced if the Constitution were amended to guarantee economic rights, to work and to income, for everyone, but since the many people who have argued for an economic Bill of Rights in the twentieth century had no success, it would be rash to predict a constitutional amendment to this effect for the twenty-first century.

Name Index

Subject Index